# PROPHET
# JOHN WROE

VIRGINS, SCANDALS AND VISIONS

EDWARD GREEN

SUTTON PUBLISHING

Sutton Publishing Limited
Phoenix Mill · Thrupp · Stroud
Gloucestershire · GL5 2BU

First published 2005

British Library Cataloguing in Publication Data
A catalogue for this book is available from the British Library.

ISBN 0-7509-4077-8

Typeset in 11/14.5pt Sabon
Typesetting and origination by
Sutton Publishing Limited.
Printed and bound in England by
J.H. Haynes & Co. Ltd, Sparkford.

# Contents

Acknowledgements                                                                iv
Preface                                                                          v
Introduction                                                                     vii

One        A Prophet is Born                                                     1
Two        The Southcottians                                                    17
Three      The Rise to Leadership                                              33
Four       Baptism of Blood                                                     54
Five       Building the New Jerusalem                                          69
Six        Scandals and Banishment                                             91
Seven      Return of the Native                                               115
Eight      Preaching to All Nations                                           130
Nine       Prophet Wroe's Mansion                                             149
Ten        Death and its Aftermath                                            165
Eleven     The Demise of the Christian Israelites in England                  179
Twelve     The Last of the Wroes                                              196

Genealogical Table                                                             206
Appendix 1:    Allegations from
               *The Voice of the People*                                       207
Appendix 2:    John Wroe in Literature                                         214
Appendix 3:    Saving the Odd Whim                                             215
Select Bibliography                                                            218
Notes                                                                          225
Index                                                                          240

# Acknowledgements

The depth of information in this book would not have been possible without the encouragement and contributions of several people. As no biography of Wroe has been written before, I am indebted to the staff and archivists at the following libraries, records offices and archives: Wakefield Library Headquarters; Tameside Local Studies and Archives Centre; Bradford Central Library; Leeds Central Library; Manchester Public Library; Gravesend Public Library; Portsmouth Public Library; Frewen Library at Portsmouth University; West Yorkshire Archives, Wakefield; Bradford Local Records Office; the British Library; the Family History Centre, London; the National Archive, Kew.

Special thanks to Sandra Hargreaves for all her help and interest in this project and for locating most of the primary source material in Australia. Also to Gay-Jeanne Oliver of Stalybridge, Cheshire, whose extensive family history research has proved invaluable in unravelling the relationships of Wroe's wealthy supporters at Ashton-under-Lyne in the 1820s and '30s.

I am also particularly grateful to Dr Brad Beaven for his assistance and perseverance as my history dissertation tutor and to the late Professor Robbie Gray, whose interest in this subject area encouraged me to research aspects of it as part of my MA at Portsmouth University.

Finally I would like to thank Christopher Feeney, Senior Commissioning Editor at Sutton Publishing for his interest and useful advice on reading the first draft.

# *Preface*

Few motorists driving to Wakefield from junction 41 of the M1 could begin to imagine the colourful life story of the character whose mansion stands just an apt stone's throw (or mud pelt) away. The property, briefly glimpsed through the trees, now part of an office complex, was originally built as the stately residence of the founder of the Christian Israelite Church, the strange and charismatic 'Prophet' John Wroe. The prophecies and outrageous behaviour of this much-travelled Yorkshireman first brought him to public attention in the 1820s. Aspects of his life have made him a firm part of local folklore, but the real John Wroe, the millennial leader, has been virtually forgotten by history.

My interest in Wroe's life story dates back to childhood, as I was brought up in Wrenthorpe, the West Yorkshire village where Wroe built his mansion, Melbourne House. The building was a most incongruous-looking place – which we would pass on our cross-country runs from the nearby comprehensive school – situated in part of the region's famous 'rhubarb triangle', which locally was rapidly being eroded by the burgeoning Wakefield 41 Business Park.

The stories relating to Wroe were fascinating, and I was most intrigued at how even then, in the 1980s, some elderly residents in the area found it an uneasy topic of conversation. My appetite for this subject was whetted still further while in the sixth form. Doing some community work at a senior citizens' lunch club I met Mrs Edith Hemingway, who had lived in one of the mansion's lodges for twenty-six years from the 1920s onwards. She told me descendants of Wroe who had still lived in the mansion during her time there, and of visits from Christian Israelite delegates from all over the world.

When I tried to find out more about our village's most famous former resident I was frustrated to discover that there was something of a dearth of easily accessible information about the Prophet. No biography existed, and what information on Wroe there was had to be gleaned from various local history books, which repeated the same stories, many of which as it turned out were merely copied from Wroe's own publications without acknowledging the fact. This dearth of information on Wroe was in stark contrast to Wakefield's other major nineteenth century eccentric, the pioneer naturalist Squire Charles Waterton of Walton Hall. Waterton was an exact contemporary of Wroe, both men having been born in 1782, and several books have been devoted to the first conservationist.

After ploughing through all the secondary sources I could find on Wroe in the early 1990s, when I included a chapter on him in a history book of Wrenthorpe, I knew that when time allowed I would have to come back to this fascinating subject and give it the thorough research it deserved. In the intervening years I slowly accumulated three files of notes and several books relating to both the Prophet and millennial religion. As I tracked down the primary source material I soon realised that many of the local historians had hopelessly mixed up the chronology of stories involving Wroe.

This book will, for the first time, pull together the many facets of Wroe's long and controversial life – information that has previously been hidden in obscure primary source material and confined to the pages of antiquarian local history books, reports in contemporary local newspapers and the briefest of footnotes in commentaries on nineteenth-century religion. It will reveal the truth behind several of the many myths surrounding this character. It will also attempt to explain why this strange phenomenon occurred at this period of English history, and why, despite the death of Joanna Southcott, existing socio-economic conditions and the state of the Church of England contributed to Wroe's success. These aspects of millenarian-ism were investigated in my history MA dissertation, which was titled 'Factors Accounting for the Popularity of the Christian Israelites from the 1820s'.

In a letter to the *Ashton-under-Lyne Reporter* in January 1955, Harold Wood, one of the then few remaining Christian Israelite adherents in England, wrote that 'it would be quite impossible for anyone to write the whole truth relating to the history of this Church from outside sources alone'. At times during the arduous research for this book, I have almost been inclined to agree with him.

# Introduction

On 29 February 1824, 30,000 spectators lined the banks of the River Aire to watch Yorkshire's self-styled 'Prophet' John Wroe perform a miracle by dividing the waters and walking on the dry riverbed. When no such feat took place he was pelted with mud and stones and forced to make a hasty retreat with his followers. On Christmas Day the following year Wroe opened the extravagant Christian Israelite Sanctuary in the South Lancashire industrial town of Ashton-under-Lyne. It was here that his sect, the Society of Christian Israelites, believed the New Jerusalem would be established on Earth. This was to be the Holy City where the 144,000 elect would gather at the Apocalypse. The Sanctuary cost in excess of £9,000 to construct, over twice as much as Ashton Town Hall, which was built some twenty-five years later.

Such an ambitious construction scheme is, of course redolent of William Blake's poem 'Jerusalem', as Ashton, a centre of the cotton-weaving industry, possessed many 'dark satanic mills'. The analogy is entirely appropriate, as Blake, writing in the 1790s, was looking across the English Channel at recent events in France's violent transition from monarchy to republic. The Revolution had brought about new millennial anticipation in Britain, where it was feared by some that what had happened in France signified the end of the world was close at hand. In the midst of this political turbulence, a nervous population consulted the Bible in an attempt to make sense of what was happening. Had these events somehow been prophesied?

The anticipated millennium was (and in some quarters still is) based on the belief that, after a struggle between good and evil, Christ will reign on Earth for 1,000 years. During this period Satan would be imprisoned and the Earth exist in peace, ruled by Christ and his saints. At the end of the 1,000 years would come the Day of Judgement and the end of the world. Such beliefs stemmed from Revelation 20, yet contemporary critics argued that millenarians such as the Southcottians interpreted too literally the Biblical definition of a thousand-year interregnum.

A profound interest in the fate of the Jews opened this bizarre episode in English social history, which would briefly bring to fame Richard Brothers, Joanna Southcott and John Wroe. Brothers believed that as many as ten of the twelve lost tribes of Israel could be found in Britain. He meticulously planned their return to Jerusalem, an undertaking in which he himself would lead them. Like Blake, Brothers was a radical, and the authorities, fearful of his republican tendencies, managed to silence him by committing him to an asylum.

Brothers's mantle was taken up by a Devon farmer's daughter, Joanna Southcott, the second in an eccentric chain of millennial leaders. (Brothers and Southcott were regarded by their followers as the first two of the seven angelic messengers of Revelation 10: 7.) Southcott was the Exeter prophetess, a former servant girl, who at the age of 42 said that she heard a voice she believed to be of divine origin, and recorded prophecies in doggerel verse. She is now best known for her famous box of predictions, which will only be opened by the Panacea Society in the presence of twenty-four Church of England bishops.

In 1814, in her 65th year, Joanna announced that she would give birth to Shiloh, a messianic figure who she and her followers believed was alluded to in Genesis 49: 10. Southcott's announcement caught the attention of the press and the hostility of non-believers. The very idea that the 64-year-old virgin would give birth seemed quite absurd. To Joanna's deep disappointment no physical birth took place, and she died in December of that year. Her followers quickly claimed that Shiloh had been born as a spirit and taken up to heaven, thus fulfilling Revelation 12: 5.

Although Joanna Southcott had died, her promise unfulfilled, her followers and certain struggling sections of the population still looked to millennial religion for an explanation of the unprecedented turmoil they were experiencing in their lives. Ordered society in France had unravelled in the 1790s at the time that Brothers and Southcott had shot to prominence. Now, in the mid-1810s, in England industrialisation was gathering pace, and traditional ways of life were being disrupted beyond recognition. Rural labourers migrated to jobs in the rapidly expanding towns where new mechanised manufacturing processes led to the painful demise of various cottage or domestic industries. The Church of England found it hard to address the spiritual concerns of these displaced workers, who in their despair turned to millenarianism.

Following the death of Joanna Southcott, a large proportion of her supporters, particularly in the North of England, recognised George Turner, a merchant from Leeds as their new leader. Turner's failed predictions, extravagant lifestyle and bouts in an asylum weakened his authority. His death in 1821 paved the way for another Yorkshireman, John Wroe, to lead a substantial portion of the sect. The Moses of the West Riding, Wroe literally wielded a rod of iron and with fresh vigour, was clearly keen to take up the initiative of Brothers's lost tribes in calling his sect the Society of Christian Israelites.

John Wroe's doctrine was markedly different from that being preached by the contemporary Established Church. Most notably, he made use of prophecies, many of which targeted the anxieties of those who had worked in the declining domestic industries of the time, such as the handloom weavers, stocking makers and wool-combers. A distinctive facet of millennial religion, these prophecies also frequently echo concerns of the broader masses in the 1820s.

Wroe's popularity was due in part to his gift for showmanship and a clever use of publicity. At the height of his religious career, the 'Prophet' had several thousand followers and demonstrated the uncanny ability to attract support from influential industrialists. This profitable relationship was badly damaged following his alleged depraved activities, which directly contributed to the spectacular demise of his authority. Although this precipitated a decline in membership of the sect in England, Wroe was nonetheless able to reach out to new congregations in America and Australia. Whether true prophet or charlatan, his abilities were obviously considerable and his life story is thus still a hugely entertaining one, encompassing as it does an era of intense social change and political unrest.

# 1

# A Prophet is Born

A small, ugly, hunchbacked man with shaggy hair and a haggard face, who spoke with the broadest of Yorkshire accents, seems the most unlikely person to have headed a religious sect in the early nineteenth century. Yet this native of Bradford was not only to wrest leadership, but would give his schism from the Southcottians media coverage the older sect had not received since the death of Joanna Southcott, their founder. Wroe's prophecies, speeches and various antics brought him much notoriety during his long life, though it was not until he was in his late 30s that he started on the road to fame with dramatic fits and trances lasting for many hours, in which he encountered the strangest of visions. All this seemed unlikely in the winter of 1819, when Wroe lay ill, his unremarkable life seemingly about to end, his name just one of many Wroes recorded in the pages of the Bradford parish registers.

John Wroe (or Roe) was born on 19 September 1782 at the family farmhouse in Rooley Lane, West Bowling, Bradford. Today this 'lane' is a busy three-lane dual carriageway taking traffic from the M606 to Bradford city centre. Then it would have been nothing more than a country road in a rural hamlet close to the Yorkshire mill town. John was the eldest surviving son of Joseph Wroe, a farmer who also had financial interests in local coal mines and the Bradford worsted woollen industry. Despite his comfortable family background, he received little education. A near neighbour at Bowling, Samuel Muff, recalled that Wroe's teacher 'never could teach him to spell or read, or even to speak plainly'.[1] Despite attending a school at Bretton, near Wakefield for a year, he progressed slowly, and, as he himself admitted, his reading barely improved, his

1

The farmhouse at Rooley Lane, Bradford *c.* 1888, where Wroe was born more than a century before. (Bradford Central Library)

master commenting that he would learn nothing no matter how long he stayed.[2]

There is very little information about the first thirty-six years of Wroe's life, and what there is comes from one primary source, *Divine Communications*, which is ostensibly his autobiography, published by the Society of Christian Israelites in three volumes.[3] These books are analysed closely in Chapter 7, and when compared with other available primary sources relating to events in Wroe's life, their accounts seem accurate. Certain important incidents, however, are missing from the pages of *Divine Communications*. The first eighteen pages of volume 1 give an account of the Prophet's life prior to 1818. His existence was far from remarkable, but the narrative does give some important indications as to Wroe's future character. A number of important themes emerge, fitting into the 'signs and portents' tradition, according to which people with great spiritual gifts have often been the runt of the litter.

Firstly, Wroe talks about being victimised by his father, and also his father's apparent favouritism towards his younger brother Joseph, in a strange parallel with the way the biblical Jacob favoured his own Joseph above his other children.[4] As a child, Wroe was 'put to all kinds of drudgery and kicked and cuffed about' by his father. Mr Wroe taunted his son, calling him Tom Bland after 'an idiot' in the nearby Bowling Workhouse. While carrying out repairs on some houses that his father had bought, Wroe was nearly bent double from carrying a window lintel to the second floor. This, according to Wroe, accounted for his characteristic hunched back. He was further taunted for his deafness, which had come about after he was thrown into an ice-covered pond. This condition was cured in young adulthood by the Whitworth doctors, one of whom syringed his ears.

Secondly, we learn of the family's Church of England background; they were staunch Anglicans, reflecting their comfortable status. Wroe was baptised in Bradford Parish Church on 8 December 1782. More importantly, we also discover the family's belief in prophecies. Wroe's grandfather had once announced that the 'Lord would raise up a priest from the fruits of his loin'.[5] Mr and Mrs Wroe took this announcement seriously and named their youngest son Thomas after his grandfather. He was trained to go into the Church, but was advised against the ministry by the vicar of Bradford and the Archbishop of York because of his stammer.

Wroe's critics, including the well-known Victorian Anglican vicar the Revd Sabine Baring-Gould, regard his account of the early years of his life as deeply self-piteous.[6] They attempt to explain Wroe's treatment by his father as being a consequence of Wroe's own stupidity, claiming that he was aimless, work-shy and unable to apply himself at school. This seems at odds with the shrewd person they later describe as devious and cunning. Wroe's supposed near illiteracy is also highly questionable. There is evidence that he could write. Was Wroe's lack of education overstressed by both his supporters and critics to show on the one hand what a remarkable person they thought him to be, and on the other to portray him as a stupid and worthless individual?

As for the rest of the family, we know that Wroe had a sister, although he does not mention her name. Neither, perhaps significantly, does Wroe make a direct mention of his mother in the pages of *Divine Communications*. She was Susanna, the daughter of

3

Thomas Fearnley. Susanna married Joseph Wroe on 8 June 1778 at Bradford.

At first the young Wroe worked for his father but his brother Joseph was put in charge of him and the brothers often quarrelled and fought. When Wroe was about 15, his uncle John tried to intervene regarding his father's treatment of him. Wroe's uncle tried to persuade his brother to let Wroe become an apprentice in his own trade. Joseph would not give his permission, but Wroe left anyway, to live with his cousin and to become an apprentice wool-comber. Wool-combing is the process of carding the tangled fibres of raw wool into roughly parallel strands and the removal of the short stable wool. The finished product is wool of sufficiently high quality to be used in the manufacture of worsted cloth. The worsted woollen trade was centred in and around Bradford, which hugely expanded in the early 1800s, the town's population rocketing from 13,264 in 1801 to 43,527 by 1831.

Joseph Wroe, however, persuaded his eldest son to terminate his apprenticeship and return home. He drew up a partnership agreement which was never signed. It was not until John Wroe had reached the age of 24 that he set up in business for himself as a wool-comber, at first staying with his cousin before taking up the tenancy of a small farm at Street House, Tong Street, south of Bradford.[7] This was to be his main home until 1831. When Wroe first took out the tenancy his father again tried to interfere in his affairs, sending Wroe on an errand to Liverpool. Wroe claimed that his father had taken advantage of him and cheated him out of the tenancy, taking ownership of the farm behind his back.

Within three years Wroe had possession of the farm. He took on a number of apprentices in his wool-combing business, but the conduct of one of the young men caused him severe losses of several hundred pounds. The apprentice, Benjamin Lockwood, had built up large debts with many local traders, in particular James Rusher, a wool merchant from Wakefield. The young man had wanted to save the money to go to America but instead almost ruined Wroe's business, as Wroe and his wife's family ended up paying bills plus legal expenses that together amounted to a sum in excess of £500.

To add to his woes, one night, at the time of Bradford's winter fair, the hapless young Wroe was attacked by two men at Adwalton who robbed him of 18 guineas. Although the men were convicted and found guilty of the robbery Wroe never recovered the money, and the circumstances of the crime caused him a great amount of trouble and expense.

Wroe's brother Joseph had married Mary Firth, and at about this time John let his brother and his brother-in-law Peter have goods and money to the value of £70 on loan. This was never returned, and such was Wroe's anger towards his brother that in the winter of 1817 he procured a pistol, determined to kill Joseph.[8] Wroe set off for his brother's house, carrying a piece of paper with words he had transcribed from Psalm 55 written on it:

For it was not an enemy that reproached me, then I could have borne it; neither was it he that hated me that did magnify himself against me, then I would have hid myself from him. But it was thou, a man, mine equal, my guide, and mine acquaintance. The words of his mouth were smoother than butter, but war was in his heart; his words were softer than oil, yet were they drawn swords.

The intention was to push the piece of paper under Joseph's front door, give him time to read it and then shoot at him through the window. On the way to his brother's house, however, Wroe relented and decided not to carry out his plan.

Bradford parish registers show that John Wroe married Mary Appleby at the parish church on 22 April 1816. She was the daughter of Benjamin Appleby of Farnley Mills, Leeds. Farnley is the next village to Tong in an easterly direction. The couple remained married until Mrs Wroe's death over thirty-seven years later. They had at least seven children although three died in infancy. Of the other four, Joseph, Susanna and Sarai survived their father.

So far there was little, if anything, in this somewhat mundane life to suggest that Wroe was destined for a strange career of fame and notoriety, but everything would change, dramatically so, following Wroe's long illness. In the autumn of 1819 Wroe became sick with fever, which over a few weeks had 'reduced him to a mere skeleton'. Wroe was visited by two doctors, Dr Blake of Bradford and Dr Field of Tong Street. Death was surely close at hand, a grim prognosis confirmed when Dr Blake advised Mrs Wroe to make the necessary final arrangements. Wroe's thoughts turned to his spiritual requirements. Interestingly, he requested that his wife should call for Methodist ministers to come and pray with him at his deathbed, but they refused. Mrs Wroe suggested calling for the local vicar, but Wroe thought by that time that it was too late and asked his wife to read him a couple of chapters from the Bible as a means of comfort.

To everyone's surprise Wroe actually recovered from his grave illness. While he convalesced he was often to be found by the roadside between Tong Street and Tong, a Bible in his hand, sitting under hedges, asking passers-by to help him read out certain passages. Soon, however, illness returned, and John Wroe started to encounter visions he believed were of heavenly origin. The first occurred when he was wandering in the fields near his home. As he later wrote in *Divine Communications*, 'I saw a vision with my eyes open; a woman came unto me who tossed me up and down in the field.' He realised it was a vision, as he 'strove to get hold of her, but got hold of nothing'. He therefore knew she was a spirit.[9] Later editions of *Divine Communications* include a bizarre footnote at this point, which states that 'Some part of this history has been published before in pamphlets wherein it is said he got hold of the woman by the breast, which is a misrepresentation of the writers.'

Wroe took to his bed once more and was shortly afterwards struck blind and lost the power of speech, at the same time falling into a trance. He encountered many visions, the first of which took place at about 2 a.m. on 12 November 1819.[10] On regaining consciousness Wroe wrote an account of his vision on a blackboard, which was later transcribed:

The sun and the moon appeared to me, after which there appeared a very large piece of glass, and looking through it I saw a very beautiful place, which I entered into; and I saw numbers of persons who were bearing the cross of Christ; and I saw angels ascending and descending; and there came an angel who was my guide. There then appeared a great altar, and I looked up and beheld, as it were, the Son of God; and looking down, I saw both the Father and the Son, and angels standing on both sides and playing music; and my guide said to me, 'Now thou seest the Father and the Son, and the glory thereof'.

Looking round me, I saw a large number of people, which no man could number; after that the angel, or my guide, said to me, 'Thy prayers have been heard, but not accepted; for thou wert not like Abraham when he offered up his son Isaac for a sacrifice; thou hast withholden thine heart back from the Lord thy God, but now thou art cleansed – Spirit, return to thy rest.' And as sudden as lightning these words struck forcibly upon me: 'Though I walk through the valley of the shadow of death, I fear no evil, as long as thy rod and thy staff abideth with me.'

Throughout the twelve-hour duration of the vision, Wroe was conscious of those around him in the room, around his sickbed. Many shook his hand, fearing he was about to die.

Two days later, at 10 o'clock in the morning he was again struck blind and experienced another vision, lasting this time for seven hours. On this occasion he recalled that he walked down a lane where there were huge numbers of oxen. He was met by his angel guide, who explained that he would tell him the meaning of the beasts. The angel took Wroe into a large place, where he saw a great quantity of books placed on their edges. The books had gilt letters on them which he was not able to read. There then appeared a huge altar full of gilt letters. Wroe begged that he might be able to read the writing and understand what he had seen. There then appeared another book with the word 'Jeremiah' on the top of it, and the letter 'L'. As Wroe was experiencing this vision he wrote the word 'Jeremiah' on the wall with his finger. He attempted to speak, but his tongue was still stuck fast in his mouth, so he was handed a piece of chalk, with which he wrote 'Jeremiah 50th chapter'. In the vision the guide told Wroe that he would explain the meaning of the chapter to him. 'I had never read this chapter, or heard it read, or seen it before, to my recollection; but when I came to myself I could, without looking at it, repeat every word in it, which indeed I did.'[11]

Further visions encountered by Wroe over these two days were surely the most remarkable of his entire religious career, as they point to some of the paraphernalia with which Wroe became obsessed. As well as showing Wroe Christ on the Cross, Moses, Aaron and the twelve Patriarchs, Wroe's angel guide also showed him 'thousands more things' in the vision. These included the throne of God, which appeared in a place 'arched with precious stones, which shone with such lustre that my eyes could scarcely behold it'. Wroe continues, 'my guide showed me the Father and the Son in the midst of it: there then was the sweetest music I ever heard.' Architecture and music were to feature strongly in Wroe's Christian Israelite religion.

Further fits and visions were to follow. About two weeks later, on 29 November, Wroe had another fit, accompanied by visions, which lasted twelve hours. A further, particularly severe episode followed another two weeks later, on 14 December. Wroe was again struck blind, but this time 'remained more like a corpse than a living man for twenty-four hours, when by degrees I came to myself', although he was to remain blind for a further five days, slipping in and out of visionary trances. During these six days Wroe's wife read out the words of a hymn.[12] Once she had finished, he asked her to repeat it, but before she could begin he fainted again, experiencing the following remarkable vision:

I saw the elements part, and there appeared a large open square, and I saw our Saviour nailed upon the cross, and the tears trickling down his face; and at that time I thought he was weeping for the wicked people upon the earth; there then appeared an angel holding a man by a single hair of his head, and he had a very large sword in his hand, and he waved it backwards and forwards; I then saw large scales let down to the earth, and I saw a large bundle put into one end of the scales, I thought that bundle was the sins of the people; and I saw a very large quantity of weights put into the other end, and they put the beam to a balance, and the bundle was so much heavier that the weights bounced out; the scales were then drawn up into heaven. I then saw the man which was holden by the hair of his head by the angel, and he brandished his sword six or seven times as before, then they disappeared. I afterwards saw Moses and Aaron, and a large number of people with them, accompanied by a number of angels; and I heard such delightful music which is impossible for me to relate.

Wroe's mammoth six days of blindness ended somewhat abruptly when, to the astonishment of those present, his father arrived at the house and placed his right thumb on his son's right eye and the fourth finger of his left hand on his left eye. As soon as Wroe received his sight back, those present wanted to know if he really could see. He took the Bible and read out a chapter to prove that he could. The sight in one eye was fully restored, but the sight in the other was poor, owing, he thought, to someone having tried to force that eye open three days before. The visit of Mr Wroe had not been unexpected by his son, as during his vision an angel spoke to him saying that his father would come to him and restore his sight. This was to remind Wroe Senior of his 'former sins and wickedness' against his son. Some thought this was miraculous, the result of a prophecy. Others were more sceptical, including Baring-Gould, who cites Wroe's cousin Joseph, saying that Mr Wroe was carrying out his son's wishes.[13] Was this Wroe's attempt at getting his own back on his tyrannical father, by forcing him to perform this strange action at his son's bidding? Was his hatred of his father a major motivating influence behind his religious career?

Local spectators of the six days of blindness included Samuel Muff and the aforementioned Joseph Wroe. Muff, from White Lane, Wibsey-Bankfoot, was later a follower of Wroe. His account of the visions is as follows:[14]

In the course of the time that John Wroe was in this trance, reports of it came several times to my house, and that he was not

9

unlikely to die; I went to see him and he came to himself while I was in the house, but could see nothing; hearing me speak, he made known to me several things which I cannot at present recollect, but I recollect him saying that he was blind, but that he should see afterwards. It was made known to him that he should be six days blind, so should the nation be six years blind; but as his eyes were opened at the end of the six days, so should the eyes of the nation be opened at the end of six years. In the course of his six days' blindness he wrote me a few lines, desiring me to come at the time his eyes were to be opened – at the end of the six days, and sent it by one of my neighbours, who said he saw him write it; and blind as he was, it was the best piece of writing of his that I ever saw in my life.

Baring-Gould believed that several of the trance incidents involving Wroe were fakes. In his *Yorkshire Oddities*, which was published over a decade after Wroe's death, he relates an account of a trance which supposedly lasted ten or twelve days. Wroe lay at home on his bed, and his wife received visitors into the room, provided they placed some money in a basket at the foot of the bed. Neighbours grew suspicious, and one young man had an opportunity to look inside the house unhindered when Mrs Wroe went out and foolishly forgot to lock the door behind her. To the neighbour's surprise, Wroe was not in a trance at all, but sitting up eating beefsteak, pickled cabbage and oatcake. Baring-Gould was keen to point out this man's name, J. Holt, and to say he was still living in Bradford when the first edition of *Yorkshire Oddities* was published.[15] The following day Wroe was to be found again on his bed, deep in his trance. One visitor wanted to press a needle under Wroe's fingernail, to see whether he really was unconscious, but Mrs Wroe would not allow it.

The early years of Wroe's marriage and the start of Wroe's vivid religious experiences coincided with the aftermath of the Napoleonic Wars and a wave of uncertainty and unrest in England. The peace had brought uncertainty to farming and a decline in the local domestic wool-combing industry. Wroe's business skills had proved somewhat precarious before the economic downturn, so his gradual move to prophecy from more conventional means of earning a living proved lucrative. Not only did it at least offer the opportunity for him to escape harsh economic conditions, it also at last enabled him to free himself from the overbearing influence of his autocratic father.

Doubtless the prophecies spread rapidly around Bradford, and Wroe's notoriety was soon carried further afield. The coverage of these early days of religious conversion in *Divine Communications* implies that his rise to prominence was almost spontaneous, happening purely according to chance circumstances. Yet there is evidence that it was very cleverly manufactured by Wroe, even at this early stage. As well as a charge to visitors, Wroe had his early visions published in pamphlets, from as early as 1820, with the title of *Vision of an Angel*. By the mid-1820s such published prophecies, and also the sale of books, would have seemed profitable when set against the collapse of the local wool-combing industry.

Wroe's cousin Joseph spoke about the commencement of Wroe's religious career, recalling a conversation he had had with him in the street in Bradford. 'I hear thou hast begun preaching,' said Joseph. 'Well, I do not know much about preaching, but I have begun talking, and people may call it what they please,' was Wroe's reply. On the following Sunday Joseph went to Wroe's house and accompanied him to the home of a near neighbour, Abraham Holmes, the first of Wroe's scribes, who recorded his early visions.[16]

On 26 December 1819, Wroe gave an explanation of the 'six years' revealed to him when he had been struck blind for six days. Each year represented a thousand years, denoting the glorious time that was to come. The six days of blindness alluded to three years of plenty followed by three years of scarcity. He said, 'the first three years from that date would be plenty, but particularly the third year, for in Bradford, and at all other places, the best beef would be sold for 4*d* per pound; and all other things would be equally cheap.'[17] A footnote points out the more prosperous years of the early 1820s and the cruel years of 1823–5, the latter period being particularly harsh for the wool-combers of Bradford.

On the same day as Wroe's explanation of the 'six years', William Muff of Little Horton wrote a letter to Joseph Wroe of Bowling and John Tillotson of Great Horton, which in effect was Wroe's first prophecy.[18] It spoke of massive advancements in transportation, including ships without sails travelling against the wind, carriages in the high road without horses and horseless ploughs.

On the night of 27 December Wroe prayed for guidance towards a church or religious sect which he should support. He awoke in the early hours of the following morning to see a board at the foot of his bed, on which the words 'A.A. Rabbi, Rabbi, Rabbi' appeared in gilt letters.[19] At first he thought that Rabbi was the name of a place, but eventually concluded that it was a sign to go and testify to the Jews. Still later he decided to testify to the Jews in England for three years and after that time to join the Jews.

Wroe was next struck blind on 1 February 1820. The bout lasted for seven hours, but this time Mrs Wroe must have been sceptical of her husband's illness, as she sent for one of the neighbours, George Hill, to cut his hair and shave his head, though to no avail. Again Wroe was in a trance as if dead, having 'no more use of my limbs at that time than a dead man'. He encountered many visions during the seven-hour period and again the same angel acted as his guide. Among the things he was shown were three trees which grew blossoms that ripened into all manner of fruits. Three new trees sprung up and grew beside them. These blossomed too, but the blossoms withered, the bark of the trees peeled off and they were plucked up by the roots. Wroe's angel guide explained the meaning of this vision, in that the trees that died represented the wicked who shall be taken from the face of the earth, whereas the three that bore fruit represented the righteous 'which shall remain and inherit the earth'.[20]

Acting on his decision to testify to the Jews, Wroe left home on 20 June 1820 to travel to Liverpool via Huddersfield. This was the first leg of his many travels. He particularly wanted to visit the synagogue at Liverpool because he had seen it transfigured before him in a vision 'both inside and out'. The synagogue at Seal Street was a well-known landmark and Tobias Goodman was the first Jewish preacher to preach in English.[21] Wroe may well have seen this building when he visited Liverpool on business at the request of his father.

Wroe left Bradford on his journey with no money and 'without anything but what covered my nakedness'.[22] He walked to Huddersfield, where he was given money by three Methodist preachers, before walking on to Manchester, where he lodged in a house. His reputation had gone before him, as when the landlord, a Mr Morrison, heard he came from Bradford he asked if he knew John Wroe. 'What sort of man is he?' asked Morrison. 'Some men give him a very indifferent character, but time proveth all things', Wroe replied cautiously. Morrison looked at Wroe and asked him if he was the man they had been talking about. When Wroe confirmed his suspicions, Morrison let him stay at the house free of charge and told him visions he had himself encountered.

In the evening Wroe visited a watchmaker's shop at Shude Hill, where he met two Jewish men. He informed them that the God of Israel had told him to travel for three years and to tell the Jewish people that 'He [God] would set his hand the second time to the covenant which He made with Abraham, and He would cause those which were joined amongst the Gentiles to come and join them'. The men scoffed at what Wroe had to say, adding that they could arrange for Wroe to be circumcised. He told them of seeing the Liverpool Synagogue transfigured before him and stressed that he had never seen the place before.

One of the Jews gave Wroe a shilling and Mr Morrison gave him five shillings before Wroe left Manchester by boat for Runcorn on his way to Liverpool. On the journey Wroe stood up in the middle of the boat and declared the words which the Lord had given him, 'and many of the people marvelled'. At Liverpool Wroe stayed with the Jews for four days, but on the Saturday night he argued with the rabbi in the synagogue, claiming that the man had deceived him. Wroe returned home.

Just two months later Wroe received another vision at home. This time it came in the form of a great rushing of wind with a voice which called out, 'Go thou to the Jews at London, and declare my words which I shall give thee.'[23] A few days later Wroe leaped off a fence and fell into a beck near his home, where he encountered another vision. The House of Lords appeared before him and he saw Queen Caroline (the wife of George IV), who was being tried. People were going backwards and forwards carrying letters and reading them out.

Wroe left for London via Manchester, where the Jews paid his coach fare to the capital. He arrived at the famous old coaching inn *The Swan with Two Necks* in Lad Lane. He alighted and told some men he met there that he was going to meet the Queen. They laughed at him, saying he was being ridiculous. The next day, however, Wroe went to parliament and on hearing that the Queen was in the Lords, being tried for adultery, he waited outside for most of the day in heavy rain for her to leave. The Queen left parliament at about 4 o'clock in the afternoon and went to her residence, the house of Lady Anne Hamilton.[24] Wroe described what happened next:

> On each side of the steps leading into Lady Anne Hamilton's house were Bow Street officers, and the people pressed hard, and the officers struck at them with their staves: the Queen put her head out of the window of her carriage, and reproved the officers several times, then they let the people do as they would, and they made way for her. When she got up the steps she turned herself about to make obeisance to the persons who had attended her, and the people gave a great shout.

It was a further two days before Wroe was able to deliver his message to the Queen. On 30 August 1820, the daring Wroe followed the Queen up the steps into Lady Hamilton's house. 'I have a message unto thee, O Queen.' 'Unto me?' replied the Queen, clearly startled as she threw back her veil. Wroe merely said 'Aye,' and handed her his message and a copy of each of his books of visions. As Wroe handed her the books, the Queen 'turned as pale as a whited wall, and trembled like an aspen leaf'. On his way out one of the guards tried to seize Wroe, but missed, and he slipped away into the crowd.

At this time, Wroe's fame was spreading rapidly because of some of the predictions he had made. One such prophecy, dating from the spring of 1820, was the hasty demise of his own brother-in-law, Joseph Appleby of Farnley Mills. Wroe was 'commanded' to tell his wife Mary to tell her brother about it. She went to his home, where she found him ill in bed. Her mother was there and when she heard why Mary had come she would not let her see Joseph, as it would be sure to frighten him. Joseph recovered, but some time later (*Divine Communications* does not give a specific date), when he was at the Bramley feast, Joseph was mocked about his brother-in-law and his prediction, his taunters calling Wroe a false prophet. That evening Joseph was taken ill at dinner and rushed home, but he died the same night. It is impossible to determine the accuracy of this story from the first quarter of the nineteenth century. Farnley burial records within the parish of Leeds record the burial of a Joseph Appleby on 27 July 1820, aged 45.[25] He seems to be the likely candidate.

A similar incident occurred in the winter of the following year. At the time Wroe was working as a wool-comber for his cousin, another John Wroe of Bradford. Wroe got into an argument with his nephew William, who had kept him waiting and refused to accept any more of his work, saying that he was 'fitter to preach for his living than to work for it'. William refused to pay Wroe his wages until he had gone home to collect his combs. Wroe returned on the Monday and the two continued to argue. During the altercation Wroe had a fit and fell against a bale of wool. He encountered an instant vision, which he imparted to the people in the warehouse: 'Take notice of this young man, he will never either take any more work in, or pay any more wages.' According to *Divine Communications*, the man became ill shortly afterwards and was dead within nine months.[26] The foreman, who had also insulted Wroe, also died within a year.

Even if Wroe received some form of satisfaction from the fulfilment of these macabre prophecies, the harsh economic realities of the declining domestic system of wool-combing were clearly beginning to bite. He had therefore increasingly to turn to his other means of conventional income, namely his farm. If *Divine Communications* is to be believed, he was assisted by a minor miracle. In 1821 his corn crop was destroyed by strong winds, but during the following year each stalk of his corn produced three ears – a threefold crop from the same kind of seed that had been sown by Wroe and his father for years. This episode is reminiscent of Pharaoh's dream in Genesis 41: 22–23, interpreted by Joseph, in which there were a more generous seven ears of corn per stalk. Several people took ears of Wroe's corn and planted the grain, curious as to whether it would produce such high yields again, but it only came up with one ear per stalk. Such were the profits arising from Wroe's crop of corn that he was able to pay off all his debts, allowing him to devote more time to his strange spiritual gifts.

In June 1820, on the day that he had originally intended to set off for Liverpool, Wroe was taken ill, struck blind yet again, encountering a vision in which it was made known to him that the followers of Joanna Southcott, who believed her to be the woman spoken of in Revelation 12, were correct. He saw an image of 'the woman transfigured before me with the child in her left arm, in the open firmament in the day time', he explained, 'and I saw this sight as plainly as ever I saw anything in my life'.[27] Wroe did not approach the Southcottians, however, as he still thought it was the Jews whom he was supposed to join.

George Turner, the Leeds businessman who had taken on the leadership of a large proportion of the Southcottians after Southcott's death, visited Bradford on 8 August 1820. Wroe had an interview with Turner, informing him that, whereas Turner had been sent exclusively to the elect of the Southcottians, Wroe's visions were not for the believers but for the world. *Divine Communications* recounts how George Turner left the room, but 'afterwards returned and shook hands with John in a friendly manner'. Turner had predicted the date of the appearance of Shiloh on Earth on 14 October of that year. The announcement was too great an invitation to Wroe, who shrewdly decided to turn it to his advancement, in the knowledge that some of Turner's wild prophecies had previously proved to be dismal flops.

# 2

# *The Southcottians*

Before Wroe's audacious rise to the leadership of many of the Southcottians is outlined, and his subsequent founding of the Society of Christian Israelites, it is worth explaining why this form of millennial religion was popular during the late eighteenth and early nineteenth centuries, and how the farmer's son from Bowling, Bradford fits into this unusual chronicle, which is now little more than a footnote in the history of Christianity in England. The shock waves emanating from the loss of the American colonies and especially the French Revolution were the main reason for the revival of popular millennial religion.[1] Superstitious populations fearful of rapid change in society looked to the Bible for possible explanations for the overturning of what had been the established order.[2] It was thought that prophecies within the books of Daniel in the Old Testament and Revelation in the New were starting to be fulfilled. One element believed to be of particular importance was the fate of the Jews.

The story of this particular succession of millennial leaders begins with Richard Brothers, who focused on the Israelite aspect of the faith. Brothers, a Royal Navy Lieutenant retired on half pension, thought that as many as ten of the twelve lost tribes of Ancient Israel could be found among British families. He believed that these 'Jews' would return to the Holy Land and that the New Jerusalem would be established in the Old Jerusalem. Brothers meticulously planned the Holy City to have 320 streets, 56 squares, 16 markets, 47 palaces, 20 colleges and 4 temples.

Born at Placentia, Newfoundland on 25 December 1757, he joined the navy when he came to England in 1771. In 1782, Brothers took part in the Battle of the Saintes in the Caribbean under Admiral

Rodney. In the only information about his early career that he provides in his books, Brothers mentions how he was narrowly missed by a cannonball which killed the young man by his side. After his retirement from the navy Brothers lived a solitary life in London on his comfortable pension of £54 p.a. In 1789 he refused to draw this money and soon got into debt. Brothers was unwilling to swear an oath that half-pay officers were supposed to repeat every six months, namely that during the same period he had not held any other employment under the Crown. Brothers objected both to swearing an oath and to the fact that the oath was supposedly voluntary, at least in its wording. Arrears on his landlady's rent led him to the workhouse in 1791, as he was £33 in debt. Brothers's landlady, a Mrs Green, noted his strange behaviour. He would lie on his bed praying for several days, drank nothing but tea, milk and water and ate very little meat. He had also cut off his hair and broken his naval sword, saying that he could no longer draw the weapon against his brother.

The Guardians managed to persuade the Admiralty to release the back-pay belonging to Brothers, and the former Lieutenant was released in early 1792. During his incarceration Brothers spent most of his time writing, work which eventually would form part of his first book, *A Revealed Knowledge of the Prophecies and Times, Wrote under the direction of the Lord God and published by His sacred command*, published in 1794.

It might seem astounding that Brothers's book proved to be a massive hit, though it must be remembered that this was a period of intense political excitement. The book was reprinted, and during the following year Brothers's pamphlets circulated widely throughout Britain. Brothers gained some support from industrialists such as Peter Morrison, a cotton printer from Liverpool, and George Turner, a merchant from Leeds. He also drew a smattering of support from the Establishment, including three clergymen in the Church of England, (the Revds T. Foley, S. Bruce and T. Webster), and one member of the House of Commons, Nathaniel Halhead, the MP for Lymington. Some of these individuals later transferred their allegiance to Joanna Southcott.

Brothers considered himself to be the 'Prince' of the lost tribes, a descendant of King David, and indeed went as far as styling himself the 'Nephew of the Almighty'. As well as obsessively town-planning for the New Jerusalem, he made painstaking calculations to ascertain the number of years that the world had existed since the Creation. According to Brothers's sums, the Earth would be 5,914 years old in 1795, the very year in which on 4 June, the date of the King's official birthday, London would be destroyed. Brothers was no longer a free man by the time of this supposedly fateful date. His frantic publishing of pamphlets had continued apace and, in a book he published in March, he demanded that the King gave up his crown to him. Such revolutionary sentiment was too much for the authorities to stomach. He was arrested and confined to a lunatic asylum, in which he remained for eleven years. Although a seemingly harmless eccentric, Brothers had spoken out against the war with France. The government, unable to comprehend Brothers's growing popularity, feared that revolutionaries were using him as a cat's paw.[3]

By the time of his release, Brothers had been almost forgotten. The failure of his prophecies had left him discredited among the faithful, not least because he had saddled himself with too short a period of time in which the predicted events should come to pass. For instance, on 19 November 1795, he should have been crowned in Jerusalem.

Richard Brothers died in 1824 and is buried at St John's Wood in London, in the same cemetery where Joanna Southcott had been laid to rest ten years earlier. His influence spread almost entirely through his writings, in particular the notion that most the lost tribes of Israel were to be found in Britain, a theory that was later taken up by George Turner, John Wroe and James Jezreel. But Brothers was not the only receiver of visions, in this period of turbulent change and uncertainty within Britain, he was overtaken by the best known of this strange succession of millennial leaders, Joanna Southcott.[4]

Southcott was born at Ottery St Mary in Devon in 1750. The daughter of an unsuccessful farmer, she led a somewhat sheltered existence, spending most of her working life as a domestic servant.

At the age of 42 she started to receive what she considered to be divine communications, which she wrote down in doggerel verse. As with Brothers, events on the other side of the Channel featured strongly in Southcott's writings. Led by a voice and by visions, Joanna became convinced that the Second Coming was imminent.

In 1801, Joanna published *The Strange Effects of Faith*. Again, as with Brothers a few years earlier, the publication of such a book of her experiences and prophecies catapulted her to fame. A delegation of seven readers visited her in Exeter. These included the Revds Stanhope Bruce, Thomas Foley and Thomas Webster, the engraver William Sharp, as well as Peter Morrison, George Turner and John Wilson, most of whom had been followers of Richard Brothers. One of the seven returned to London with several of Joanna's prophecies, and placed them in a box. It is this box for which Joanna Southcott is still best known today. For many years during the mid-twentieth century Southcott's believers in the Panacea Society demanded its opening in the presence of twenty-four Church of England bishops.

From 1794, Joanna began to seal sets of her prophecies, making sure they were securely stored. For this she used a seal she had found while sweeping the floor of a shop belonging to her employers, a Mr and Mrs Taylor. The seal bore the initials 'I.C.' and two stars. From 1802, Southcott also began the sealing of believers, as the Book of Revelation also makes reference to sealed people as well as sealed writings. Each believer received a square piece of paper on which was drawn a circle containing the inscription: 'The Sealed of the Lord the Elect and Precious, Man's Redemption to Inherit the Tree of Life, to be made Heirs of God and Joint Heirs with Jesus Christ.' The paper was signed by the believer and then sealed. It was intended to seal 144,000 each, an interpretation of Revelation 7: 4.

As Joanna's fame grew, she undertook what were known as three trials. These were public examinations of her prophecies taking place between 1801 and 1804. Each trial lasted for seven days and was intended as an inquiry into her claims. None of the invited clergy attended.

From 1804, Southcott spent ten peaceful years in the seclusion of a house at Blockley in the Cotswolds. Here, in the company of her two most faithful companions, Miss Jane Townley and her maid Ann Underwood, she continued her most prodigious output of books of prophecies. A total of sixty-five books were published during her lifetime and the remaining unpublished manuscripts would fill many more volumes.

The final and most remarkable stage of Southcott's life took place in 1814. The 64-year-old virgin announced that she was to give birth to Shiloh, 'by the power of the Most High'. Shiloh was the 'third representative of Divinity', so named because of an obscure reference in Genesis. In what was the standard history on this sequence of millennial religious leaders,[5] a Church of England clergyman, the Revd G.R. Balleine, explained what he called 'The Shiloh Myth'. He pointed out that Southcott's belief in the coming of Shiloh was based on Genesis 49: 10, which reads, 'The sceptre shall not depart from Judah, nor a lawgiver from between his feet, until Shiloh come; and unto him shall the gathering of the people be.' The misunderstanding, according to Balleine, came about because there are many references in the Bible to Shiloh, a town in Central Palestine. This reference in Genesis is the only suggestion that Shiloh is a person. Balleine looked to the original Hebrew for an answer and concluded that it was so obscure as to be 'almost untranslatable'. Followers of Southcott reject this hypothesis.

Joanna moved to London in preparation for the great event. She faced ridicule in the press, but, of the twenty-one doctors who examined her, seventeen announced that she was pregnant. These included a Dr Richard Reece, a most eminent doctor, whose *Medical Guide* was a standard text. The predicted time of Shiloh's birth came – and went. By December it was clear that Joanna was very ill and death was surely not far away. She died on 27 December 1814. In accordance with her strict instructions, her body was kept warm for four days after her death, before the *post-mortem* examination could commence. It was conducted by Reece in the presence of fourteen other doctors. There was nothing to suggest Joanna had been pregnant. The seeming non-appearance of Shiloh did not present a problem to many of Southcott's followers. Joanna was regarded as being mentioned in Revelation 12 as 'the woman clothed with the sun', and it was thought that her child had been 'caught up unto God' (Revelation 12: 5), snatched back up to heaven to save it from the dragon.

Joanna Southcott was buried at St John's Wood cemetery on 1 January 1815, the start of what was to be a landmark year in European history. Despite her spectacular failure, this chapter of millennial religion was far from closed. The sect continued to draw an audience, many of whom were still anxiously anticipating the arrival of Shiloh. Just as in the 1790s Richard Brothers had risen to prominence during a decade of intense political excitement, the ideas expounded by the Southcottians remained fresh in the latter part of the 1810s, as society endured an uneasy period of social and economic change. Despite the death of Southcott, the rapid pace of industrialisation was to give millennial religion a new spurt of growth.

Less than six months after Southcott's death, Britain was victorious at the Battle of Waterloo. Although this meant the war in Europe was now at an end, the peace brought renewed vigour to this uneasy period of social unrest which had begun with the Luddite riots of 1811 and culminated in the Peterloo Massacre in 1819. The Establishment was still stunned by the events in France in 1789 and anxious that a similar situation should not occur on this side of the Channel. The emerging working classes were anxious too, about the retention of their jobs, low wages, poor housing conditions, poor working conditions and rising prices. The grim catalogue of contemporary discontent and unrest meant conditions were ripe for attracting followers to millennial sects. Increasing numbers of people were seeking new ideas, both political and theological.

The distress and discontent felt by working people following the end of hostilities with the French was due to three main factors: the after-effects of the Napoleonic Wars, the continuation of industrialisation, and repressive government intervention. Although there had been a short boom following the end of the war, rapid demobilisation threw approximately 300,000 men onto the labour market. This in turn led to the closure of many munitions and other factories, and brought depression to areas such as the ports which had benefited from increased trade during the war. Prices fell, particularly the price of corn, leading to the bankruptcy of many smaller farmers. Bad harvests in the years 1816–19 led to a rise in the price of bread. Producers responded to the slump by laying off workers, cutting wages or 'importing' cheaper labour. Britain's trade was poor, as war-ravaged Europe was unable to buy her goods. In 1816, Britain's overseas trade was two-thirds of the 1814 figure. Unemployment remained widespread until after 1822. This economic distress was accompanied by renewed agitation for reform from both the manufacturers and workers alike.[6] Samuel Bamford stated that 'whilst the laurels were not yet cool on the brows of our victorious soldiers . . . the elements of convulsion were at work amongst the masses of our labouring population'.[7]

The Southcottians (and later the Society of Christian Israelites) had congregations in areas suffering from the consequences of demobilisation after 1815, such as Gravesend and Devonport. They reaped their greatest following, however, in localities undergoing the turmoil of transition from cottage, or domestic, industries to the new factory system. Under the old system men usually working at home operated in scattered industrial villages and hamlets. Although working conditions were often poor, the workers had enjoyed many freedoms and benefits, and various apprentice systems regulated the flow of new labour into the industry, thus ensuring higher wages.[8]

Evidence as to the geographical location of both Southcottian and later, Christian Israelite congregations comes from two main primary sources: registers of Southcottian believers from the late 1810s,[9] and the *Life and Journal of John Wroe*, which was written from 1822 onwards.[10] Taking Yorkshire as an example, some very small locations which feature in John Wroe's career had proportionately large Southcottian congregations. These included the communities of Idle and Idle Thorpe, north of Bradford, and the hamlet of Potovens or Wrenthorpe near Wakefield. The former had benefited from its close proximity to water power in the first wave of industrialisation, but was now in decline. The latter had been the location of a once-prosperous domestic pottery trade which declined rapidly from the 1770s with the opening of new pottery factories at nearby Rothwell and Leeds. The first volume of *Divine Communications* proves the most fruitful source of information. In the early 1820s Wroe, challenging for the leadership of the Southcottians, undertook a visitation, travelling to many of the congregations in Britain.[11] From this information a clear pattern emerges of where the Southcottians enjoyed their greatest support. The sect had a strong following in areas where the traditional cottage, or domestic, industrial workforce declined from the mid-1810s onwards.

It is possible to identify three particular instances of key groups of workers in areas of decline following the peace with France. There are the stocking makers of Nottinghamshire, the wool-combers of Bradford and the cotton-loom weavers of Lancashire. Before the rapid transition to the factory system of manufacture, these workers enjoyed a fairly comfortable status because of their particular skills. Working patterns were also very similar across the different trades, with much of the work taking place in the home.

The hand-frame stocking makers of the East Midlands were the first group to lose out, some years before the end of the wars. The stocking-frame knitting machine had been invented in 1589 by the Revd William Lee.[12] The industry had flourished during the eighteenth century, but was badly in decline by 1810, due to cheaper production methods. Wide frames had been introduced, capable of turning out pieces that could be cut into gloves, socks, stockings and other garments, inferior items that soon flooded the market.[13] Under the domestic system, the merchant hosier rented out frames to the master stockinger, who in turn employed the frame-work knitters to carry out his work. The masters who used the regular stocking frame disliked the invention as much as the men.

At the start of the period of Luddite Riots (1811–17), almost 1,000 frames, valued at over £6,000, were destroyed. The so-called Derbyshire Insurrection took place in 1817, when that county witnessed a desperate outbreak of rioting from unemployed frame-knitters.[14] Three were hanged and eleven transported for life. Similar incidents mainly involving stocking makers occurred in other parts of the Midlands and in Yorkshire. The worst disturbances took place in a triangular area bounded by Nottingham, Derby and Leicester. The dispute arose over frame rents, wages and the number of apprentices employed. The Pentrich Rising of 1817 was the march of armed working men from a remote Derbyshire village, where the domestic system was in decline, to Nottingham. It was brutally suppressed and the ringleaders were hanged.

The traditional hand-frame stocking industry collapsed because of the introduction of new machinery. The domestic handloom weavers lost out not only to new manufacturing techniques, but also because of new working practices.[15] The lapsing of the Apprenticeship Acts and their eventual repeal in 1813–14, flooded the trade with cheap labour. Weaving was a relatively unskilled job and easy for anyone to learn. This cheap labour came into the Lancashire towns from the depressed countryside and from Ireland, with the result that the number of handloom weavers increased from 50,000 in 1769 to 240,000 in 1820.[16]

The job of handloom-weaving was replaced by the power-loom, but the introduction of machinery was slow. The power-loom had been invented by Edmund Cartwright, who patented the device in 1785. By 1806, more than twenty years later, there were perhaps only four in England, and by 1813 there were barely a dozen.[17] However, the process of industrialisation accelerated after the end of the Napoleonic Wars, and in 1817 cotton weavers took to the streets in a desperate attempt to fight for their jobs. In the March of the Blanketeers a group of Lancashire cotton weavers set out to march to London to present a petition to the Prince Regent. The leaders of the march were arrested and the march disbanded before it had left the neighbouring county. The nearby South Lancashire town of Ashton-under-Lyne was a centre of the declining trade, where handloom-weaving still lingered over two decades later.[18]

Of all the groups of domestic workers, the wool-combers were the most privileged; indeed, they have been referred to as the 'aristocracy of the worsted workers'.[19] Like the stocking makers and cotton-loom weavers, the wool-combers also operated as part of a 'putting-out system' that characterised many cottage industries. Their ancient occupation formed one part of the process of worsted manufacture and its practitioners were heavily concentrated in Wroe's home town of Bradford. Wool-combing was highly skilled and usually involved a seven-year apprenticeship. The wool-combers' industrial muscle was expressed at the annual Bishop Blaize parade, St Blaize being the patron saint of wool-combing. Industrialisation came in the form of the wool-combing machine, again invented by Cartwright and patented in 1793. Mass protests against the possible introduction of such machinery took place during the following year, and such was the power of the traditional wool-combers that they managed to get a bill introduced into parliament.[20] The bill was defeated on its second reading, but the introduction of the machinery was slow due to the inferior quality of cloth produced.

The demise of the domestic system and the subsequent futile pattern of disturbances and unrest are important but inevitable characteristics in the evolution of the factory system.[21] 'The boom of domestic industry and proliferation of small-scale individual settlements are of immense importance. Domestic industry was transient because it was a rudimentary phenomenon in the evolution of the factory system.'[22] The government's response to the distress and discontent was typically laissez-faire, but when it did intervene it aggravated the situation. The introduction of the Corn Laws in 1815 outlawed the import of foreign grain until the price of domestically grown wheat had risen to a set price considered profitable enough for farmers and landowners to keep all their labourers in work. This move was disastrous for those who were unemployed or on low income. Although income tax was abolished in 1816, the tax burden was merely shifted from direct to indirect taxation. Tax was now levied on a wide range of popular goods including tea, sugar, tobacco, beer, paper, soap and candles. These regressive taxes hit the poor harshly – a section of society who had previously paid no income tax.[23] Uprisings and disturbances merely presented the government with the opportunity of introducing further repressive measures or enforcing existing legislation, such as the notorious Combination Acts of 1799 and 1800, which had prohibited any trade-union activity. Two pieces of legislation were particularly severe: the 1817 Gagging Acts, which were introduced in the wake of the Spa Field Riots, and the brutal Six Acts, the government's response to Peterloo.

Whatever the motives of the rioters, whether revolutionary or not, there is a consensus of opinion among historians that the actions of the rioters were doomed, that their defeat was inevitable.[24] The lack of success of those involved in the disturbances in either retaining their jobs and improving working and living conditions, or changing the political system, is a significant contributory factor in the rise in popularity of Nonconformist Churches. The failure of popular disturbances gave alternative churches and sects a new fillip, as elements of the emerging working class turned away from popular protest. After 1820 the popular political momentum that had led to Peterloo was no longer maintained.[25] Energy was diverted first into religion – there were Methodist revivals in Lancashire and Cumbria, and in 1823 there were 2,000 conversions in Cornwall in a fortnight[26] – and then into trade unionism, where 'strikes rather than riots [were attempted] to obtain improvements in living standards'.[27] Strike action was more effective in the new factory system, but not a feasible means of protest under the domestic system, where the workforce was widely scattered.[28] The 'old' domestic industries had trade clubs, not trade unions, and were weak.

The popularity of Nonconformist religion among the working class is seen as a sign of their desperation, a phenomenon described as the 'Transforming Power of the Cross'.[29] The confident working class followed radical political movements. The despairing working class – their hopes shattered by the disappearance of their former status – became 'religious' and joined either the Methodists or apocalyptical sects to seek spiritual satisfaction (for example, the success of Primitive Methodism in Nottinghamshire in 1817–18 due to the collapse of the revolutionary hopes of workers in this area).[30] In Bradford, the rapidly expanding textile industry witnessed an emerging class of industrial workers 'facing a new class of distant employers who had few incentives to protect traditional standards and relationships'.[31] Such harsh working and living climates created new working-class communities which at first channelled their energies into 'abortive insurgency' from which millenarian outbursts tended to issue, which 'corresponded chronologically with political radicalism's defeat'.[32] The early twentieth-century American historian Elmer Clark describes this trend rather more succinctly:[33]

> Pre-millenarianism is essentially a 'defence mechanism' of the disinherited; despairing of obtaining substantial blessings through social processes, they turn on the world which has withheld its benefits and look to its destruction in a cosmic cataclysm which will exalt them and cast down the rich and powerful.

Writing in the 1840s, over a century before the phenomenon was analysed by E.P. Thompson in *The Making of the English Working Class*, James Smith, a former Scottish Presbyterian minister and contemporary of Wroe, pinpointed the decline of the domestic industrial system as a major contributing factor in the rise of the Christian Israelites. Smith worked with the Christian Israelites in the late 1820s as a teacher of Hebrew and was an important figure within the Society of Christian Israelites prior to 1831. He later wrote a book, *The Coming Man*, which was published posthumously some twenty years after his death in 1857. Most of the book takes the form of a novel which features characters including Wroe – 'John the Jew'. Chapter 31, however, is explanatory in nature and postulates the economic factors behind the rise of the Christian Israelites. In his proficient analysis Smith talks of a population 'collected in masses', who were 'acquiring a new species of intelligence, a taste for political discussion'.[34] He argues that Wroe 'belonged to the old domestic industry', and continues:[35]

> But a new system had arisen within the memory of man, a system which might be called the social system, under which all the manufacturing labour was conducted in large factories by hundreds and thousands of males and females, adults and children away from home and apart from all its domestic endearments. The one system was apparently subduing the other, and as the

change progressed the character of the population was undergoing an evident and corresponding revolution.

As well as being places of acute deprivation during the demise of the domestic system, Ashton and Bradford were also typical areas of intense industrialisation. The new industrial towns, although booming, contained unpleasant living and working conditions. Here workers endured long hours at the factory, forgoing many freedoms they had taken for granted in the countryside or under the domestic system. Wages fell as cheap labour came in from the rural areas, resulting in even more overcrowding and the spread of disease. The dangerous conditions of the new industrial areas were a major theme of the nineteenth century. This phase of industrialisation, driven by harsh market forces, resulted in class formation, as there was now a sharp distinction between the labouring classes and the industrial middle classes. It also produced new working-class cultural and political movements, such as the Chartists, the trade unions and ultimately the Independent Labour Party.

This process of class formation involved the transfer of control over the manufacturing process from the worker to the employer.[36] The once economically powerful craft and artisan workers of the early stages of English industrialisation were crushed; yet Christian Israelites were amongst those bringing about this socio-economic change. The industrial interests of the Lees family at Ashton-under-Lyne, for example, included the ownership of power-looms, which helped to oust the domestic handloom weavers.[37] This incongruity is further compounded when the doctrines of Christian Israelites are examined, in particular with regard to the wool-combers' dispute. At a meeting in Bradford on Sunday 18 October 1824, Wroe described the strike as 'evil', stating that 'they would not gain their end, but the masters would surely overcome them'.[38] Although the following day he privately condemned the employers as well, Wroe's insensitivity towards the displaced domestic workforce would appear to be counterproductive.

\* \* \*

Following the death of Joanna Southcott, the Southcottians experienced their first major schism, as a result of pronouncements expounded by George Turner. The Leeds businessman had attended Joanna's 'trial' in 1804, along with such followers as the Revd T.P. Foley, the Anglican clergyman, and the engraver William Sharp. He had also acted as her host whenever she visited Yorkshire and had hoped to become her husband. Turner was so disturbed at the sudden death of Joanna and the non-appearance of Shiloh that he had began to experience visions. Southcott appeared before him and accused Miss Townley of disobeying her will. Townley refused to accept that Turner had inherited the mantle of prophecy and as a result of this argument many of the provincial congregations in the north split away from the Southcottians in London and the rural south.[39] The Turnerites were concentrated in rapidly expanding industrial locations in Yorkshire and South Lancashire as well as in the South-West.

The Southcottians fragmented still further, taking some very strange turns. At Staverton in Devon, Mary Boon, a peasant woman with one eye and a cleft lip, declared that she heard the voice of Joanna. Boon was illiterate and her communications were written down by John Field, the village stonemason.[40] In the capital Samuel Charles Woodward Sibley formed a congregation known as the Household of Faith. He took the more conventional view of Joanna's pregnancy that Shiloh had been caught up to God, but the coming of Shiloh was nonetheless imminent. Sibley's chapel in Smithfield attracted an attendance of 500 in the mid-1820s.[41] Alexander Lindsay led another faction and opened a chapel in Southwark in 1825. Significantly, he converted William Tozer, the high-ranking follower of Joanna, and many of his faithful at his Duke Street Chapel transferred their allegiance. Another group was led by 'Zebulon', or Joseph Allman, who divided his followers into twelve tribes. None of these individuals was recognised by Jane Townley, Miss Underwood, Mr Foley or William Sharp. The only person that the Southcottians did recognise was the little-known William Shaw. He prophesied between the year 1819 and his death in 1822, yet as his communications were only circulated in manuscript, little can now be ascertained about his character.

Despite his close association with Southcott, Turner's wild prophecies were more akin to those of Richard Brothers. He predicted that the earthquake foretold in Revelation 6: 12 would occur on 28 January 1817. The stars would fall and the sun turn black and all who had mocked him would perish. He granted salaries of £20,000 per annum to himself and his close friends and uttered the most peculiar declaration about what would shortly come to pass. There were to be no rents, no postal costs, no turnpikes, in fact no taxes at all.[42] On the evening of 27 January men in London threw all their money out of windows, believing it would soon be worthless. During the following day the carriage bearing the Prince Regent to the State Opening of Parliament was struck by a projectile that passed through one of the carriage windows. This event overshadowed any demonstration which Turner and his supporters may have carried out in London during that day. Daily life continued unchanged.

Shortly after the fracas in London, Turner was placed in the Retreat, the famous Quaker asylum in York, where he remained for two years. The parallel with Brothers is obvious: revolutionary ideas at a time of social unrest, meticulous planning and a stretch in an asylum. While at York, Turner set about planning for the appearance of Shiloh on Earth. His palace in Jerusalem was to have walls of pure gold decorated with precious stones, similar to visions experienced by Wroe late in 1819. There were to be 70,000 male musicians and 70,000 women singers. Turner was to have 300,000 servants, modest compared with Shiloh, who was to have half a million servants. He was also most interested in Brothers's notion that ten of the lost tribes of Israel were to be found amongst the British population. His hopes of accumulating the tribes in time for Shiloh's appearance were dashed, however, when the woman who claimed to be able to distinguish which tribe an individual belonged to left the Turnerites for a rival sect.

Had Turner not been released from the asylum in 1820, he would probably have died an old man, largely forgotten. Although the doctors had certified him cured, their judgement was surely soon questioned because of the most extraordinary behaviour he exhibited on his release. Turner called for the most preposterous marriage ceremonies to be enacted. It was revealed to Turner that he was to carry out 'spiritual marriages' to the women of the faithful. During the ridiculous proceedings, each woman stated that she desired 'to be married to the Lord'. She then gave Turner a kiss, to show that she accepted the Lord had now 'healed her of the Fall'. Turner kissed her in return to show that the Lord had accepted her. He then placed his hands on her knee, which meant she was now to bow to the Lord's commands. Over five weeks Turner travelled 2,500 miles and the ceremony was enacted 1,556 times. The pathetic yearnings of an elderly man were no doubt satisfied. At the end of his tour, on 30 August, Turner threw a huge marriage supper at Westminster. It was shortly after this event that Turner announced that on 14 October, Shiloh would at last make his appearance.

3

# The Rise to Leadership

George Turner's announcement that Shiloh would make his appearance on Earth on 14 October 1820 was exactly the sort of opportunity Wroe needed to further his own career. As he returned home from his August meeting with Turner, it was 'revealed' to him that George Turner 'was not the man that would lead the people till the kingdom was established, for he would die before the time and that the believers had made more of him than they ought to have done'.[1] He told this to his cousin, Joseph Wroe of Little Horton, and decided to pass on the communication to the Bradford believers, who were keenly looking forward to Shiloh's arrival. Wroe was becoming convinced it was the Southcottians, and not the Jews, that he was supposed to join. At a meeting of the Bradford Southcottians on a Wednesday evening in September, Wroe was given permission to speak to the congregation.[2] He spoke shrewdly:

> Friends, you are looking for great things, and you are looking for Shiloh to appear and be amongst you on such a day, but I will tell you he will not appear at that time, and many of the believers will fall off . . . not that I am doubting George Turner's visitation, and as a testimony of it I'll give my name amongst you.

The fourteenth of October arrived. According to the 'Voice' which Turner had heard, Shiloh would appear in London, as a boy aged 6, who would be 'tall for his age'. His disciples gathered on the evening of the 13th in keen anticipation of the great event. No one knew at what time of day he would make his appearance, but as the hours

33

ticked by the believers gathered in the hall that Turner had hired grew steadily more anxious. The place was packed: the entire complement of Southcottian believers from Chatham and Maidstone had come up to London.[3] As the clock struck the third stroke of twelve there were audible moans of disappointment as the credulous followers of Turner realised that nothing had happened. The coach that had been ordered to take Shiloh throughout England was cancelled.

Despite the bitter disillusionment of 14 October, the credulous continued to believe in Turner, stating that 'God has disappointed us to test our love for Him'.[4] Much heartened, Turner had another go. Fresh hopes of Shiloh's imminent arrival were raised when Turner predicted that the boy would appear once the winter was over. This time Turner's followers prepared a large house, employing servants and even providing clothes, in case Shiloh should arrive naked. Money and gifts poured in; it was as if they had not done enough to anticipate such an important arrival the previous October. Turner's confidence grew, as one of his pronouncements was that the Lord had commanded him 'to marry a common strumpet', which he did. Then the 'Voice' came up with a new and definite date for the arrival of Shiloh, 10 April 1821. This time, however, it was Turner himself who was to prove the most disappointed by Shiloh's non-appearance. Deeply shaken, he took to his bed and refused to be comforted. He died in September of that year.

In the following year, on 14 August 1822, the final call to Wroe to go to the Jews was received in the strangest of circumstances.[5] He was sitting at home with three men who were not believers when he heard a voice, which cried out, 'Go! Go! Go to my people Israel, and speak the words that I command thee to deliver unto them.' The strangeness of this oral manifestation is that it came from out of the bar of the second fire grate. The voice continued to speak for about a quarter of an hour before turning into heavenly music, 'which seemed so loud that it might be heard a great distance from the house'. The men were alarmed, as they heard the voice too. *Divine Communications* records their names as John Hill, Robert Fox and Samuel Binns, and describes how it thundered so loudly that 'the groundwork of the house, and even the very glasses in the cupboard, shook'.

Wroe asked the men from where they thought the voice had come. 'Out of the fire,' said one. Another thought it had come from the chimney. Wroe said he believed that the voice had come not for his sake, but for the sake of the witnesses. His critics put the voice down to a clever deception.

A little under a year after Turner's death, Wroe started his bold and impudent bid for leadership of the Southcottians.[6] At a Sunday evening meeting of the Bradford Southcottians in the same month of August 1822, Wroe encountered a vision in which he was commissioned to act as a prophet. Only two of the Bradford committee believed him; others opposed him so fiercely that he was not permitted to speak at their meetings. Over the next few weeks Wroe managed to convince five of the committee, a majority, which gave him the freedom to speak at meetings; but still a great many were against him.

On the evening of Sunday 24 October 1822, Wroe and his supporters set about their brash and dramatic ploy to convert the majority of the Bradford congregation to believe in Wroe's visitation. William Muff borrowed two swords from his employer and Wroe arranged for two men to stand with the swords aloft at one of three archways that divided the meeting room. The swords were held together at their points and everyone who entered the meeting room had to walk beneath them. Wroe attempted to enter after the rest of the congregation, but as he did so the men held the swords against him, exclaiming that 'the sword of the Lord is against thee!' Wroe fell to his knees and cried out that the swords should cut him to pieces if his mission was not of divine origin.

After prayer, Wroe stood up and proceeded to the second archway, the men stepping backwards at the same time, their swords still pointing at his chest. At this point he stood and preached to the stupefied congregation, many of whom were 'drowned in tears'. After his sermon, Wroe directed all those who now believed in his mission to pass under the swords. The majority did, although others, including James Shand, a later supporter, felt intimidated and refused to go under the swords. The piece of theatre had worked.

Following Wroe's success in Bradford he used his charisma in an attempt to assert his leadership over the whole of the Southcottian sect. Although Turner had died discredited in 1821, he had left the Southcottians with a well-structured organisation, consisting of a number of branches or meetings, with their own businesslike system of self-government. Each meeting had its own elected committee, and Wroe directed members of the committee at Bradford to write to other Southcottian branches. Each branch was invited to send delegates to Bradford in order to examine Wroe and evaluate his claims.

Southcottians at Almondbury near Huddersfield, as well as Idle and other congregations near Bradford, had already given Wroe their allegiance. Sheffield and Stockport were against him, but within a year both had fallen into line. The letter to the Society at Ashton-under-Lyne went missing in the post, so it was several weeks before they sent their two delegates to meet Wroe at Bradford. The men arrived on 20 November, but one of them was sceptical of Wroe's claims. Wroe addressed him directly, saying that there would be a 'sign' for him that would meet him as soon as he returned home to Ashton. That sign would prove the 'greatest trial to you that ever you had in your life, and you will take to your bed upon it, and seek for death'.

While the men were in Bradford, the Southcottians at Ashton-under-Lyne discovered that the sceptical delegate, who was married and of advanced years, had been having an affair with a young woman. When he returned home he was indeed 'faced with the greatest trial to him that ever he had in his life.' Wroe had in effect charged the old man with adultery. The Ashton congregation were astonished because it was true. On 24 November Robert Blackwell of the Ashton committee wrote a long letter to Wroe at Bradford, stating that they had 'no doubt of thy visitation being from God'.[7] Wroe's mission had been accepted by an influential congregation who were to have a massive impact on his millennial career.

Once Wroe had wrested control of a large proportion of the Southcottians he reverted to ideas expounded by Richard Brothers, incorporating many aspects of the Jewish faith. On 14 December

1822, he renamed the sect the Society of Christian Israelites, and claimed his mission was to continue for 40 years from that date. However, not all the Southcottian congregations recognised Wroe, particularly those in London.

Wroe began to organise his flock through the gradual introduction of a number of tests. These revolved around introducing the whole of the Mosaic Laws, plus additional obsessive observances of his own devising. The laws were backed up by severe penalties, including corporal punishment, administered by Christian Israelite women. The regulations included the following: Christian Israelites were to consume only animals that chewed the cud and fish with fins or scales; they were also forbidden to take tobacco, snuff or spirits; shaving and the cutting of hair was prohibited; a clear dress code was laid out in very precise details, with a particularly strict code for women, who were only permitted to wear certain colours; sect members were not permitted to possess portraits or images of any kind, as this was regarded as a breach of the Decalogue; the holy days of both Friday and Sunday were to be observed, because the Sect's members were both Christians and Israelites; the practice of male circumcision was introduced.

Circumcision was instituted as a sign of God's covenant with Abraham (Genesis 17: 10), but apart from circumcision the growing of beards was the most controversial of the laws that Wroe introduced. This stemmed from Numbers 6: 5 and was a particularly important test, as at this time beards were seen as comic, even disgusting. Many commentators stress how unusual beards were in Britain before the time of the Crimean War,[8] with the result that this custom caused more prejudice than virtually any other. A report in the *Glasgow Weekly Mail* tells of a Christian Israelite worker in the city who was dismissed from his job by his employer for refusing to shave.[9] The beards and uncut hair made the Christian Israelites easily distinguishable from the Southcottians.

Although shaving was forbidden at first, a special dispensation was eventually granted to those more wealthy members of the Society who had to attend the Manchester Stock Exchange due to business commitments.[10] A contemporary article in the *Leeds*

*Patriot* reported that the 'better sort were allowed a privilege, and the poorer complained, saying that they were taken for Jews, and were subject to insulting epithets'.[11] Conversely, Jews in Manchester were sometimes mistaken for Christian Israelites.[12] Even Friedrich Engels was once mistaken for a Christian Israelite because he had a beard.[13]

In his book *The Coming Man*, James Elishama Smith described how he became a member of the Christian Israelite Society.[14] In the following passage taken from Smith's work, the character of Benjamin is really James Smith and the place described as Salem is really Ashton-under-Lyne.

It was a fine May morning when Benjamin first made his appearance in Salem, and presented himself before John the Jew. The prophet was a stern, elderly man, of forbidding aspect, by no means like Moses, nor much in the habit of controlling his feelings. His beard was full-grown, and his mouth was covered with strong, grizzled moustaches; he had a white or undyed broad-rimmed hat upon his head, a Quaker's coat without collar, a sort of wine colour, and a silk velvet waistcoat. He was in the vestry belonging to the sanctuary, and he held a rod of iron in his hand. Several of his chief men, some of them gentlemen to appearance, others rather clownish-looking, sat or stood around him.

'Well, young man,' said the prophet to Benjamin, 'what has brought a man like you amongst a people like we?'

'I come,' said Benjamin, 'to learn what I do not know.'

'Well, if you come with an honest heart you shall be welcome, but you must not expect to come here without bearing a burden like the rest of your brethren.'

'I expect to carry my share of the burden.'

'Are you willing to obey?'

'I hope so. I think obedience the first duty a man ought to learn.'

'Well said, young man. Are you willing to hold your tongue when commanded to be silent?'

'That is a part of the duty of obedience.'

'It is; "He learned obedience by the things that He suffered." "When He was reviled He reviled not again." Can you bear to be abused? Can you bear to be robbed? Should the Lord desire your silver or your gold, would you give it up? Will you cast all your jewels into the treasury? I see a ring on your little finger, will you give up that?'

'Oh, willingly.'

''Tis enough; I do not want it; I want the heart, but the heart must be tried. "Obedience is better than sacrifice, and to hearken than the fat of rams." Are you willing to submit to the baptism of blood – the rite that was imposed upon Abraham and all the males of his house? For without this you can only come into the outer court, and not the inner court of the sanctuary; neither can you hold office amongst us.'

'I am willing.'

''Tis well, then; we accept thee as a brother, and if thou prove a false one, the evil lie at thine own door. I say thee and thou to thee now, for so we speak to one another, but we "you" to the world.'

Benjamin was now a member of one of the most disreputable and outcast of all the sects in England – a sect that had no communion or fellowship of feeling with any other sect, but was cut off from the main body of the Church like the Jews themselves, whose better name of Israelite it had adopted. He began now to feel that he must be despised by gentlemen and ladies, by people of fashion and men of the world; that he must appear in a dress that would expose him to the contempt of the Christian sects and the infidel wanderers, to the sneer of the well-dressed passenger in the street, the scoff of the profane, and the jest of the young and the thoughtless. He must now know what it is to be reckoned vile. Yet so far from being disheartened he felt unusually cheerful, and seemed to say with David, 'I will yet be more vile than thee, and will be base in mine own sight.'

He very cheerfully submitted to all that was enjoined. He suffered his beard to grow. He gave away his black hat and his black clothing, and faithfully removed every thread of cotton from his attire. Even his worsted stockings he gave away to a poor man, and substituted linen in their stead. Nothing but linen clothing touched his person. This was the law, and he scrupulously obeyed it. During the first month he looked rather an odd figure with stubble of his growing beard, his white broad-rimmed, low-crowned hat, his Quaker claret-coloured coat with large buttons, and waistcoat of similar colour; and he was advised by his Israelitish brethren to keep frequently rubbing the upper lip, from the middle outwards, in order to give the hair a set, for they who neglected this had a most uncomely moustache, which hung over the mouth and dipped into liquor whenever they attempted to drink. As he particularly disliked this falling moustache, which he was told was occasioned by the set which was given to the hair in shaving downwards, he for several weeks was most assiduously employed in using means to prevent the evil – means which he was happy to find at last were crowned with success, for he had a free clean mouth when the beard was grown.

Smith states that Wroe divided his followers into twelve tribes and called them Israel or the House of Joseph.[15] The House of Joseph was divided into two houses – Manasseh and Ephraim.[16] Manasseh at first contained two tribes and Ephraim ten, but these were later split evenly into six tribes each. The tribes were led by twelve males and twelve females, including his own son, Benjamin. According to Smith, Wroe's young son Benjamin was the male head of one of the tribes, and 'wonders were promised' of him. He was to complete the work his father had begun after Wroe's forty-year mission was ended. Smith says that 'he was the Coming Man, and was looked up to with a sort of reverence; for the Spirit had said, "There is a prince amongst the twelve".' But Benjamin was spoiled and 'turned out wild'. He died young, but Wroe apparently overcame the calamity by simply transferring the name to another son.

Wroe's second eldest son, Benjamin died at Wakefield in March 1834 in his 14th year. It really does seem that the name 'Benjamin' was merely transferred to the next eldest son, who would have been 8 years old at the time of his brother's premature death. On his wedding certificate Benjamin's name is recorded as 'Benjamin

Appleby Asriel' Wroe, which suggests that he was being groomed to take over from his father at the end of Prophet Wroe's forty-year mission. This Benjamin however also died before his father, at the age of 34. His young son James became the Prophet's principal heir.

An article in the Australian newspaper the *Dunolly and Betbetshire Express*, which briefly outlines the history and faith of the Society of Christian Israelites, briefly summarises their beliefs:[17]

1. We believe in God.
2. That his is three persons, yet one, consisting of God and Father, God the Son, and God the Holy Ghost, or Jerusalem above.
3. We believe in the first coming of Jesus, who is now coming a second time as Jesus Christ.
4. We believe that Jesus came and suffered for man.
5. We believe that at his first coming the people of Israel were a scattered people.
6. We believe that he is now coming a second time, and is called 'THE SHILOH', unto whom the gathering of the people shall be; for he, with the Spirit of Truth – the Holy Ghost – the Jerusalem above, with the Father, the Great I AM, can only gather the scattered people of Israel.
7. We believe in a first and final resurrection of the dead.
8. We believe in an everlasting punishment upon the souls that repent not, and who believe not in the Lord Jesus Christ as their Saviour, but we do not believe in an eternal damnation upon the soul, but that it is upon the bodies of those who go to the grave who undergo the sentence of dust unto dust.
9. We believe in the preservation of spirit, soul and body.
10. We believe in the union of the law with the gospel to be the means by which the preservation of spirit, soul and body shall be obtained. 1. Thess. v. 23.
11. We believe that from the Gentiles is not required the law given by Moses, because that is not given unto them, but only unto Israel; yet we believe in the universal salvation of

the souls of all the human race, which is to be fully accomplished at the final resurrection through Christ Jesus the Lord.

12. We believe in the establishment of the kingdom of God upon earth, being the restoration of the kingdom unto Israel, and for which they are now being gathered; not by the power of man alone, but through the threefold power of God, the immortal King who will reign in them, and by them, and unto whose kingdom they now subscribe and surname themselves Israel.

Following Wroe's establishment of the Society of Christian Israelites at Bradford in December 1822, Wroe and members of the Bradford committee visited Christian Israelite and Southcottian congregations in the North of England, in response to the following directions he had received in a communication that he should[18]

go to the different bodies of the believers in the visitation of Joanna Southcott and George Turner, and to the Jews, and into all nations, and preach the everlasting gospel; and speak with his hat on his head, and a man should travel with him as a witness, and to pay his expenses, as he was commanded not to touch money himself.

At 2 a.m. on the same day that Wroe founded the Christian Israelites he had intended to set out on a journey in northern England. The date, 14 December 1822, was the third anniversary of the day in 1819 when he had been struck blind for six days. The meeting had started at midnight and was to continue until noon the following day, representing the 36-hour vision he had encountered on 20 June 1820. Wroe's journey was interrupted by illness – inflammation of the kidneys – and it was not until 13 December that he set off, accompanied by William Muff.[19] The men had barely left the Bradford meeting room when Wroe got into trouble. A man from Little Horton to whom he owed coal money challenged him to pay up. Wroe pointed out that the payment was not due until Christmas. His cousin Joseph Wroe said he would pay the bill the following morning, but the man was not satisfied. A crowd gathered and Wroe was encouraged to break the peace, as a means of getting him locked up. He resisted, doubtless conscious of what had happened to Brothers, who spent many years in an asylum.

Muff and Wroe continued on their journey, over the next few days visiting Southcottian communities in Colne and Ashton, via Preston and Liverpool. Here they visited the Jews' synagogue, where the Rabbi remembered Wroe from three years earlier. 'Well, Wroe have you been dreaming again?' he asked. John said he had not, but had a message for them all and started to preach. The Rabbi left the room and rebuked those who stopped to listen.

Wroe visited Ashton-under-Lyne for the first time on Christmas Day. He spoke at the Southcottians' meeting room at Charlestown. The speech was poor, with many blunders and mistakes, but he met with acclaim from many of the Ashton body, most of whom believed in his visitation. Only the Southcottians at Failsworth withdrew from the Ashton meetings and continued to give their allegiance to the London committee.

From his travels, speeches, visions and the incidents of healing (which are recorded in the pages of *Divine Communications*), Wroe was seen to be putting the former Southcottians back into the media spotlight. His prophecies continued to bring him public notoriety. These markedly set this religious society apart from other Christian Churches that were in the ascendancy at this time, particularly the Methodists. Many of these prophecies were related to contemporary events.

The energy and effectiveness with which Wroe pursued his goal continued throughout the 1820s. As soon as Wroe achieved leadership of a large proportion of the Southcottians, he was quick to exploit his new authority, by not only visiting many of the congregations in England and Wales, but embarking on a European tour in his mission to the Jews. Wroe and Robert Harling of Thornhill near Wakefield left Liverpool in the brig *Doris* on 27 April 1823, bound for Gibraltar.[20] On the day after their arrival, however, Harling's courage had begun to fail him and he complained of a pain in his leg. Wroe too had been very sick for much of the voyage.

Harling lost no time in finding a vessel to take him back to England. This unreliable behaviour did not bode well for Harling's voyage to America in November of that year (discussed in detail in Chapter 8) a mission that failed principally because of his actions.

Wroe found Gibraltar fascinating. In a letter home he wrote (or dictated) that the rock 'is a strange place, but here are the handy works of the Lord set forth in a wonderful manner'.[21] He was particularly drawn to St Michael's Cave, a location in which he received a communication on 29 May. According to Wroe, the cave was 'much like a church in its interior parts'. He continued, 'no one has ever been able to find its end; many have tried, but they could not accomplish it; they have gone as far as they could carry lights without their being extinguished by foul air'.

Apart from Gibraltar's geographical features, Wroe was also intrigued by the cosmopolitan mix of the population in such a small area. He wrote, 'there are all kinds of people gathered together – Jews, Turks, Greeks, Moors, Portuguese, Italians, French, Dutch, Spanish, Germans – and sin and iniquity in abundance the devil being their head, he leads them into all manner of vice, iniquity and unbelief'. At the time of Wroe's visit the colony's population was experiencing instability because of events over the border. Spain had recently been invaded by the French, who wanted to depose the country's liberal government, which Britain supported, and put the absolute monarchist King Ferdinand VII back into power. The liberal armies were badly defeated during the summer and many soldiers sought refuge in Gibraltar. This turmoil created fertile soil for the propagation of millennial religion.

Wroe remained in Gibraltar until 27 July. The visit met with little success, with the remarkable exception of the conversion of a Methodist preacher, William Cooke. The authorities refused Wroe permission to preach in the colony, because they considered this would provoke a riot. When Wroe did attempt to address two regiments of soldiers, the meeting was broken up after he had been speaking for about half an hour.

During his ten-week stay Wroe visited three synagogues, where he received a hostile reception. He fared no better at the Roman

Catholic Church, where he met fourteen Spanish priests and their bishop. He recounted, 'some of them heard me with patience, and others gnashed their teeth at me, especially their bishop'. Wroe told them that if they did not take down their images then the Lord would 'chase them as the hounds chase a fox, into the holes and caves of the earth'.

The following day Wroe deposited a communication at the altar of the Spanish church in Gibraltar, as well as distributing a number of copies in Spain, after he and Cooke had managed to make it over the border. The tract, which was translated into Spanish by John Querell began:

> I, Jesus from heaven, command thee [John Wroe] to warn the kingdom of Spain, that if they return not from their wicked ways of worshipping images made with men's hands, and bowing before them, I will draw my two-edged sword against them, and it shall turn every way till I have destroyed them; but who is this that has caused them to err? They have hearkened unto their priests instead of hearkening unto me.

During his visit to Gibraltar Wroe faced intimidation on a daily basis. He was threatened by a pistol, and one woman threw a pitcher out of a window at his head. It missed. As Cooke commented, 'the people want him out of this place'. Wroe was horrified by the news of the brutal murder of a postman and his wife from St Roch, across the border in Spain. They had been killed by soldiers at Algeciras after his mail was found to contain correspondence addressed to the French Army. The man's body was stripped naked and left by the roadside. On a more mundane note, Wroe was plagued by mosquitoes: 'they bite me very sore; my right hand is all swollen with them and my left eye, and face, and hand, are all covered with blotches'.

On the same day that Robert Harling deserted him, Prophet Wroe received a divine communication, part of which concerned the youngest brother of Wroe's then-keenest supporters at Ashton-under-Lyne:[22]

And the youngest son of Hannah Lees is to come to a Methodist preacher in Gibraltar, and I will order the Methodist preacher to send him unto thee. Now let him be strong and valiant; have not I the Lord commanded him to come forth unto thee? Now I tell thee I am taking the weak instrument to confound the strong instrument, for he is only a youth, yet shall he come forth, and have my servant David's spirit, for I will deliver him from the paw of the lion, and out of the mouth of the bear. Now I tell thee, if his mother refuse to deliver him up unto me the Lord, I will return evil unto her, as I had thought to return good unto her.

The young William Lees did not arrive, but later that year Wroe returned to Continental Europe, this time accompanied by William. The pair arrived at Paris on 16 October and Wroe began to preach his mission to the Jews in the Palais Royal. A full account of these visits, including the transcripts of several of the divine messages received and tracts distributed, is contained within the pages of *Divine Communications*.

From Paris the men travelled on to Strasbourg, where they attended a meeting in a synagogue. No one there could speak English, so the men were taken to the rabbi's house – his daughter spoke a little English, though not enough to understand his message. Wroe left a written copy of the communication. *Divine Communications* reports that 'they behaved very well to us', but by the following day their attitude had completely changed. On the following day, a Sunday, Wroe was too ill to receive the response from the Jewish congregation, so William Lees made contact with an English-speaking man who had the message read to the rabbi. Lees was told of the rabbi's anger. The rabbi assured the Englishmen that he had the power to imprison them for two years, but nevertheless took pity on Lees and Wroe because he thought they were deranged. He mocked them still further, saying that he had read all the English newspapers yet had never heard of John Wroe; but if Wroe could divide the sea between Calais and Dover, make the sun stand still, or some other such miracle, then he would believe.

At Trieste they visited the Rabbi Abram Eliezer Levi, an elderly man, who was very civil. The rabbi at Venice, Samuel Rockwell, also received a divine communication from Wroe. As the men travelled from Venice to Milan they left letters in churches or handed them to priests. At Milan their letter to the priests was returned to them unanswered. As they were dining in an inn at Milan, with about forty men of various nationalities, 'the Spirit of the Lord' rested on Wroe and he 'stood up and spoke to them and gave them two letters, and they seemed much astonished'.

Wroe and Lees left Milan on 30 November and travelled via Turin, crossing the Alps at the Mount Cenis pass. From Chambéry they pressed on to Lyon and then to Chalon-sur-Saône on a packet-boat on the River Saône. It was during the very final part of their travels that Wroe and Lees were arrested. The men had continued to distribute tracts and prophecies in churches, even leaving some on the altar of the cathedral at Amiens. It was only at Calais that the police grew suspicious, suspecting the men of disseminating subversive literature. Wroe and Lees were arrested and their baggage searched for anti-government pamphlets. Once released, Wroe took the remains of his religious tracts and tore them into little pieces, scattering the litter about the streets of Calais as a testimony against the authorities.

The men left France on 17 December, on board a French-mail boat. The passage was rough, the weather so severe that the vessel was unable to get to Dover and was forced to unload both passengers and luggage at Deal beach. It was during this voyage that Wroe had prophesied that Lees would meet his future wife before reaching his Ashton home. After Deal the men called at Chatham and Gravesend, where there were strong Christian Israelite Societies.[23] It was here that Lees met the young Cordelia Clunne, who eventually became his wife in June 1828, when the couple married at Ashton Parish Church.

Wroe and Lees returned to Ashton in early January 1824. Their travels had met with little success, not least of course because neither of them spoke any foreign languages. Although the visits were seemingly pointless, they were nevertheless the sort of activity which befitted a prophet. On his travels in Europe, and as the signature to many of the 'divine communications' he received, Wroe used many different names, including Asriel Wroe, Johanan Asrael, Joannes Roes, a Latinisation of his name, and Yokkow or Yockaman, corruptions of the word 'Yorkshireman'.

Back in England, Wroe embarked on a number of publicity-seeking activities, which both spread his notoriety and helped raise funds for the Society of Christian Israelites. Many of these backfired and led to hostility from the non-believers. Other rites of the Society, although deep and meaningful to Wroe and his followers, appeared ridiculous to many others in the local population of the West Riding. Wroe's high profile in his native Bradford was heightened by the Sunday afternoon service at which he officiated. This was held in a large room in an old building known as the Bradford Cockpit, which had formerly been used as a place of worship by early Wesleyan Methodists in the town. It was not the service itself that drew so much attention, but the procession of Christian Israelites before the meeting.[24] Wroe left his Tong Street farmhouse and walked up Dudley Hill towards the town centre, followed by twelve virgins dressed in white with long white veils.

Such had been Wroe's success at converting several Southcottian congregations in England that in June 1824 he felt confident enough to visit Jane Townley and Ann Underwood, the two prominent disciples of Joanna Southcott who had not accepted his visitation. The women refused even to see him, or to receive any communication he might have cared to hand them.[25] Wroe merely replied that he had 'done his duty', that the time would come when Mrs Townley 'would be glad to see him, but would never have the chance, for she would die within a year'.

At about this time another millennial prophet made a bid for leadership of the remaining Southcottians. Calling himself 'Laban, who is Paul according to the Spirit', he summoned a meeting of the Sealed, of which about fifty attended. Townley refused to attend. Laban announced that she would die within three months, which she did. He then summoned Ann Underwood, but again within three months she befell a similar fate.[26] This peculiar prophet of doom was the aforementioned Alexander Lindsay, a cousin of the Earl of Balcarres who enjoyed the allegiance of his splinter group of Southcottians in the metropolis. In the summer of 1825, Wroe returned to London, this time to challenge Lindsay at his chapel at White Horse Court, London Bridge. Wroe's challenge had come about following a 'divine communication' that he had received at Ashton-under-Lyne on 2 July:[27]

> Thou shalt go forth unto London, and there shall be a large number gathered together; and one man will come forth and prophesy, and many of them will prophesy but one man will say he is the standard, and thou shalt stand before him, with the iron rod in thine hand, and thy rod shall swallow up their rods.
>
> And there shall come forth a man, and he shall say he is the man that carries the inkhorn; thou shalt stand bodily before him, for he is a liar, and he shall return to the dust from whence he was taken.

In obedience to the command, Wroe visited Mr Lindsay's chapel on Sunday 28 August 1825, in the company of young William Lees. Lindsay welcomed the men cordially, saying that 'Brother Wroe' had full liberty to use his chapel at any time. Wroe prayed, asking that 'Satan be rebuked within *them* walls that day', and then stood up and spoke. The meeting was largely uneventful, but as Wroe spoke Lindsay wrote down various points in red ink. He was then observed by Lees to take two ivory balls out of his pocket, which were about the size of partridge eggs. According to Lees's account, he 'drew a small stick across them, and laid them on the table, on a book; just at this time John was speaking of the white stone and new name, Lindsay pulled out something much like a glass, about the size of a large marble, but not quite round, and put it between the two ivory balls'. As Wroe spoke about circumcision Lindsay made blotches of ink.

Wroe and Lees went to lunch at a cookshop with Lindsay and several members of the congregation before returning to the chapel in the afternoon. This time Wroe spoke more aggressively. 'Thus saith the Lord.' He openly challenged Lindsay: 'If you will sign for

Satan's destruction, let a man be deputed to Ashton on the 17th of next month. There will be many dreams interpreted at Ashton; let the same be sent to those who profess to be visited, and see who will get an answer in truth.'

While Wroe spoke, Lindsay walked back and forth in and out of the room, yet said nothing. He was clearly greatly agitated by what Wroe had to say, but devised his own scheme to trick his rival into admitting he was the impostor. He told Wroe that they had both been ordered to go and see the 'Living Skeleton' at 3 o'clock the following day, and that 'one must take his clarionette [*sic*] and play a tune before the skeleton', but admitted, 'for what purpose I know not'. John Wroe answered, 'If the Lord hath commanded me to go, I will go; if not, I cannot go.'

The 'Living Skeleton' was Claude Ambroise Seurat, a Frenchman in his late 20s who consisted merely of skin, bone and blood. This poor emaciated man (who died during the following year) was being publicly exhibited at the Chinese Pavilion in Pall Mall. Baring-Gould quotes a contemporary account of Seurat by Mr Hones, who said that he seemed like

> another 'Lazarus come forth', without his grave-clothes . . . My eye then first caught the arm as the most remarkable limb; from the shoulder to the elbow it is like an ivory German flute, somewhat deepened in colour by age; it is not larger, and the skin is of that hue, and not having a trace of muscle . . . Amazed by the wasted limbs, I was still more amazed by the extraordinary depression of the chest.

Seurat caused a sensation in London, his extreme emaciation seeming to suggest that his very existence had some deeper significance. A millenarian such as Lindsay would have seen Seurat as an omen pointing to the peculiar fulfilment of prophecy. Wroe too showed superstitious tendencies in that he sometimes drew lots to decide which action to take.

It seems that Seurat was to have acted as the judge of the two men – Lindsay and Wroe – deciding who was the 'true prophet' and who was the impostor. Wroe did not go through with the ordeal. Instead he decided to confront Lindsay's second in command, William Tozer.[28] At 10 o'clock on the Monday, Wroe approached Tozer and told him the words of a divine communication he had received:

Go thou . . . to Tozer, and stand before him, and prophesy, with thy rod in thy hand; and thou shalt say, 'Thus saith the Lord: the Lord thy God has showed thee many things, and for this end wast thou born. The seal thou hast received thou shalt be able to contain it; but thy body shall go to dust, and thou shalt put on incorruption at the first resurrection . . . Thou shalt be a witness for Joanna, and thou shalt come with her, and at that day thou shalt be great unto the ends of the earth.

Tozer was more resentful of Wroe's challenge than Lindsay had been. He was Lindsay's scribe and claimed to be the man 'clothed with linen, with a writer's inkhorn by his side,' spoken of by the Prophet Ezekiel (Ezekiel 9: 2). When Lees appeared with Wroe, dressed in a white surplus and carrying a bottle of ink, he saw Lees as a mischievous challenger.

Wroe returned to Lindsay's chapel again the following Sunday, and the contest of the rival prophets really got underway, each challenging and defying the other. 'I say . . . in the name of God, you shall shave!' demanded Lindsay of Wroe. Then Wroe took his prophetic rod and, thrusting it towards Lindsay, cried out, 'Dost thou come to defy Israel? By ordering them to break the commands of God? The Lord rebuke thee, Satan.'

Lindsay was at first somewhat taken aback by the harshness of Wroe's rebuke, but soon recovered and turned his 'prophetic thunder' against William Lees. 'This is thy servant, thus saith the Lord; he shall shave, and prophesy against his master.'

'When will he shave off his beard?' asked Wroe, indignantly.

'When thine is plucked up by the roots.' retorted Lindsay.

Although not remarked on in *Divine Communications*, following Wroe's fall from grace at Ashton in 1831 William Lees did indeed leave the Christian Israelites and shaved his beard. Wroe had handfuls of his own beard ripped out by rioters during the serious disturbances in Bradford in April of that year. But at this point, in 1825, Lindsay was angered at Wroe's non-appearance before the Living Skeleton on the premise that he was ill. The pair nevertheless decided to accept their differences of opinion, Lindsay stating, 'You see we are agreed; the spirits may seem to differ a little sometimes, it is only us that do not understand it.'[29] The whole futile episode of Wroe's challenge remained unresolved.

Despite his rapid rise to leadership, his European tours and his ability to convert members of many Southcottian congregations to believe in his visitation, to many Wroe was simply renowned for his strange antics. He may well have been a great showman, and he understood how to use the publicity stunt to good effect, but his eccentricity and alleged depravity are what have preserved his character in the local folklore of both Yorkshire and Lancashire. For example, one strange incident involving the Prophet, which seems to have been a one-off, occurred in January 1823.[30] When Wroe was on his way from Idle to Leeds, accompanied by Samuel Walker, he had a dream which contained the following communication: 'I will take thee from the sight of men for forty days, and thou shalt eat such meat as I shall command thee; thou shalt eat no kind of animal's flesh, for butter, milk and honey shall be thy meat; and no hat shall come upon thy head for forty days.'

In response to the command, Samuel Walker returned to his home at Bradford, taking with him Wroe's hat. For the next forty days the Prophet was confined in a darkened room at the home of Joseph Hudson, at Woodhouse Carr near Leeds. For the first thirty days Wroe ate nothing but butter, milk and honey. At the end of the forty day period, on 26 February, Wroe returned to Idle to preach to the public. His hat was returned.

Wroe's eccentric nature is further epitomised by one of his remedies for the common cold. The Prophet would 'put a pillow in the oven, lay his head on it, and have the oven heated as hot as he could bear it'.[31] But the man who preached at the Palais Royal in Paris is only remembered by many in the West Riding from the following incident, which earned him the nickname of 'Pudding

Wroe' from the street urchins, of Wakefield and Bradford. It derived from a conversation which took place after one of his long trances. Asked by an acquaintance about his health and what he would like to eat, he replied, 'Nowt but pudding!' in his broad Yorkshire accent. One day, after being taunted by cries of 'Nowt but pudding!' and 'Pudding Wroe!' by local children, Wroe returned home and, standing at the door, saw his wife and children sitting ready in their places at the dinner table. 'What's for dinner today?' asked Wroe. 'Nowt but pudding!' shouted his children, and the Prophet flew into a rage, saying to his wife, 'I'll tell thee what, lass, I wi'nt have yon stuff called "pudding" any more.' 'Why lad, what are t' bairns to call it then?' enquired Mrs Wroe. 'They mun call it "soft meat".'

## 4

## *Baptism of Blood*

The following year, 1824, was another extraordinary one for Wroe, but this time the strange events did not take place overseas. In February Wroe announced that he would be publicly baptised in the River Aire at Apperley Bridge, a hamlet approximately 3½ miles north-east of Bradford. Between 12 noon and 1 o'clock on the appointed day, Wroe's followers left William Smith's house at Thorp Garth, Idle and walked to the river in a procession. Wroe followed, walking alone. Idle had been a local stronghold of the Southcottian faith, an area reeling at the rapid decline of the domestic industrial system. There were sixty-three Southcottian followers at Idle and Idle Thorpe in the late 1810s – proportionally more when compared with nearby Bradford and substantially greater than congregations in other Yorkshire towns such as Halifax, where a paltry five followers are recorded.[1]

The baptism ceremony had been well publicised throughout the Bradford area, and enormous crowds turned out to view the fun.[2] They were not to go home disappointed. The following is a copy of the placard which Wroe caused to be posted about the neighbourhood of Bradford at that time:

The public are respectfully informed
that
JOHN WROE
the Prophet of the Lord,
will be
Publicly Baptised
in the River Aire

near Idle Thorpe
At half-past one o'clock
on Sunday, the 29th day of the 2nd month, 1824, at
which holy ordinance appropriate hymns (accompanied
by a select band of music) will be sung, and immediately after
WILLIAM TWIGG,
one of the witnesses mentioned in Rev., Chap. II, will
preach the everlasting Gospel, as revealed by the
Redeemer of the World.

The banks of the Aire were packed with spectators. Crowds estimated at 30,000 lined both sides of the river. The weather was wet – a rainy day had been preceded by two days of severe frost and much snow – so the water level was high. Not surprisingly Wroe was apprehensive about entering the water. He faltered, intending to find a location a little further upstream. The hostile crowd, thinking him to be afraid, shouted: 'He dussn't go in! He's runnin' away!'

Despite the pressing crowd, Wroe found another place to enter the river and, as he stepped into the water, the sun miraculously began to shine 'very beautifully . . . with unusual heat for the season' and 'the sky became quite clear' – at least, that's how the event is chronicled in *Divine Communications*. The musicians and singers performed as the ceremony commenced. The baptism was carried out by John Brunton of Bradford. There was also heat from the hostile crowd, who cried out, 'Drown him!'

Wroe's most vocal critics among the crowd were a group of seven young men who were viewing the proceedings from the branches of a tree on the water's edge. One of them, John Hudson, had been an apprentice with Wroe before his bankruptcy and cursed him from his vantage point. Wroe commanded them in the name of the Lord to come down. Accounts tell how, without warning, the part of the bank on which the tree was growing suddenly gave way. They all fell into the water with the tree, and were rapidly swept downstream. Although fortunately none of the young men were drowned, they all had a 5- or 6-mile walk home in their wet clothes. Hudson died a few days later.

The unfortunate wetting of the young men did not divert the crowd's attention for long. Many had turned up half-expecting a miracle and to their mocking delight, though not complete surprise, no such miracle occurred. There are two versions of the supposed nature of the miracle that the crowd was expecting Wroe to perform that day. The first and more widely held view was that Wroe would divide the waters of the Aire and walk across the dry riverbed, as Moses had done with the Red Sea. Others were expecting him to walk on the rapidly flowing waters.

Members of the crowd expressed their disappointment by ducking Wroe in the river, attacking him with sticks and pelting him with mud and stones, succeeding in pushing him onto the ground. The account of the events in *Divine Communications* describes how Wroe and his friends escaped the melee unhurt, but how a man who looked like Wroe was severely beaten by the mob.

Late nineteenth-century Bradford local historian William Cudworth outlined the events of 29 February 1824 in his book *Round about Bradford*.[3] Cudworth, a severe critic of Wroe, describing him as 'not merely a gross impostor himself', but also a person who 'represented in a marked degree human folly and credulity', relates the disappointment of a follower who was expecting Wroe to 'demonstrate his superhuman powers by walking on the water without wetting his clothes'. The follower, indignant at the fraud, removed his broad-brimmed hat and coat, and seizing Wroe assisted in ducking him in the river. This narrative is copied virtually word for word from a review of Wroe's career published in the *Leeds Times* in June 1857, which recalled the events that had taken place at Apperley Bridge a third of a century earlier.[4] In a short letter subsequently published in the *Leeds Times*, two patriarchs of the Christian Israelite Church strongly refuted that Wroe had ever pretended that he would walk on the waters of the Aire.

Wroe's baptism at Apperley Bridge has become part of Yorkshire folklore, but as is often the case with such stories the bare facts of the event are unclear, and it is difficult to ascertain what actually happened on that day. The longest record of the events is from Wroe's autobiography, from which local authors such as Baring-

Gould and Cudworth have merely lifted their accounts of the proceedings. Bradford's first newspaper, the *Bradford Courier and West Riding Advertiser*, did not publish its first issue until July of the following year, so it is to the *Leeds Mercury* that we must turn for a contemporary account of events; but, frustratingly, again there's no report of this unusual event.

Visiting the places associated with Wroe's baptism today, it is still possible to imagine the events of leap day 1824. There is still a street in Idle called Thorpe Garth, which is not all that far from the amusingly named Idle Working Men's Club in the High Street. From the war memorial at Greengates, the busy Harrogate Road runs down a steep hill into Apperley Bridge. Nowadays, the main bridge over the Aire used by traffic is a modern structure, but fortunately the old double-arched stone bridge survives a little way upstream, carrying Apperley Lane across the river. On the Greengates (south) side of the river, next to the bridge, is The George and Dragon, a large public house with a date stone of 1704. Bushes and trees line the banks of the river north of the old bridge, by the actual spot where Wroe was baptised. Perhaps some of these trees are descendants of the one that collapsed, carrying the hapless Hudson down the river and precipitating his death.

Wroe's baptism in February 1824 was actually more of a rebaptism, a rite that he and other members of the Christian Israelites resorted to whenever they felt the need for cleansing. It was baptism of total immersion in water performed outside, in a river or even the sea. Wroe had been baptised in August of the previous year at Park Bridge near Ashton-under-Lyne, close to the residence of one of his wealthiest backers, the Lees family.[5] On this occasion the attitude of the crowd had been more favourable, as hundreds of the faithful witnessed the ceremony from the wooded banks. On leaving the river, he stood with one foot in the water, the other on the bank, and lifting his hands heavenwards he swore: 'by Him that liveth for evermore that there shall be time no longer', like the angel in Revelation 10: 5–6.

The event was later parodied in an old edition of the *Penny Post* to be found in the Foley Collection at Worcester Record Office.[6] 'A certain gentleman of position, moved by a prophecy of the impostor Roe [*sic*], essayed to walk upon the water of the canal which flowed past his house. In the presence of expectant crowds he stepped forth upon the water, and sank. The failure was ascribed to his want of faith.'

\* \* \*

On the morning of Saturday 27 March 1824, Wroe's youngest child, Mary, was found dead in bed. She was about 9 months old.[7] The death, according to *Divine Communications* 'was not unexpected, as John always said from the baby's birth that it would die'. Not surprisingly, however, neighbours grew suspicious, particularly as the girl had apparently been in good health the day before her death. The Wroes were nevertheless exonerated after the infant's body had been examined by Dr Field.

In a command 'given by the Lord', Mary's grave was marked by a stone which rested on seven pillars, 18 inches high. Unfortunately, *Divine Communications* gives no indication of the location of the grave (which was probably at Tong), but notes its inscription:

> Behold, ye sons of Esau, as ye now pass by,
> The time is come that your two houses they shall die;
> For as your father did, your birthright you have sold
> For filthy wisdom, that shall perish like your gold.
> And I, the mighty one of Israel, now have said,
> That my last covenant is with my two houses made:
> Which are my Israel true, in whom is found no guile,
> My Judah and my Joseph they for joy shall smile;
> Whilst all the sons of Esau shall supplanted be,
> And all my Jacobs shall possess my kingdom free.

\* \* \*

However, it was not the death of Wroe's daughter that produced the biggest controversy for the Christian Israelites in 1824, but the

death of another, even younger child, which caused uproar throughout South Lancashire and far beyond, as news of 'the outrages of
these pseudo-Semitic cranks' spread. The extravaganza of Wroe's
baptism had been spectacular enough, but in April 1824 his
followers were able to view an even more astounding proceeding,
Wroe's 'baptism of blood'.[8] The most contentious of the laws
introduced by Wroe was the practice of circumcision, and he led the
way, being publicly circumcised 'in the midst of the people' on the
evening of Saturday 17 April.[9] The circumcision took place on the
Oldham Road, Ashton, in a new building, which belonged to
wealthy local industrialists John Stanley and Henry Lees. The pair
traded as Messrs John Stanley & Henry Lees, Iron & Brass
Founders and Machine Makers, supplying parts to the burgeoning
cotton industry. That day's events had begun at sunrise with a
parade of Christian Israelite musicians who had marched in uniform
from their new meeting room in Charlestown into Ashton, playing
all the while.

On the afternoon of the following day, Wroe preached to a large
congregation in a field next to the building in which the operation
had been performed. As he preached he told the crowd about his
circumcision and predicted that 'a light shall break forth out of this
place where I stand, which shall enlighten the whole town; with a
light also to enlighten the Gentiles'. A footnote in some editions of
*Divine Communications* explains how this prediction was actually
fulfilled some years later 'by the erection of the gas house, and part
of an edifice connected therewith being converted into a Methodist
chapel'.[10] The gasworks and the building in which Wroe had been
circumcised were demolished in 1972, and the site is now occupied
by the Ashton Swimming Baths.[11]

Musical accompaniment featured strongly in the ceremony of
circumcision, with between thirty and forty musicians taking part.
Cynical contemporary commentators described the role of the music
as a means of drowning out the infants' screams. The operations
were carried out by enthusiasts among the faithful, particularly
Henry Lees, one of Wroe's wealthiest supporters in Ashton-under-
Lyne. Lees, the above-mentioned machine maker, held the office of

circumciser within the sect. On the night of Thursday 16 September 1824, Lees circumcised three infants, including 8-day-old Daniel, the son of Martha and Robert Grimshaw, a coal miner from Hurst Brook. Daniel died exactly a week later and on the Saturday an inquest was held into his death at The Colliers' Arms in Hurst Brook. The inquiry was adjourned until Friday 1 October, when the jury returned a verdict of manslaughter.[12] Lees was committed to Lancaster Castle by Mr Milne, the Coroner.

The trial took place at the Lancaster Assizes on 14 March of the following year. Lees was indicted for manslaughter, allegedly having caused the death of the infant Grimshaw by circumcising him with either a knife or a pair of scissors – it was uncertain which had been used. The case for the prosecution was opened by a Mr Raincock, who observed that it was indeed a case of an extraordinary nature, almost, if not completely, unprecedented.

A contemporary report of the proceedings states that 'many of the followers of the sect were also in court, and attracted much attention by their appearance and garb . . . like the Patriarchs of old, wearing beards of great length; others dressed in a uniform of blue cloth of Quaker cut, with bright buttons'.[13] Lees was dressed in such attire, but did not have a beard. It was thought that he was permitted to shave on payment of a fine to the Christian Israelites. The *Lancaster*

Mid to late nineteenth-century caricature sketch of Prophet Wroe. (From an original drawing stuck in the back of a copy of *Divine Communications* at Bradford Central Library)

*Gazette* opened its account of the trial by describing Lees as 'a young man of very respectable appearance'.[14] *The Times* said he 'appeared to be 30 or 33 years of age, and of a rather dark countenance'.

Raincock admitted that Lees did not intend to do any grievous bodily harm to the child, and there was no accusation of malice whatsoever. Indeed, Daniel's parents (described as 'deluded') had fully consented to the operation. Mr Grimshaw explained that he had had the procedure carried out on himself. Controversially and incorrectly, however, Raincock described the act of circumcision as illegal, saying that 'even if an adult were so deluded to consent to the operation, no one possessed the right of performing it'.

Mr Thomas Ogden, Surgeon at Ashton-under-Lyne had carried out a *post mortem* on Daniel the day after he died. Ogden attributed the death not to the circumcision itself, but to the after-treatment, in particular the application of a ligature. Furthermore, the child's grandmother revealed in court that Daniel had been born prematurely and had neither fingernails nor toenails.[15] Mr Justice Bayley accepted Ogden's evidence and acquitted Lees, recommending that in future he should abstain from circumcising children. Nevertheless, Henry Lees continued to perform the 'holy surgery' on Christian Israelites for some years. Because of his high status in Ashton, where he was a Poor Law Guardian and Mayor of the Borough of Ashton in 1852–3, local historians and commentators kept his name secret when recounting the death of Daniel Grimshaw. Lees was anonymously referred to as 'a gentleman' until after his death in 1884, aged 87.

Radical publisher, humanist and free-press campaigner Richard Carlile seized on the case of Henry Lees. Writing in *The Republican* from his cell in Dorchester Prison, Carlile rounded on the legal system, denouncing the fact that justice could not be administered because the law was 'so hampered by other religious associations'.[16] He nevertheless expressed his pleasure with the Lees trial, as it was 'impossible, that any one branch of Christianity can be denounced without affecting the whole'. Carlile reserved his strongest criticism for Mr Justice Bayley, the judge who, in 1819, had sentenced Carlile to six years imprisonment:

You, Mr Justice Bailey [*sic*], have written, as if you looked for the second coming of Jesus, and is it not reasonable, that the followers of Johanna Southcote [*sic*] should expect to have his birth from a member of their sect, as that you should expect him to spring from any other sect . . . All the nonsense practised and held by these Southcottians is drawn from the general source of delusion, the Bible. They are nothing inferior to you and your sect, on the score of delusion; with at least the advantage of consistency, of acting up every injunction and instruction of the sacred book.

Across the Pennines, Bradford physician Dr James Simpson, writing in his journal on 13 March 1825, commented on the popularity of the Christian Israelites (or Jerusalemites, as he called them) in Wroe's native town. He observed that some deaths had occurred due to the practice of circumcision.[17] Even further afield, the practice brought controversy. As the creed of the Christian Israelites gained a foothold in the United States of America, a leading authority in the Church there suffered the same tragedy which had befallen Lees almost thirty-five years before. The father of this child, circumcised by John Bishop in 1858, was remanded on bail for a heavy sum.[18] Wroe too conducted circumcision, for instance, in September 1824 he carried out the operation on an infirm young man in Barnsley.[19] It is unclear, however, how many circumcisions he performed, though he too carried out the procedure on infants.

\* \* \*

Almost as strange as the trances at the very outset of his religious career, not to mention Wroe's forty days of eating only milk, butter and honey in a darkened room, were the occasions when he wandered in the fields for fourteen days, existing on the local wild vegetation: blackberries, haws, hips, herbs, nettles, nuts – in fact anything suitable that he could find to eat. He would doubtless have feasted on locusts and wild honey had these been in abundance in the West Riding and South Lancashire of the 1820s. Wroe's first fortnight in the field emanated from a voice he heard at Ashton-under-Lyne on the morning of 10 September 1824.[20] Its words are transcribed in *Divine Communications*:

> Awake, thou son of man, and go out into the fields and the highways for fourteen days, and thou shalt beg thy bread like a hungry man; for hunger and thirst shall be upon thee, and water shalt thou drink out of the brooks. And as thou does, so shall they and their children do; they shall go out into the fields seeking the blackberries, nuts and wheat-ears, for very hunger.

A footnote in *Divine Communications* points out how this prophecy was 'literally fulfilled' in the autumn of the following year, 1825, at the time of the Bradford wool-combers' mass strike.

The day following the vision, obeying the command Wroe set out from Ashton and walked in heavy rain to Black Hill Foot (the Black Hills) in the Peak District. He sought shelter, but on finding refuge in a barn he was approached by the owner's wife, asking what business he had there. Wroe asked if he could lodge in the barn, but was turned away, the lady suggesting that a public house might be a more appropriate place for him to stay. 'What must I go with, for I have no money?' he asked. 'Pawn your clothes,' came the reply. He said, 'The clothes on my back are not my own. Am I to pawn another's property? Neither have I anything to call my own.' Fortunately for Wroe an onlooker took pity on his plight and allowed him to shelter in his barn instead.

From the Black Hills he travelled on to Huddersfield, during which time 'green sauce and hips were his meat' for two days. From Huddersfield he walked to Oakenshaw and then to Shirtliff [Shetcliffe] Lane in the neighbourhood of his own Bradford home. His presence attracted a large number of people, including his wife. He told her of a command he had received from God, that she should 'destroy out of her house all likenesses of anything that God had created, or caused to grow, [whether] of iron, wood, stone, paper or clothing'. Mrs Wroe obeyed.[21] Interestingly, this command was not obeyed by Wroe's son Joseph, whose will, proved in March

1890, mentions only one specific item – a framed photograph of himself.

The command explains the friction between Wroe and his wife three years later, in April 1827, when Mrs Wroe bought some earthenware pots with pictures of herbs on them.[22] She was ordered to destroy them. It also explains why no painting or portrait of Wroe survives. A caricature depicting him riding a donkey may well be the only picture of the Prophet that exists. He is described by contemporaries as having a 'savage look and hump back', a haggard face with a 'very prominent nose', shaggy hair and a broad-brimmed beaver. William Stott Banks describes his speech as being 'not better than the vulgar'.

During the second week of his wanderings a couple of incidents of healing are recorded in *Divine Communications*.[23] At Thornhill near Wakefield on 17 September he called on John Dobson, a tailor of about 80 years of age who was a follower of Wroe. Dobson was so badly afflicted with 'a shaking of his head and hands' that he could not hold his pen to write. Wroe performed a healing and then visited another sick man, Joseph Clarkson, at nearby Bretton. This time no healing took place. Wroe warned that there would be no healing in Clarkson's house until 'all their strange gods' were put away, and then that 'that should be a sign to them that God would heal them; but they put them not away'. Clarkson died shortly afterwards.

Wroe visited John Dobson at Thornhill again on 25 September, at the end of his fourteen days of wandering. On this occasion Dobson exclaimed that he had been cured of his shaking since Wroe had visited him and that 'the Lord has done this for receiving [him] into the house'. Mysteriously, Wroe replied, 'Well, but before thou see my face again, thou wilt be cured of some inward complaint.'

On Sunday 26 September, Wroe marked his return to a more conventional lifestyle by addressing a congregation in a Bradford chapel. The strange events that had occurred over the previous two weeks had ensured that Wroe received much public attention. The chapel was crowded, and many of those present were deeply hostile to him. The streets outside were packed too, many swore they would kill him once he came out. After the service Wroe waited inside, hoping the mob would disperse, but a riot ensued in which Wroe and his principal followers were assaulted.

After a struggle Wroe managed to get out of the building, but was pursued by a mob said to number thousands. He was accompanied by two women followers, Mary Brear and her sister Elizabeth Elsworth. The trio attempted to reach The Sun Inn where horses were kept waiting, ready for Wroe and Joseph Brear to make their escape. From Scarlet Heights near Halifax, Elizabeth Elsworth recorded the events of the evening of 26 September.[24] She described how they were pursued through what is now inner-city Bradford to Horton:

When we had gone about two hundred yards someone pushed my sister away; someone struck at me, and pushed me away and pushed John several yards. We got into the house, and many of the mob attempted to get in, but the landlord kept them out. There were a number of people in the house, and they said we were his women, and he was picking the poor people's pockets, and used many malicious and abusive sayings. The horses being got ready in the yard, those in the house ran out, and said, 'Now lads, now lads; he's going, he's going,' and the mob closed the gate of the yard, and kept it closed, but he afterwards got out another gate. Being got on the road to Great Horton, they cried out, 'Now lads, kill him – kill him; that's the devil who says he has been living on hips and haws, and wheat and nuts, fourteen days.' And they closed him in on every side, there being many thousands. My brother Joseph went before John to clear the way, and he then got forwards a few yards, and they pulled at the horse, and tore his coat; he got a little further, and my brother cleared the way again; my brother was knocked off his horse with a stone, but got on again. John then got about twenty yards further, and he turned him about and said something, which I cannot recollect, and they pulled the horse down, and pulled him off, and struck him, and broke the bridle and saddle girth to pieces.

Forced from his horse, Wroe was compelled to continue on foot with stones and clods of earth being thrown at him as he fled. At Great Horton, Wroe and Brear cowered in a corner of Zaccheus Robinson's garden. Wroe assumed that they were about to be killed. Yet the mob was dispersed by a heavy cloudburst, which probably saved Wroe from death. It gave enough time for the local constables to be alerted and for Wroe to make it to the safety of Brear's home. Here he showed his wounds to William Muff. Almost his entire body was black from bruising, he had a black eye and his face had been cut by a stone.

On the following morning John Brunton, John Mallinson, Samuel Muff and James Clayton obtained warrants from Mr Stocks the local magistrate against nineteen of the rioters. On the Tuesday they were bound over to keep the peace for twelve months and ordered to pay expenses.

The disturbances of 26 September were the most serious protests against Wroe during his career, except for the unrest following the virgins incident at Ashton-under-Lyne and the ensuing Bradford riots in April 1831. Nevertheless, little over three weeks later Wroe was again preaching at the Bradford meeting room. On this occasion his address was particularly controversial, as it coincided with the start of a strike by the Bradford wool-combers for more pay. Wroe described the strike as evil, saying that the masters 'would surely overcome them'. His prophecy pleased neither side.[25] The strikers threatened to pull down his house; the masters mocked: 'We may as well give up, for Wroe has prophesied that we shall overcome them, and anything that he prophesies is sure to come contrary.'

The next day, however, four 'decently dressed men' came to visit Wroe at home. They had supposedly come from Wakefield, wanting to know if the wool-combers' strike would end in failure. They too received little comfort from Wroe, who prophesied that 'the Lord would bring distress upon their masters as well as them, and then "hav-at your banks"'.

The strength of the wool-combers was indeed finally broken during the following year, after a disastrous 22-week strike for increased wages by combers who had formed a union. In Bradford, fifty masters met and pledged themselves not to employ any wool-combers or handloom weavers who were union members.[26] During the strike an estimated 20,000 workers were unemployed.[27] A contemporary account describes particularly harsh effects of the strike in and around Bradford, where 'numbers of people were seen in the fields gathering blackberries, nuts, nettles, or anything they could eat; some begged grains, and some were starved to death in consequence of commercial distress'.[28] The strike had the effect of rapidly increasing the rate of industrialisation in the wool-combing industry, although the domestic workers still lingered until about 1850.

The owners fared almost as badly. In the autumn of 1825 a financial crisis erupted in London as a result of overinvestment in South America. In less than three weeks seventy-three banks had failed, including the Wakefield banking firm Wentworth, Chaloner and Rishworth, which had opened a branch in Bradford in 1819. Bradford's only other bank survived the crisis, but many of the town's businesses had been ruined.

Wroe's second bout of wandering took place at a time of year when there was no hedge fruit to be found, as the Pennines and Peak District were covered in thick frost. In early January 1826, Wroe left Park Bridge near Ashton to wander again in the fields for fourteen days.[29] Again he led a vagrant lifestyle, travelling through various parts of Lancashire, Cheshire and Derbyshire, and was frequently out all night. Over the fortnight he had very little to eat, as on this occasion he could only beg food from people who were not Christian Israelite followers. Strong anti-Semitic sentiment was also evident during this time. One morning he called at a house near Kettleshulme in Derbyshire, asking for some water to drink. He was offered a basin of blood from a pig that had just been killed.

The final wandering incident took place at Pudsey, near Leeds in July 1831.[30] The result was even more disastrous. Once again Wroe announced to his followers that he had received a 'Divine Command' to go on a mission and that he would be away for several days, but on this occasion Wroe abandoned the idea of a John the Baptist existence and his believers raised a considerable sum to cover any expenses. A few days after Wroe had left, however, some locals became suspicious of Mrs Wroe's apparent new daily routine. They decided to follow her, only to discover that she was secretly supplying her husband with food. The spies followed Mrs Wroe at a distance and saw her walk into a field of corn. She gave a discreet signal upon which Wroe crept out from the corn carrying a horse-rug, which he placed on the ground anticipating a meal. The indignant Pudseyites, assuming Wroe had pocketed the funds, seized him and placed him on a donkey. He was then paraded through the streets of the town. A rope was then tied around him and he was thrown into and dragged out of a horse-pond several times, until he was nearly exhausted and some women onlookers begged his persecutors to spare him.

The incident at Pudsey occurred only months after Wroe's spectacular fall from grace at Ashton-under-Lyne. But although the Prophet was not recognised in his 'own country' of Bradford in the West Riding, he had nevertheless achieved an impressive following in a cotton boom town on the other side of the Pennines. Here the Christian Israelites enjoyed several advantages and even prestige, thanks to the backing of wealthy new industrialists and the indifference of the despised absentee vicar, who lived in a tiny rural parish over 150 miles south of Ashton. It was here, at Ashton, during the mid-1820s, that Wroe was able to put his extravagant building schemes into practice. The Christian Israelites believed that Ashton-under-Lyne would be the New Jerusalem, where the 144,000 elect would gather at the time of the Apocalypse.

## 5

# Building the New Jerusalem

The decline in the influence of the Established Church in the new industrialised parts of Britain was a significant factor behind the success of the Society of Christian Israelites. Until the late eighteenth century, the vast majority of the English population belonged to the Church of England, fitting the traditional model of the rural parish. In the rapidly expanding new industrial areas, however, the influence of the Anglican Church was in sharp decline, and new religious movements saw their opportunity to move in and fulfil the spiritual needs of the poor. The period of 1740–1830 has been described as an 'era of disaster' for the Church of England.[1] Within that 90-year time-span the Church had gone from having a virtual monopoly over English religious practice to being on the point of becoming a minority religious establishment.

The religious factors which led to the rise of the Society of Christian Israelites were closely associated with the decline of the Church of England. Industrialisation had brought about a massive shift in population from rural to new urban areas, yet this huge demographic expansion was not accompanied by an increase in church building that was anywhere near adequate to accommodate this new population of parishioners. The Church of England was slow to realise the desperate need for a massive programme of church building. A serious attempt to rectify the situation was not made until the early 1820s, with the construction of the so-called Commissioners', Waterloo or Million churches, a programme which has since been described as one of the four major church-building episodes since the close of the Middle Ages.[2] The Incorporated Church Building Society, founded in 1818 and incorporated by Act of Parliament in 1826, provided nearly £200,000 in its first twenty years for the new churches.[3] Parliament had voted £1 million in 1819, and this sum was increased by half as much again in 1824, when the government received the unexpected windfall of the repayment of a £2 million war loan from Austria. At first, populous parishes of at least 4,000 inhabitants were targeted, where the existing parish church had accommodation for fewer than 1,000 worshippers.[4] Of the one hundred churches initially proposed, ninety-seven are known to have been built, a large proportion of which were in the West Riding and South Lancashire.

The simplistic reason of lack of space for congregations goes only part of the way to explaining why the Anglican Church declined in this period; historians have focused on factors other than the mere question of accommodation space.[5] For instance, did the problem lie with the structure of the Anglican parishes themselves? The structural weakness of the parochial system was shown only too clearly by the new economic settlement patterns caused by the first wave of industrialisation in England. The post-medieval village or town had been dominated by its church – both physically and symbolically. The edifice was usually built in a commanding position within the parish, where it symbolised the authority of the Established Church. Within a community this social power was rooted in the clearly structured rural society that had evolved gradually since the Reformation.[6] Rural Anglican clergy were easily able to keep the 'flock' in check. There was also social pressure from members of the congregation and extended family structures. Such a parochial system was most suited to the small, compact communities of pre-industrial society in lowland rural England, but the system broke down in the large, outsized parishes of the new urban areas.

Other factors dissuading potential worshippers from attending church included the system of pew rents, whereby pews in churches (and some chapels) were allocated under a system of paid ownership. Many were treated as freehold property, prices varying according to the vantage point within the church. The failure of the pew system was one of the reasons for the alienation of the poor from church attendance, reasons that were searched for desperately three decades later by Horace Mann in his introduction to the *1851 Census of Worship*. Mann also put the problem of low church attendance by the labouring population down to their 'feeling of inferiority'.[8] He was keen to see the churches expand into the urban areas and to see improvements in housing conditions in the industrial areas. The primary need for such improvements, however, was not, according to Mann, the eradication of squalor and disease, but rather the creation of an atmosphere of 'solitude' and 'reflection' for the labouring classes. The report clearly illustrates the points raised by contemporary writers such as Disraeli, who commented that the classes had little or no understanding of each other.[9] In truth, Mann's anxieties were rooted in the issue of how authority over the industrial working class could be regained and secured.[10] He was still harking back to the golden age of a rurally rooted Church of England presiding over parishes of precise social hierarchy.

Lack of empathy was another important factor. The clergyman was highly likely to come from a privileged background and to be Oxbridge educated.[11] How could such an individual possibly have any understanding of the anxieties of the downtrodden industrial worker? Furthermore, another problem for the Church of England was its close association with the governing classes. Anglican establishments frequently operated under strong control from the local squire, with often a close connection between the clergy and the local aristocracy. Absentee clergymen, like absentee landowners, were particularly resented. This was 'an obvious connection between areas susceptible to Nonconformist encroachment'.[12]

Of all the locations where the Christian Israelites had a congregation, they gained their greatest prominence in the industrial South Lancashire town of Ashton-under-Lyne. Here socio-economic, demographic and 'religious' factors combined with peculiar local circumstances to give their Church not merely a foothold, but an impressive following, particularly visible in one of the most fashionable parts of the town. The most important explanation of the Christian Israelites' success in Ashton was the comparative weakness of both the Church of England and the obstacles faced by other Nonconformist churches. The principal landowner, the 6th Earl of Stamford, was hostile to Methodism and would not allow the erection of dissenting chapels on his land. Consequently, by the time the Christian Israelites became popular in the mid-1820s there were only three Nonconformist chapels in Ashton, namely the Wesleyan, the New Connexion, and the Refuge Chapel of the Congregationalists. A major reason for the Establishment's aggression towards the up-and-coming churches was that the Anglican Church's living would lose some of its value if its potential congregation was allowed to fall by having it spirited away to other churches.

The Revd John Hutchinson had been inducted as Rector of St Michael's, Ashton in March 1810, but resigned in 1816 to allow the living to be given to the Revd George Chetwode, who was a nephew of the Earl of Stamford and the second son of Sir John Chetwode, the 4th Baronet. This new rector was particularly unpopular in the parish. He received a stipend of £1,500 p.a. plus the parsonage. From this income Chetwode paid two curates each the sum of £125 p.a. and lent them the parsonage. He also ascribed £5 p.a. to the churchwardens' expenses and gave £2 to the school fund. This expenditure left Chetwode a disposable income of £1,243, or 82% of the initial amount. Additional money also came from the sale of coal reserves beneath the church's glebe-land.

As if the crude financial benefits enjoyed by Chetwode were not enough to anger his Ashton parishioners, their hostility was heightened by the astounding fact that he seldom visited the town. Chetwode spent almost all his time at his other living of Chilton in Buckinghamshire, where he resided at Chilton House, a large mid-eighteenth century country mansion. The 1831 census shows that there were a mere 315 souls living in his Buckinghamshire parish, compared with 14,673 in Ashton town and in excess of 33,500 in Ashton parish. Towards the end of the hated Chetwode's life, in November 1869, it was reported that the Reverend had not been near the church at Ashton for ten years, and had not officiated there for thirty years. Was he too old, too infirm to travel? No. He was described as generally enjoying good health and as being a 'hale old man of near 80'. The Revd Chetwode died in August 1870, a wealthy old man in his 79th year who had been married four times and left an estate valued at approximately £16,000.[13] Had he lived a little more than three years later, he would have inherited his brother's title. Ironically, at over fifty-four years, the Revd Chetwode was 'officially' the longest-serving rector of Ashton-under-Lyne since at least the fourteenth century. The *Ashton Reporter* of 6 August 1870 showed its indifference, carrying a tiny paragraph mentioning Chetwode's death, saying that he had 'lived at Thame in princely style'. Perhaps this helped give rise to the misapprehension among Ashton's local historians that Chetwode had been the vicar of Thame, Oxfordshire, which is the nearest town to Chilton.

Through his greed Chetwode had unwittingly contributed to the Christian Israelites' success. The Revd Hutchinson acted as curate of the parish and when a new commissioners' church (St Peter's) was built in Ashton in 1821, he was made Curate-in-Charge. He worked hard and was well respected, but due to illness was forced to retire, living at Sandal Magna, near Wakefield for many years, where he died in May 1847.[14]

Historically, Nonconformity was extremely popular in Ashton and even more so in the neighbouring town of Dukinfield just over the border in Cheshire. Dukinfield did not even have an Anglican church, but lay on the edge of the large and ancient parish of Stockport. In the mid-seventeenth century the Lord of the Manor, Colonel Robert Dukinfield had been a staunch Nonconformist and republican. As early as the 1640s, after hearing Samuel Eaton preach a fiery sermon at Chester, Colonel Dukinfield made him his chaplain in the chapel attached to Dukinfield Hall. This was the first congregational church in the country. George Fox made his first speech at Dukinfield in 1647, before his involvement with the Quaker movement, and the Dukinfield family later sponsored Samuel Angier, a Presbyterian, who from 1677 held services in a barn until Dukinfield Old Chapel was built in 1707. The Moravians too set up their first community in Dukinfield in the mid-1740s, before moving to their present Fairfield Settlement at Droylsden, south-west of Ashton, in 1785. Planned and built by its own people as a self-contained and self-governed community, Fairfield had its own shop, bakery, public house, laundry, farm, doctor, fire engine and even its own inspector of weights and measures.

In a letter to the *Morning Chronicle* almost two decades after the Christian Israelites were at their height in Ashton, a correspondent described the town's population as having 'the reputation of being turbulent and fanatical . . . The most ultra-political and theological opinions run riot amongst the population.' Even today, the modern visitor to Ashton-under-Lyne cannot fail to notice the splendid Gothic revival Albion Congregational Church, which looks as, if not more, imposing than the medieval parish church on the opposite roundabout. Pevsner comments that 'with its size and its spire, it places itself in deliberate competition with St Michael's Church'.[15] It is the second-largest congregational chapel in the country, the product of the support of wealthy Liberal mill owners, built in 1890–5, three-quarters of a century after Wroe first came to Ashton.

Of all the dissenting religious groups in Ashton, it was the Primitive Methodists who fared the worst. This group had broken away from the Methodist Church in 1812, and its preacher in the town was persecuted by the authorities. On 8 July 1821, Walter Carver, a Primitive Methodist, preached on the steps of the cross in Ashton marketplace to a crowd of attentive listeners. As Carver spoke, his name was taken down by a local constable who, acting under the orders of the Revd Chetwode and the Earl of Stamford, proceeded to assault him, knocking him down the steps. The constable then attempted to arrest Carver, but was prevented from doing so by the hostility of the crowd, who demanded that he carried on preaching. Carver was later summoned to appear before magistrates, but they refused to imprison him. Not all preachers were so lucky. Chetwode had managed to imprison another Primitive Methodist, Samuel Weller, in June of that year. A Manchester cotton-spinner, Weller was jailed for 'holding a meeting in the King's Highway at Ashton Cross'.

The comparative weakness of the Nonconformist Churches and the neglect, obstinacy and deluded complacency of the Established Church and its hated rector had prepared fertile ground for any third party seeking to found a new Church in Ashton. They were further helped in that the Earl of Stamford's steward had been sympathetic towards the followers of Joanna Southcott.

The Ashton entry in *Pigot & Company's National Commercial Directory* for 1828–9 concludes its entry about the Churches in Ashton by stating that 'there is a tabernacle erected by a sect calling themselves Israelites; the deluded followers of that extraordinary impostor, the late Joanna Southcote [*sic*]'. The controversial 1851 Religious Census of congregations at all services lists 160 Christian Israelites in Ashton-under-Lyne, some twenty years after the Church had fallen from favour following Wroe's trial.[16] The sect was described as 'flourishing' there from 1825 to 1833–5, and it has been estimated that there were at least 500 active members of the Christian Israelites in the town in the 1820s.

Like Bradford, Ashton-under-Lyne was reeling at the decline of its domestic industry, in this case, handloom weaving. Crucially, however, at Ashton the Christian Israelites were fortunate to enjoy the backing of three leading industrialists in the town. These wealthy industrialists supported the Society of Christian Israelites not out of fear or despair, which were traditional motivating factors for supporters of millennial sects, but for reasons of prestige, a way of gaining influence in a town that was largely controlled by a member of the aristocracy. Although economically wealthy, these middle-class industrialists had no political power before the Great Reform Act of 1832. The conventional natural church for such wealthy families would have been the Anglican Church. Yet clearly the Church of England was as unsuccessful in attending to the spiritual needs of these industrialists as it was with the displaced domestic workers.

These prosperous followers were able to bankroll extravagant building projects and could also help carry the considerable expense of printing religious literature, as well as assisting with the establishment of such churches elsewhere. These wealthy supporters were machine maker John Stanley, coal owner Samuel Swire, and the Lees family, who owned ironworks at nearby Park Bridge. There were almost certainly other affluent supporters too, as former Chief Constable Chadwick comments in his memoirs that 'at one time they had many wealthy people connected with them [the sect] in Ashton, and as these had to attend the Manchester Exchange, a dispensation was granted them whereby they were initially permitted to shave'.[17] Was the interest of the emerging middle class in millennial religion a way of keeping the working class in check, or were both the working and middle classes in solidarity, given that both were without political representation until 1832?

John Strongi'th'arm Stanley (yes, that really was his full name) was born in 1786, and thus was more or less a contemporary of Wroe. Stanley, who is buried in St Peter's churchyard, remained faithful to the Christian Israelite Church right up to his death in 1855. His second wife and widow, Mary, however, had all four of her children rebaptised in January 1857 at Ashton Parish Church, eighteen months after her husband had died.[18] John's nephew, Robert Stanley, was Mayor of Stalybridge in 1874–6. Samuel Swire was also a high priest of the Society of Christian Israelites and an even more important civic figure in Ashton than John Stanley, being Mayor of the Manor in 1840–1. As the brother-in-law of circumciser Henry Lees, Swire was related to the third of the wealthy Ashton families who supported Wroe.

We have already seen that Wroe exerted a strange influence over the Lees family. It was William Lees who was called for when Wroe was causing upheaval during his tour of Gibraltar, and whose marriage to Cordelia Clunne came about as the result of a prediction from Wroe. It was William's brother Henry who was charged with manslaughter after the death of circumcised infant Daniel Grimshaw. William and Henry were two of the eight children of Samuel and Hannah Lees – four boys and four girls. The Lees family had started production at their ironworks in the mid-1700s.[19] In the early years of the nineteenth century, however, the business was run by Samuel's widow and then by two of his children.[20]

Daughter Hannah took charge at first; then Henry, the second son, guided the company. Edward, the eldest son, was an apprentice hatter in Macclesfield. The family firm experienced difficulties during the harsh immediate post-Waterloo years, and Henry suffered a breakdown. Hannah assumed responsibility again, after which the third son, Samuel, took charge. However, it was another of the Lees sisters, Sarah, who was to be honoured by the sect. Her 'marriage' to Wroe took place in 1823 at the Christian Israelites' Chapel, and it was later announced that she would give birth to Shiloh during the following year.

Doubtless, the believers at Ashton-under-Lyne busied themselves with preparations for the birth of the 'Promised Shiloh', just as the followers of Joanna Southcott had done almost a decade before, when over £100 had been spent on pap spoons alone. Little is known about the preparations for the Ashton Shiloh, but a crib was brought to the Lees's Ashton town home of 1, Henry Square, to be ready for the birth. For many years the cradle supposedly intended for Joanna's Shiloh was on display at the Peel Park Museum at nearby Salford, before it was acquired by the Panacea Society in Bedford in the 1920s. The incongruity of the cradle in a museum so close to Ashton, led the mid-twentieth century local historian Winifred Bowman JP to question whether this crib was actually the one made for Joanna Southcott's baby, rather than Sarah Lees's baby.[21] In any case, the momentous event occurred on 17 July 1824. Unfortunately, in the thinking of those less enlightened times, the baby, the 'Promised Shiloh', turned out to be a girl. The prophecy had failed.

The name of Sarah Lees's child never made it into the local history books, her identity remaining a secret for several decades after her death. In her second history of Ashton-under-Lyne (1960), Mrs Bowman refers to the memories of those who had known Sarah Lees's child in old age. She does not, however, dare mention the name, confining herself to saying that she was a 'respected and capable lady'. It was Manchester University postgraduate student P.J. Tobin who first put the Lees child's name into the public domain. In the 1970s, while researching for his MA religious studies thesis *The Southcottians in England*, Tobin was fortunate enough to have sight of the Lees family papers. These included a letter dated 6 April 1950, in which a family descendant, Horace Lees – the custodian of the papers – reveals that the child was another Sarah Lees, who later took the surname Hague from her stepfather, William Hague.

The parish registers of St Michael's Church, Ashton record the marriage of Sarah Lees to William Hague on 16 May 1832. The registers of three years later show the baptism of Sarah Lees's daughter as Sarah Hague Lees on 1 April 1835, giving her date of birth as 17 July 1824. Fortunately, it was common practice in the parish of Ashton to record the date of birth when baptism did not take place within the usual short time-span after birth. No father is recorded, but the mother's name is given as Sarah Lees.

By the time of the 1871 census, Sarah has become legitimised as Sarah Lees Hague. The census returns of that year show the unmarried Sarah living with her 80-year-old widowed mother on an annuity in Currier Lane, Ashton. Sarah's mother had died by the time of the next census, ten years later, but further proof that Sarah Lees Hague was the correct person to identify as 'Shiloh' is shown on the 1881 census. On enumeration night she has a visitor, 64-year-old Sarah Clunne of Gravesend, Kent, who is almost certainly the sister of Cordelia Lees (née Clunne), Sarah's aunt, and the widow of William Lees.

The pregnancy of Sarah Lees, as recounted by local historians, has been the most confused of the sexual scandals involving Wroe. They have either mixed up the chronology of Sarah Lees's birth with the later incident of the seven virgins, or they have neglected to include the story of the female Shiloh. Baring-Gould, Burnley, Howcroft and even Mrs Bowman have all confused the story, wrongly implying a date of birth of 1831, not 1824. Tobin too, despite achieving the coup of discovering the identity of Sarah Lees Hague, wrongly assumes that her mother was one of the seven virgins and plumps for 1831. He cites Horace Lees's letter, which quotes the erroneous birth date of 19 February of that year. Tobin did not have the advantage of easily being able to cross-reference this information with the census returns of 1881 and 1901. He was further thrown off the scent by the contents of another document in the Lees's family papers, an agreement dated 1832 between Sarah Lees and two of her brothers, Edward and Samuel. The brothers decide to help support and educate Sarah's daughter, who is clearly illegitimate, as mother and uncles share the same surname. They agree to pay Sarah £50 once she marries, provided that she renounces all claims to the family property. The agreement's date, 16 May 1832, is the day that Sarah Lees married William Hague. A further item in the Lees papers is a letter written in April 1881 by the widow of Samuel Lees. She writes of Sarah Hague's distress at the death of her mother, Sarah Lees, and further proposes an annuity of £20–25 for Sarah, who is by now in her mid-50s.

The birth of the supposed Ashton Shiloh does get some coverage in contemporary news in the 1820s. For example the report of Henry Lees's trial in *The Times* in March 1825, reproduced by Carlile in *The Republican*, contains a preamble outlining some of the antics of the Christian Israelites in Ashton-under-Lyne.[22] It states that Lees had been 'induced to sanction a mock marriage of his own sister, at the chapel of their sect, to one of the pretended Prophets of their community, in the expectation that from the marriage the real Shiloh was to arise'.[23] The reporter, who, like Carlile, does not implicate Wroe by name, continues: 'The lady in due course, presented an appearance likely to realise all the hopes formed of her, except one! when oh! sad and second disappointment, the new stranger proved to be a girl. The Prophet being soon afterwards detected in a house of ill-fame in Manchester.'

Although Baring-Gould, Burnley and Howcroft may have got the date wrong, they do mention that Wroe was tracked down to a Manchester pub, where he was drinking 'hot whiskey and water' in the company of two prostitutes.[24] They also state, however, that it was Lees's father who sought out Wroe. Yet Sarah Lees's father had died some years before. Baring-Gould – who was writing in 1874, fifty years after the event – goes even further, telling of how Lees, 'exasperated at the dishonour of his daughter . . . stationed himself behind a chimney and fired a gun at Wroe. The ball whizzed past his hat.'

Sarah Lees Hague lived into old age, surviving on her annuity. In the 1901 census she was living at 53, Henrietta Street, Ashton, a fairly genteel Victorian terraced house just north of Ashton-under-Lyne railway station. She was living with a widow, Charlotte Austin, and her family as a boarder, so clearly the annuity was running low.

Sarah Lees Hague died of apoplexy in December 1907 at 152, Albermarle Terrace, Ashton. The 83-year-old had never married. Her death certificate humanely records 'William Hague, General Produce Dealer (deceased)' as her father.

The astonishing credulity of many of the Ashton believers was borne out by what happened to their 'Prophet' John Wroe in the wake of the birth of Sarah Lees. They believed, as reported in *The Times*, that 'the Lord himself has permitted him to fall for a season'. Despite the nature of this most outrageous scandal, the more the Christian Israelites were persecuted and ridiculed, the more this strengthened their resolve. Curiously, there is no mention of this Shiloh scandal in *Divine Communications*. The absence of any reference to it is worth noting in the light of the book's coverage of both the 1827 sexual depravity accusations at Tong Street near Bradford and the virgins' allegations at Bradford and Ashton in 1830–1. By contrast, that later outrage receives plenty of coverage, Wroe's closest supporters having put up a strong rebuttal against the allegations.

The high point of the 1820s for the Christian Israelites in Ashton came three years to the day after Wroe had first visited the town. Their new place of worship, the Sanctuary, was opened on Christmas Day 1825, in the then-fashionable Church Street area. The huge brick building was plain on the outside, with no windows, the whole interior being illuminated by natural daylight through two very large glass domes on the roof. Over the main entrances were huge stone slabs. One depicted the Star of Judah, which was a symbol of the Church. The other was inscribed with the words 'Israelite Society' in Hebrew characters.

In contrast to the stark appearance of the outside of the Sanctuary, its interior was particularly sumptuous. The polygonal organ cost well in excess of £600.[25] Each of its twelve sides supposedly represented one of the tribes of Israel, and each was topped with a carved mahogany crown. All the seating in the Sanctuary was made from oak, the galleries and all other furnishings being entirely constructed of St Domingo mahogany. All the fittings were of silver and bronze. On each side of the chapel was a pulpit rising from the

The Christian Israelites' Sanctuary, Church Street, Ashton-under-Lyne. (Glover, W. *History of Ashton-under-Lyne*, ed. Andrew, J. (Ashton: 1884), p. 310)

ground floor right up to the height of the galleries. There was an 'unclean' pew, and beneath the pulpit was the 'cleansing' room. As the later plan shows, many of the pews on the ground floor were semicircular.

The Sanctuary cost £9,500 to build, paid for entirely by one of Wroe's rich industrial supporters in the town, John Stanley. The level of extravagance can be easily assessed when compared with Ashton Town Hall, which cost less than half that amount when it was constructed twenty-five years later. Wroe prophesied great worldly success for Stanley, who indeed subsequently became even more wealthy.

Such a lavish building project gave the Christian Israelites distinction, individuality and prestige within the town. The Sanctuary had been built in a prominent position, on a major route to the parish church.[26] Many Christian Israelites lived quite close to their new place of worship, in a fashionable terrace overlooking the river and the green fields beyond. The sect was new, seemingly fashionable

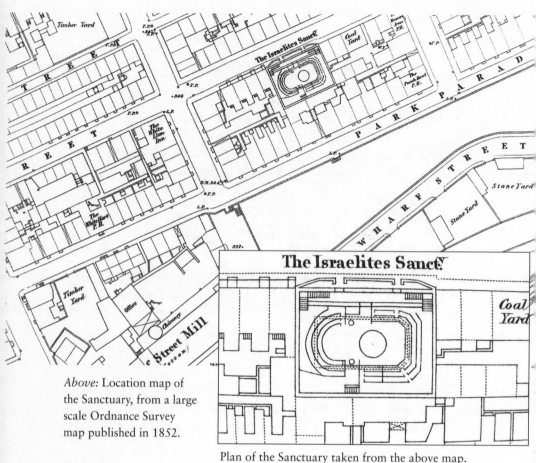

*Above:* Location map of the Sanctuary, from a large scale Ordnance Survey map published in 1852.

Plan of the Sanctuary taken from the above map.

and relevant to people's lives, unlike the Church of England in Ashton.

On 28 January 1826, at the end of his fourteen days wandering in the Peak District, Wroe received a vision at his Yorkshire home at Street House, Tong Street (between Bradford and Tong). The penultimate part of the communication states that 'within seven months (that is seven years) the Lord's temporal house at Jerusalem shall both be built and established, and that is the day that your millennium shall take place'.[27]

Plans were drawn up to build four gatehouses at the chief entrance points to the town. These buildings marked the four 'Gates to the

Temple of the Children of Israel'.[28] The description of these buildings as gatehouses, implying single-storey lodge-type buildings, is quite a misnomer. As the photographs show, they were substantial detached properties, constructed of red brick and having typical late Georgian features. The architectural scheme, of course, was firmly connected with the beliefs of the Christian Israelites. Ashton-under-Lyne was to be the 'New Jerusalem', the 'Holy City' where the 144,000 elect were to gather.[29] The Sanctuary would be its central citadel.

It was originally intended that walls would be constructed from gate to gate, enclosing a massive temple area with the Sanctuary its centre. This plan would be abandoned after the decline in popularity of the Christian Israelites following the scandals of 1831. It is not recorded what other citizens of Ashton thought of the scheme. Its feasibility must be called into question, as unfortunately the Earl of Stamford had already mapped out the area to the west of the old town on a grid system, naming its streets after members of his own family.[30] Stamford family names in Ashton streets include: Bentinck, Burlington, Cavendish, Delamere, Katherine, Margaret, Portland, Stamford, Warrington and Welbeck.

Tracing the sites of these gatehouses, the most noticeable thing about their locations is the distance between them. Two are particularly remote from the built-up areas of 1820s Ashton. Neither is the plan at all square; the seemingly haphazard locations of the gatehouses would produce a walled city of peculiar shape, with the Sanctuary not literally in the middle of the scheme. The following four gatehouses were built:

- Moss Lodge. The gatehouse off the Manchester Road, at Moss Close, about a mile west of the centre of the town in the Moss district of Ashton. This building survived until as recently as the early 1990s, being used as a residential home in its later years, when it was known as Grasmere Lodge. The area was cleared for the construction of the last section of the M60 motorway. Photographs taken during its demolition show that it bore a striking resemblance to the Odd Whim.

- Taunton Lodge. This large house was situated just off the Taunton Road, at Waterloo, on a site just north of the Waterloo Primary School. It was demolished in about 1890. The building was also known as Waterloo House and was once the home of John Stanley jnr,. whose father had paid for the construction of the Sanctuary.

- The Odd Whim. The only gatehouse which is partially extant. It stands on Mossley Road, just north-west of Park Square. This well-known Ashton public house closed in May 2004.

- A fourth gatehouse, the 'southern gatehouse', stood at Shepley, in close proximity to Dukinfield Hall, and was the first of the four to be demolished. The legacy of the four-gatehouse scheme is preserved in the name Gate Street, which was formerly called Southgate Street, located in the vicinity of the Shepley gatehouse. For many years the surrounding area was known locally as Jerusalem.

These large gatehouse residences were the homes of the high priests and other influential members of the Society of Christian Israelites. For example, William Skin lived at the house which for many years was known as the Odd Whim. And Mrs Wroe lived at the Shepley property in some style from 1830 until the spring of 1831.

In addition to these houses, a Doric-pillar-fronted mansion was built for Wroe in about 1828, close to the banks of the River Tame to the west of the County Bridge at Tudor Mill, Portland Basin. This mansion was an even more substantial property than Wroe's later home of Melbourne House at Wrenthorpe, near Wakefield. The Ashton mansion is best referred to as his 'official' residence; contemporary reports still describe him as living at Street House, Tong Street, just south of Bradford.

The Swire family are recorded as living at the Portland Basin mansion at the time of the 1881 census, but the property had been demolished by the early years of the twentieth century. Its site now forms part of the greenery surrounding the Portland Basin Museum.

Other houses associated with the high priests of the Christian Israelite Church have gone too. John Stanley's house was demolished in about 1960. Its site is now a bypass, which nevertheless preserves the name Park Parade. The houses in Henry Square, including number 1 – the house in which Sarah Lees gave birth to the female Shiloh in 1824 – have also been demolished. Their location, however, was familiar to millions of TV viewers in 1998–9, as its site is now occupied by Tameside Magistrates' Court, outside which many broadcasts took place during the preliminary court hearings of the Harold Shipman case.

Despite the lavishness of the Church's new architecture, and the wealth of the main benefactors to the New Jerusalem utopian town-planning scheme, the life of the typical Christian Israelite was much more austere. Members of the sect could be easily identified by others in the local population because of their peculiar mode of dress, which came about as part of the strict laws introduced by Wroe, and which never changed in style throughout the nineteenth century. Chief Constable Chadwick later remembered that the 'dresses were of a style of their own, and the bonnets were made to match'. As much as a dozen yards of coarse linen were used by the women to make a single skirt. Also, women were not allowed to wear certain colours, including red, scarlet, yellow and black. Blue and green were the most popular colours, but no mixing of colours was allowed. Similarly, Christian Israelite women were only permitted to wear clothes made from one material – all silk, all linen or all woollen, but no combination. Silk dresses had to be sewn with silk thread, and the lining could not be of cotton or wool, but had to be either linen or silk. The justification for not mixing fibres was attributed to Leviticus 19: 19. Perhaps the stipulations relating to which colours to wear came from Exodus, 28. Trimmings also had to be of a prescribed material. Finally, the women also wore veils, sometimes embroidered with Hebrew characters or signs worked so as to fall just below the eyes.

The men wore coats without collars and were only permitted seams sewn on the sides of their clothing. Their jackets were single-breasted, buttoned high to the throat over a linen shirt and ruffle.

Their hats were broad-rimmed, with drab bodies, green under the rims, yet invariably made of good-quality felt. On the days of great festivals within the Church, such as the Passover, both men and women attended the Sanctuary dressed in white linen.

Various contemporary accounts help explain not only the Christian Israelites' sense of colour and dress, but also some of their customs. The first is a report of the funeral of Samuel Swire's daughter at Ashton on 10 November 1827 and shows their aversion to the colour black:

> Mr Swire and his friends appeared in blue coats, drab trousers, and brown hats, their usual custom. The ladies were dressed in white, with Leghorn bonnets trimmed with large white satin roses . . . After the corpse was taken from the hearse, it was covered with a blue cloth pall trimmed with white satin and looped with white (ribbon) and satin roses. The ladies had on blue shoes and white shawls; the coaches were not covered, but green and yellow painted.[31]

In January of the following year, the much-travelled Richard Carlile visited Ashton-under-Lyne and attended two services in the Sanctuary. He wrote of his visit in his journal *The Lion*, which was a record of his 'Tour through the Country'.[32] As well as their mode of dress, Carlile noted the Christian Israelites' style of worship. He was particularly impressed by their music, which featured prominently in their services. Carlile 'counted twenty-one pieces of wind instruments, and some of those of the most boisterous kind, indeed, I know not one of the wind instruments commonly used in military bands that was not there.' Former Chief Constable Chadwick remembered that as many as 'sixty to seventy players accompanied the singing on such days as the Passover'.

The welfare enjoyed by members of the Christian Israelite community was something else remarked on by Carlile during his 1828 visit. For instance he notes that they 'are very polite to strangers, court their visits to the chapel, and there appears to be much good feeling among them, providing for, also like the Quakers, their own poor'. He also tells of the existence of two Israelite shops, one for food, the other for clothing. These shops, in Stamford Street, dealt in fair weights and measures and had adopted a cooperative system of trading in Ashton two decades before the Rochdale Pioneers founded the Co-op.[33] The shops, which served both members of the Christian Israelite community and the general public, closed at 6 o'clock on Friday evenings in accordance with their observance of the Sabbath. The words 'Israelites' Shops' were inscribed over the doors, but the townspeople in Ashton called them the 'Johanna Shops'.

As Hebrew was to be spoken in the New Jerusalem, classes were arranged to teach the language to the Lancashire weavers and miners. Two Hebrew schools were established in the area, one in Ashton, the other at nearby Mottram. A further extraordinary character came to Ashton in 1828 to teach at these schools. The Revd James Elishama Smith was born in Glasgow in November 1801, and converted to the Christian Israelite religion from Presbyterianism. Smith became disillusioned with the Christian Israelites following Wroe's trial and was later a licentiate of the Church of Scotland. For many years he wrote the leading article for the *Family Herald*, but it is his book *The Coming Man* that proves invaluable to anyone wanting to read about Wroe's life in Ashton in the late 1820s. Largely autobiographical, *The Coming Man* was completed in 1848, but not published until 1873 – over fifteen years after Smith's death. Wroe features in the book as 'John the Jew', and Ashton-under-Lyne is referred to as Salem.

Despite the welfare and benefits such as shops and schools provided by the Christian Israelites at the time, Smith writes of how the Ashton working-class population was 'bold and impudent', despising the Yorkshire Prophet and defying him 'to his teeth'. Locals also resented the laws imposed by Wroe, such as stipulation on dress. Ashton landlady Mrs Riddle, in conversation with one of the book's main characters, Benjamin, speaks of Wroe and her disobedience: 'He has such strange ways. I don't think the Lord concerns himself about such trifles as the number of petticoats that women wear. I thought the old fellow meant to kill us when Wroe ordered only one to be worn; and, do you know, I would not obey the last order – I wore my two.[34]

Mrs Riddle feared the consequences of her disobedience and confided in Benjamin of how she could not face Yaacov (Wroe) in the Sanctuary when, shaking a poker at them as he spoke, he chastised those who had disobeyed his commands, which were delivered by the chief women of each of the twelve tribes. The consequences for those who broke Wroe's laws were shocking, as punishment was enforced by severe penalties:

> These penalties were sometimes immersion seven times in water, sometimes corporal punishment, inflicted by the women, with rods, and the women were commanded to strike without fear on the bare shoulders, or be themselves subjected to their own peculiar penalties, which were still more trying to the feelings. In time, Wroe became a tyrant, severe and austere; and his person was dreaded by all who followed him. But though they feared him, they confessed that his law was good and made them better men.[35]

At the height of the Christian Israelites' success in Ashton-under-Lyne in the late 1820s, the sect enjoyed a huge following in the town. Their leader Wroe was able to exert a strange and powerful authority and influence on some highly educated and wealthy people. Strict laws were rigorously enforced, yet Wroe still exhibited odd behaviour at this time in his career. *Divine Communications* records apparent signs of mania in his character, witnessed clearly in a vision he received at his house at Street House near Bradford on 30 June 1827. The vision 'taken from the mouth of John Wroe' was transcribed by William Tillotson:

> And put thou on old rags and shoes, and stand in the market place at Bradford and drop letters, and tell them as it is with thee so shall it be with them. And every market town that thou enters in thy travel thou shalt put on those old rags and old shoes, without hat, with thy buttocks uncovered, and drop letters – as it is with thee so it shall be with them.

The prophetical content of the letters was conveniently delivered to Wroe during the following day, and at sunset on the evening of 12 July the Prophet set about putting the crude and most strange command into practice. He started by dropping a number of letters at different places around the two markets in Bradford. That evening Wroe began his journey to Scotland, dropping twelve letters of prophecies in Leeds, again with his buttocks exposed. On Sunday the 15th he dropped a further ten letters at Tadcaster and on Monday the 16th he dropped nine letters in York.

The former Chief Constable of Stalybridge, William Chadwick, who had grown up in the Tameside area when the Christian Israelite religion was at its height, wrote about the extremely credulous nature of some of the Ashton believers.[36] A corn merchant was so convinced that he was appointed to meet Joanna Southcott at Jerusalem that he told his neighbours that his money and goods were now of no further use to him, as he was to go on a journey to the Promised Land. The late Joanna did not turn up at Jerusalem, yet neither the man nor his family renounced their faith, despite the failure of the expedition. A more plausible story, of the trumpeter in the snow, is also recalled by Chadwick, relating to a joke played on another adherent:[37]

He resided in an old two-storey house, with very small windows and heavy flagged roof, upon the road from Mud to War Hill. One Saturday at midnight the meadows were covered with a thin silvery sheet of snow, when two young fellows who had been out playing with a band were returning home, one of whom carried a trumpet under his arm. They knew the old gentleman's failings about the journey to Jerusalem, so they determined to try his credulity to the fullest pitch. One of them accordingly mounted the wall which led to the back of the house, and placing himself nearly under the bedroom window, he blew three or four melodious blasts from his trumpet. The jokers listened attentively, and soon were rewarded by hearing the old man arousing the whole of his family from their pleasant slumbers, and anxiously inquiring how they could sleep on such a pleasant occasion. The family had to get up, and he reminded them that he had often told them there would be a sign when the time of deliverance came and lo! All had come to pass as predicted, even to the sound of the trumpet . . . It was generally reported that the faithful fellow took his family as far as Ashton, and returned a wiser and more prudent man than he went, although he continued in the faith he had become such a firm believer in.

Having already ridden out one major sexual scandal in Ashton, in late 1829 Wroe made an announcement that was to test the credulity of his followers to the very limit. The Prophet proclaimed to his followers that 'the Spirit of the Lord' had commanded him to take unto himself seven virgins, 'to cherish and comfort him'. Not surprisingly, the explicit allegations shocked the chattering classes and precipitated Wroe's downfall at Ashton.

# 6

## *Scandals and Banishment*

Approximately two miles south of the centre of Bradford, just off the road to Wakefield, lies the area of the city called Tong Street. The farmhouse tenanted by Wroe from the early 1800s was situated here, south of the junction of Dawson Lane at a place once known as Street House.[1] The place name has long since fallen from usage, but it was here that alleged incidents took place involving the Prophet that were to have such massive repercussions for Wroe at Ashton-under-Lyne and Bradford, and that permanently changed the fortunes of the Christian Israelite Church in England. The farmhouse was the scene of the alleged rape of Wroe's young apprentice girl, and later the first and most damaging of the virgins scandals, for which Wroe was brought to trial at Ashton and which led to disturbances at both Ashton and Bradford.

It barely needs noting that there is a history of charismatic leaders whose outrageous behaviour have led them to become entangled in depraved sexual scandal. When a millennial religious leader such as Wroe announces that he has received orders from heaven to take seven virgins to cherish and comfort him, the episode is bound to end in disaster. According to a contemporary Manchester paper, Wroe's virgins (who were proved to be so on strict examination) were to 'wait upon, nourish, and comfort him, and be as wives unto him, except that he should not carnally know them'.[2] These girls and some married women accompanied Wroe on his travels, acting as his servants. Rumours of scandals arose and, in the late summer of 1830, when questioned three of the virgins disclosed shocking allegations to senior members of the Society of Christian Israelites.

This was not the first sexual scandal in which Wroe had become embroiled, even excluding the case of the female Shiloh Lees. Almost three years earlier, in December 1827, rumours had spread around the Bradford area that Wroe's young apprentice, Martha Whiteley, had become pregnant by her master. Martha's apprenticeship agreement, dated 20 July 1826, survives at the Bradford Local Records Office.[3] Signed by Wroe, the document describes Martha as 'a poor child belonging to the Township of Tong', aged 11 years and 11 months. Wroe took on the young apprentice to work at his farmhouse at Street House, Tong Street. The document states that Wroe was to 'provide for the said Apprentice sufficient Meat, Drink, Washing, Lodgings, Apparel and all other Things needful or meet for an Apprentice during the said Terms'.

Doubtless the churchwardens and overseers of the poor in Tong township were appalled to hear of the alleged pregnancy, not least, in their minds, because the 13-year-old was carrying a child 'likely to be born a bastard and chargeable to the Township of Tong'.[4] On 20 December 1827, a warrant for Wroe's apprehension was drawn up, signed by Mr Hird the magistrate and addressed to the constable of the township.

Two days previously three men had entered Wroe's home to question Martha. They were Joseph Dennison, the local constable, George Field, a surgeon, and Samuel Firth, the overseer of Tong.[5] Field had examined her, and when Wroe's scribe Tillotson arrived at the house he found the doctor washing his bloody hands.[6] The poor girl had to endure two subsequent examinations and attend the magistrates' hearing against her master. Wroe too was examined by two doctors, who declared him 'free from venereal disease, as well as from any marks which might indicate his having had it'.[7] From the verbal evidence they received from Martha, the magistrates deemed that 'the answers which she gave on a certain point they said were impossible to be true'. Although the doctors had not stated that Martha was pregnant, the magistrates nevertheless placed her in the care of a woman called Greenhalgh, so that 'no deceit might be practised, lest the accusers should say she had miscarried when she had not'.[8] According to *Divine Communications*, the charges concerning Wroe's illicit behaviour towards Martha Whiteley had been made up by another member of the household, a woman servant from Barwick near Leeds.

It certainly seems that Martha Whiteley did not give birth. The bastardy records of Tong township were scrupulously kept, but there is no mention of Martha Whiteley or John Wroe in records of examination, or settlements, or affiliation orders. Neither is his name among those in the township's meticulously kept accounts books.[9] However, on the reverse of Martha Whiteley's indenture to John Wroe, there is a pen-written note that 'he hath misused and ill treated her' and that she was discharged of the apprenticeship on 7 February 1828, seven weeks after the warrant had been drawn up for Wroe's arrest.

Even though the scandal of Martha Whiteley blew over, the whiff of depravity was not to leave Wroe. The farmhouse at Street House was to be the starting point of the next, far more damaging set of allegations against him, brought by three of the seven virgins under his charge. Members of the committee of the Society of Christian Israelites supposedly became aware of the allegations after the first of the virgins feared the loss of her comfortable lifestyle. Wroe lost confidence in her trustworthiness and had threatened to demote her to be servant to his wife. The virgin took out her revenge by revealing aspect's of Wroe's behaviour to the committee. These allegations first began to surface in Ashton during September 1830, a month which would also have a profound effect on his prophecies of industrialisation, as it also marked the first journey of the *Rocket* from Liverpool to Manchester.

Certain newspapers in March 1831 explained what the function of the virgins was to be in their relationship with Wroe. *Bell's Life in London* reported that the virgins 'were to live with him in a state of innocence, and thus display a pattern of purity to the whole people'.[10] *Wheeler's Manchester Chronicle* describes what happened once the seven virgins had first been selected:[11]

The appointment of the seven to this holy calling took place on the 'feast of the full moon', when the high priest delivered a disclosure 'on the coming of Shiloh' and his reign upon earth. The 'believers' were also informed that if they had faith, they should not die, but were to inherit Shiloh's kingdom, which was near at hand, where they would behold the seven virgins 'walking amongst the seven golden candlesticks in the New Jerusalem'. The ladies were entrusted by the committee to the prophet, who was to take care that they were kept free from the world and all its impurities, and the elect were favoured with a communication every morning as to their condition and feelings.

So what is known about the seven virgins? The names of the three virgins who revealed the nature of the shocking allegations to the committee at Ashton can be easily identified. They were Ann Hall of Doncaster, the daughter of Hannah Hall; Sarah Pile of Ilfracombe, Devon (whom he probably met during his visit to that town in the summer of 1828); and Mary Quance, who was also probably from Devon.[12] Of the three Sarah Pile at least could read and write; indeed, she acted as Wroe's scribe. Her name appears in *Divine Communications* in early October 1829, over a year before the start of Wroe's trial.[13] The young woman wrote down a communication given to John Wroe at his farmhouse near Bradford, the place where all the trouble started. As has already been mentioned, some local historians have assumed the name of a fourth of the virgins was Sarah Lees, the sister of his strongest backers, Henry and William. The discovery of the 1824 birth date of her illegitimate child means that she can, obviously, be discounted.

What happened over the ensuing few months is unclear. Reports in the papers, once the full story broke in March 1831, outline a similar course of events to what must have happened in the case of Sarah Lees, some seven years earlier. Wroe allegedly told each of the three virgins that 'the the Shiloh was soon to make his appearance upon earth' and that Wroe 'was to be honoured as the holy instrument for bringing about this glorious event'.[14] Each of the virgins was told this in confidence, and threatened that if they divulged they should be visited by some awful judgement.

On Sunday 17 October 1830, Wroe received a letter from the committee of the Society of Christian Israelites at Ashton, asking that he return to the town immediately to answer serious charges that had been made against him. The Prophet had intended to sail to Ireland from Bristol, but left for Ashton the following day. Wroe made good progress, arriving at Sheffield on Tuesday the 19th, where he held a meeting with friends.

Wroe ordered William Tillotson to draw lots to decide to go via Barnsley or Doncaster for the next stage of the journey. It seems propitious that the lot chose Doncaster, as this was the home town of one of the virgins, where Wroe made sure to try and find out what he could about what Ann Hall had said. He called on Ann's mother, who, according to *Divine Communications*, agreed with Wroe that her daughter 'had not done anything amiss, but others had put words into her'.[15]

Wroe's trial by senior members of the Society of Christian Israelites convened at 2p.m. on Sunday 24 October 1830, in the Ashton eastern millennial gatehouse, which was later called the Odd Whim.[16] The court had commenced as soon as Wroe had arrived there on his way from Bradford. The account of the proceedings in *Divine Communications* tells of how on entering the house Wroe addressed those present 'as gentlemen, instead of friends or brethren', because he considered that some of them did 'not belong to the house of Israel'. He declared that he had 'come in the name of the Lord Jesus Christ to suffer the sentence they should pass on him'.[17]

The Revd James Elishama Smith was appointed as chairman of the jury, and he started the proceedings by reading out the statements by two of the three young women: Sarah Pile and Mary Quance. They had brought charges of lying and sexual misconduct against Wroe. In his defence Wroe merely solemnly declared his innocence. No conclusion could be drawn and, amid confusion over how the court should operate, the sitting was adjourned until the following day.

The court assembled again at 2 p.m. on Monday the 25th, at which point two of the jury, William Masterman and James Smith, were immediately dismissed, as it was considered that the men were determined to 'act contrary to the rules of the court'. Two other men were chosen in their place. Masterman and Smith did not, however, give up their seats on the jury without a fight, and a scuffle ensued which delayed the proceedings of the court for another day. It was not until the early hours of Tuesday morning that the court reconvened, thereafter sitting from morning to evening each day until the Saturday.

The jury, consisting of twelve men and twelve married women, heard evidence from the witnesses for the following five days. Wroe agreed not to appear before the court until all the evidence had been heard. *Divine Communications* prints the names of the twelve male members of the jury: Joseph Billington, of Ashton-under-Lyne; David Brummit, of Leeds; James Bradbury, of Stalybridge; Thomas Craven, of Wakefield; John Hague, of Sheffield; Joseph Ogden, of Ashton-under-Lyne; John Shaw, of Sheffield; Joseph Shaw, of Ashton-under-Lyne; William Skin, of Ashton-under-Lyne; John Stanley, of Ashton-under-Lyne; William Windle, Scotland Street, Sheffield; Aaron Woollacott, of Ashton-under-Lyne.

The accusations centred on Wroe's alleged behaviour towards two of the virgins while at his home at Street House, near Bradford. *Divine Communications* prints extracts from some of the evidence, mostly that which was given in Wroe's favour. The following are typical:

Mary Bullough: 'I have lived with John Wroe and family, at Street House, near Bradford, a considerable time, as servant; Sarah Pile was there part of the time; I never saw anything improper between them.'

Ann Garland: 'I have been with him both by day and night, and never saw anything amiss by him.'

Nancy Knowlson: 'I was with John Wroe and his wife as a servant for about five weeks; I never saw anything amiss in him, nor knew him tell lies.'

Esther Lees: 'About seven years ago I waited on John Wroe six weeks at Idle; he always conducted himself as a man of God.'

William Lees: 'I have travelled with John Wroe in this and in foreign lands; I never saw anything improper in his conduct; have thought his conversation rather light at times, but I never saw or had any suspicion of improper conduct or inclinations towards women.'

Sarah Masterman: (who had also lived with him as a servant at Street House): 'I have seen nothing improper in his conduct whilst living with him.'

William Muff: 'I have travelled with John Wroe, and known him from the year 1822, and I never saw him behave any way improper towards women . . .'

Robert Stewart: 'I have travelled with John Wroe, both in England and Scotland, and never saw anything in him but what became a man of God.'

The evidence against Wroe centred on an incident which had allegedly taken place in his farmhouse at Street House in October 1829, where Sarah Pile and Ann Hall were working as servants. As Sarah Pile sometimes acted as Wroe's scribe, she would wait up with Wroe late at night, ready to take down his *Divine Communications*, after the rest of the household had gone to bed. According to the allegations, which were later published in a Manchester paper,[18] 'they sat together in one chair for some time, gratifying his lustful inclinations', when the couple were suddenly disturbed by Wroe's wife, Mary entering the room. Fortunately for Wroe the light in the room was dim and a clothes horse, heavily laden with linen, obscured Mrs Wroe's view of the couple, 'otherwise', as the *Voice of the People* puts it, 'his wife must have seen their very acts'.

In an attempt to conceal his actions, Wroe merely said, 'Date it,' to Sarah Pile, as if dictating the last part of a communication. '"Date it!" is it?' stormed Mrs Wroe, as she flew into a rage. The brief report of this incident in *Divine Communications* mentions Mrs Wroe's jealousy towards the two servants at Street House. At the time, members of the Society expressed some concern, as the servants were questioned about the incident by William Muff and Sarah Wroe (probably Wroe's cousin). Muff recalled that both said that the Prophet had not behaved improperly, and were prepared to state this on oath.[19] As for Mrs Wroe's jealousy and 'rebellion' towards her husband, *Divine Communications* prints what must be the most astounding lines in the entire three volumes of Wroe's *Life and Journal*. At the time of the alleged incident at Street House, Mrs Wroe was pregnant. Wroe pronounced that either his wife or the child would die for his wife's rebellion.[20] The infant did indeed die in February 1830, aged 6 weeks.

Wroe and his supporters dismissed the statements made by Hall, Pile and Quance. They alleged that Samuel Walker had told the three young women what to say, pointing out that Ann Hall had stayed at Walker's house for two weeks prior to the trial. Walker was the chief instigator against Wroe. Although a member of the Ashton-under-Lyne committee, he was in fact from Bradford, having been one of the original believers in Wroe's visitation in 1822. He therefore would have been well aware of the Martha Whiteley allegations.

At the end of the proceedings on Saturday 30 October, Wroe continued to protest his innocence. The chairman of the jury piously concluded that they could not condemn him, stating, 'I say as Pilate said to the Jews of old, when our Lord was before him: I wash my hands from the blood of this man.' Thus the trial ended, inconclusively. He may have escaped the condemnation of the court, but the wrath of the people of Ashton was to prove almost as severe as that in his native Bradford. Wroe left for Huddersfield on the evening of the final day of the trial and spent most of the winter of 1830–1 living at Sandal near Wakefield.

Two members of the Society of Christian Israelites were far from happy at the outcome of Prophet Wroe's trial, and they bided their time over the winter months, plotting their revenge on Prophet Wroe. The details of the charges at Wroe's trial had been kept behind the closed doors of the court. William Masterman and Samuel Walker, however, were determined to bring the allegations to the attention of a wider audience. Masterman and Walker enjoyed powerful positions within the Society as they made up half of the so-called 'No. 4', the group of four individuals who managed the Society at an executive and administrative level.

Wroe remained away from Ashton-under-Lyne for almost four months. He had even received a 'communication' to 'stop thou out of Ashton till the indictment be removed'.[21] Wroe would come to rue not heeding this celestial advice. Notwithstanding, undaunted he later announced his intention to return to Ashton on 26 February to preach in the Sanctuary to members of the Society as well as to address the general public. This was the opportunity Masterman and Walker had been waiting for. The two men printed and distributed handbills around Ashton, containing the following information:[22]

The public are respectfully informed, that John Wroe alias Joannes, alias Yohannon, alias Asrael Wroe, stands charged with acts of indecency, immorality and perjury, of the most offensive and disgusting nature on the evidence, upon oath, of three respectable females, taken before a jury of twelve respectable persons in October last, for which vile conduct he has not given any satisfactory explanation; . . . to come forward and preach in the sanctuary on Sunday the 27th February, at half past two o'clock, at which time we call upon him to make his defence to the charges proved against him, and we request the public to attend and hear the same.

Ashton, February 25th 1831

W.C. Masterman
Samuel Walker

By the afternoon of Sunday 27 February 1831 the excitement in Ashton was intense. Wroe had arrived in the town at about midday, on a coach from Wakefield, accompanied by James Shand.[23] The Sanctuary was crowded to excess with an odd mixture of towns-people from all classes of local society. Wroe's supporters sat among his opponents within the Society, as well as those who were not of the Christian Israelite faith. Members of the congregation included Mr Southam, a local cotton manufacturer, Mr Astley a magistrate from Dukinfield, and even soldiers.

The service started peacefully enough. Wroe preached an uninspiring sermon, which was not interrupted by any of the congregation, so he spun it out, talking for an unusual length of time. The sermon concluded and Wroe was directed by the clerk to announce a psalm. This he did, the psalm being one of the longest in the book.[24] Masterman, growing tired of what he considered to be Wroe's procrastination, rose from his seat and started to read out the accusations. The band began to play, which temporarily stopped Masterman in mid-sentence, as Wroe descended from the pulpit amid jeers and catcalls from sections of the congregation.

'What! Are you running away?' shouted Thomas Spencer, who was another of those who had turned against Wroe. Silas Lees and others sensed that Wroe was about to make an escape but were unable to prevent it, as the Prophet's allies held them back. In the commotion that followed, Wroe made his escape through a trapdoor, along a tunnel and safely into the house of the still-faithful John Stanley in Park Parade.

Meanwhile, supporters and opponents fought and considerable damage was done to the interior of the extravagant building. Pews were torn up and smashed – being used as weapons – hymn books were thrown and the windows above the entrance doors in Church Street were smashed to pieces. Masterman escaped the wrath of Wroe's supporters and stood on a chair outside the building, continuing to read out his catalogue of allegations to those leaving the Sanctuary and anyone else who would listen.

Later in the afternoon a group of men led by Silas Lees searched the town for Wroe. They heard he was hiding at the house of William Skin (later the Odd Whim public house) and tried to force their way into the property. Those inside fought hard to prevent this and Lees received a violent blow on the head from a poker, which brought forth a torrent of blood.[25] Skirmishes erupted elsewhere in the town and some of the houses belonging to Christian Israelites were damaged.

\* \* \*

Such was the media's interest in the disturbances at the Ashton Sanctuary that the allegations published by Walker and Masterman made it into the press. It is easy to see why their accusations caused so much excitement. Of all the newspapers that reported the story, the most damning coverage of all was given by the Manchester newspaper the *Voice of the People*, which printed the allegations virtually in full in its edition of 5 March. The newspaper recounts the experiences of each of the three virgins. The explicit nature of the allegations is shocking, particularly as they appear in a paper published in 1831.

The most shocking allegations relate to Sarah Pile, who was appointed head of the seven virgins. Other than those already mentioned, the columns of the *Voice of the People* tell of a strange journey, made by Wroe, Pile and another of the virgins, in which they left Street House, Bradford in a gig, heading in the direction of Ashton. They had not got very far on their journey when they were confronted by bizarre sights including naked men dancing near a large open fire and the sound of 'a large piece of water, running with a rushing noise close by the road side'. These seem to have been illusory.

Even more alarming, however, was Pile's confession that Wroe 'used to suck on her breasts, and declared he could live on them'. He also, according to the *Voice*, caused her 'to inflict a peculiar punishment upon him, which he had appointed for disobedient and offending females'. The paper stops here with its report of this particular allegation, stating that it is 'too gross to be mentioned'. Surely this is an allusion to flagellation. The full account of the allegations (as reported by the *Voice of the People*) is reproduced in Appendix 1.

Apart from the allegations published in the *Voice of the People*, the *Sheffield Courant* and the *Manchester Chronicle* also printed the story that week, and other newspapers, including *Bell's Life in London*, took up the story during the week which followed. On the day after the most damaging allegations had appeared in the *Voice*, Wroe received the following communication, which his followers believed came 'from the Holy Spirit of God':[26]

The Spirit of the Lord is upon me . . . The world must advertise first, and bring forth all lies and abominations, that desolation may be amongst them. And I now command the twelve to advertise their evidence, and that there is not a witness against my servant. For the time is come that I will gather by the newspaper, and Israel shall know that it is I.

Later that month Wroe and his highest-ranking supporters met at Sheffield and set about a massive damage-limitation exercise, bombarding the press with letters rebuffing the allegations. In a desperate bid to clear Wroe's character, which they believed had been dragged through the mud by the newspapers, the men answered specific allegations and published parts of the evidence given at the trial which supported Wroe. Their efforts resulted in a document, an 'Address to the Public', which was sent out to many of the papers and later published in the pages of *Divine Communications*. The document begins as follows:[27]

As certain persons who were lately professed believers in the visitation of John Wroe as being of God, and also public advocates of the same, have, through blindness and disappointment in their expectations, become apostates to their late professed religion; and have also, through the enemy of mankind, Satan, taking advantage of them, and turning them into the gall of bitterness, dared to publicly defame and wantonly reprobate John Wroe's character.

Although the names of Sarah Lees and the 'female Shiloh' Sarah Lees Hague were not generally known, the names of the three virgins – Hall, Pile and Quance – were not kept secret. The *Voice of the People* did not publish the names of the three in its lengthy article; Wroe's supporters made the names widely known in their denunciations. Their rebuttals of the allegations of what went on behind the clothes horse will suffice as an example:

John Wroe's wife being examined, she declared she knew nothing of such words being said as 'date it', but said, 'She had seen a thing she did not like, neither would she bear it'; it is as follows, in her own words. 'I told her (Sarah Pile) of getting up before the rest, and part dressing herself before him', (viz. John Wroe).

Despite the furious denials of Wroe's supporters, the damage had already been done and the scandals stuck to Wroe's character. It is clear from the pages of *Divine Communications* that hardly any of the specific charges are answered by the document, and a third of the three pages (excluding footnotes) is taken up by a character-reference-type testimony from Wroe's most enduring scribe, William Tillotson. The attempt failed, as only one newspaper, the *Sheffield Courant*, printed their document in full.[28]

Other papers took little interest in what Wroe and his remaining supporters had to say in refuting the allegations. For example, their letter to the *Voice of the People* was acknowledged in the edition of that paper of 26 March 1831.[29] The *Voice* printed a small paragraph on the matter, concluding with the letter's final sentence which it considered would 'show the opinion which is still entertained of this consummate hypocrite: "We, the above mentioned, wish it to be understood that we think or judge J.A.W. to be free from error, but consider him to be as *other prophets* of the Lord God, whom he has sent with his word in former ages."'

\* \* \*

Trying to ascertain if there is any truth behind allegations of incidents which took place in the first quarter of the nineteenth century is obviously fraught with difficulty. The accuracy of some of the precise details of the allegations can only give grounds for speculation. The fact that Wroe called for seven virgins is undoubtedly true: it is referred to in Smith's *The Coming Man*, which includes what appears to be a candid account of Smith's time in Ashton as a follower of Wroe. It seems most unlikely, however, that three of the young women became pregnant by Wroe. The *Sheffield Courant* in its version of the story that Wroe was to be the 'holy instrument' for bringing about the birth of Shiloh, tells of how each of the three was kept unaware that he had also had sex with the other two. A few months later, however, according to the *Courant*, there was 'evidence that instead of one Shiloh, there would shortly be three, and a suspicion of the prophet's guilt'.[30] The *Manchester Chronicle* contains a very similar account, saying that 'instead of the one Shiloh, it was evident that three young candidates should soon appear upon earth'. Yet where is the later evidence that three (or even one) of the 'virgins' gave birth?

Had any of the women conceived even as late as September 1830, they would have been almost seven months pregnant at the time of the Sanctuary riot. If the fact that the women were pregnant had aroused the suspicion of senior members of the Society prior to the trial, then the births would have taken place before the allegations appeared in the papers, yet no births were reported. So was it instead the case that Wroe did have sexual intercourse with Mary Quance, Sarah Pile and Ann Hall, but that no conception occurred?

Although local historians refer to the birth of Sarah Lees's baby, they do not mention that any of the virgins gave birth. The confusion of the Lees baby with the case of the seven virgins has given the virgins' story greater credence, helped by the wrong assumption that Lees was one of the seven. Christian Israelite renegade Thomas Fielden takes some delight in the disturbances at Ashton and refers to a single pregnancy of a married woman by Wroe, but admits that he was not a member of the Society of Christian Israelites at the time.[32] Had the virgins given birth he would surely have included this extraordinary fact in his pamphlet. Baring-Gould also does not mention any pregnancy other than that of Sarah Lees.[33] As an Anglican vicar and local historian he took a keen interest in pillorying Wroe's character and clearly sought statements from his contemporaries, such as the young man from Bradford who had witnessed one of Wroe's trances early on in his career. He too would not have been able to resist writing about more than one birth.

The pregnancies can thus be discounted as tittle-tattle, but there is still evidence that at least one other aspect of the allegations was true. This is Sarah Pile's assertion that Wroe made her 'inflict a peculiar punishment upon him, which he had appointed for disobedient and offending females'. Alongside the reports of prophecies relating to industrialisation, freak weather and plague within the pages of *Divine Communications*, are more disturbing indications that Wroe's sexual appetite was a driving force behind his career. Other contemporary sources providing accounts of obsessive initiation ceremonies associated with Wroe make unsettling reading. It could be argued that these practices had only been adopted by the Christian Israelites as late as about 1860, when the pamphlets were published by Fielden and one other defector outlining the procedures.[34] Yet there is a similarity between their accounts and the description already cited, given in Smith's *The Coming Man*, of the punishment meted out by the females to the males. In Smith's narrative, corporal punishment was 'inflicted by the women, with rods'. This was written at least a dozen years before the defectors' pamphlets, but only published, posthumously, in 1874.

There are many unanswered questions about John Wroe, his relationship with the seven virgins, and how the allegations were reported in the press and recounted in the pages of *Divine Communications*. Not least, why was there apparent silence from the other four virgins? One or two of these women may have been among those who gave evidence in favour of Wroe's character at his trial, but there is no indication to suggest that they did. Why was the case not taken up by civil authorities at Ashton or Bradford? This point seems strange considering the speed at which the Tong magistrate had acted over the Whiteley allegation in 1827. And why did not the scandal of the birth of Sarah Lees's baby resurface in the press, whereas the unfounded Martha Whiteley allegations did?

A notebook, ostensibly written by Samuel Lees under Wroe's dictation, survives at the Tameside Local Studies and Archives Centre, Ashton-under-Lyne.[35] It dates from December 1828 to May 1830 and details the types of buckles, chains, clasps, jewellery and other means of adornment to be worn by the faithful. Running to some thirty pages in length, the regulations are somewhat repetitive. The last two pages of writing, however, reveal a sudden obsession with the clothing to be worn by pregnant women. The notebook's entries are signed, in a shaky hand, by the familiar 'Jaakov Asriel', a known pseudonym of Wroe. These last two pages may well have been written by Wroe himself. Does this notebook have a bearing on the case of the seven virgins, or is it merely an intriguing red herring, given that so much of the other primary evidence does not survive?

It has mistakenly been concluded that Wroe's obsession coincided with the pregnancy of Sarah Lees. However, what all the other historians have overlooked is that in 1830 Mrs Wroe was actually pregnant again, this time with the couple's youngest daughter Sarai. It is difficult to pin down the date of birth of Sarai Wroe. Her age as recorded on her marriage certificate and in the census returns of the late nineteenth century does not equate with the age given at the registration of her death. Sarai was born at Sandal Magna, probably in late 1830. Could this explain Wroe's obsession?

Despite the absurd strains placed on John and Mary Wroe's relationship, the couple did not separate, remaining married until Mrs Wroe's death over twenty years later, aged 74. Such an age would mean that Mrs Wroe gave birth to her youngest child when she was 51, seemingly almost miraculous. This has to cast doubt over whether Sarai really was her daughter and not a substitute; that is, until the parish registers of Mary Wroe (née Appleby's) home village are consulted. Could the answer lie in the baptism records for the chapelry of Farnley in the parish of Leeds? These registers record the baptism of Mary, daughter of Benjamin Appleby on 8 May 1785.[36] Therefore the true age at which Mary died was 66, and thus she would have been a more plausible 45 when she gave birth to Sarai. Or could it be that Mary was 6 years old when she was baptised? This would always have been left open to speculation were it not that for some reason the Farnley-by-Leeds registers also record Mary's date of birth as 10 April 1785.

* * *

As with many of the accounts in *Divine Communications*, there are several footnotes relating to the torrid events of the period from October 1830 to April 1831. Wroe and his followers regarded with particular relish what befell some of those who had 'persecuted' him, believing it to be a form of divine retribution. The first of Wroe's opponents to fall was Samuel Walker, one of the chief instigators of the allegations. On the evening of the first day of the trial he had predicted that 'the Lord shall return to Samuel Walker his master's spirit'.[37] The footnote neatly turns the tables on Walker, accusing him of fathering a child through an affair. It explains that when Walker was living at Bradford in 1824 his employer Stephen Ambler left his wife for another woman and the couple had a child. Now Walker too had 'committed whoredom', just as his master had approximately nine years before. As if that prophecy of Walker's impending downfall was not enough, on the day following Wroe's acquittal, 30 October 1830, Wroe dictated another Walker prediction to William Barraclough at Huddersfield. Walker would end up without 'a house, or a bed to lay down on'.[38] This too transpired, in 1835, when the debt-laden Walker was forced to lodge in the room of a house in Ashton, before returning to his native Bradford.

Two predictions against him may have been harsh enough, but the pages of *Divine Communications* tell of the outcome of a third.[39] This was made by Wroe at Wakefield on 30 June 1833 and is particularly disturbing, warning Walker that:

> I will prove him before the whole house of Israel, by his flesh pining from his bones; I will make him a sign to the four winds, that his name may be carried into many nations; and I will punish their souls during the life of their bodies by a grievous punishment.

Again the footnote of fulfilment helpfully explains that after Walker had fallen on hard times he became a fortune-teller in Bradford, at first with some success. In the autumn of 1838, however, he was suddenly taken ill and was dead within five days. Although *Divine Communications* does not give any references, it mentions that strange accounts of Walker's fortune-telling, visions, illness and death appeared in the press, and how after he died his flesh turned black.

Another of the perpetrators behind Wroe's downfall, Thomas Spencer, ended up in London in severe debt amounting to £1,500, and was made bankrupt at the beginning of 1835. But Wroe's final and most gloating footnote on the events of 1830–1 concerns Messrs Hampson and Hadfield, the publishers of the *Voice of the People*, the Manchester newspaper which had published the majority of the virgins' allegations and refused to print Wroe's rebuttals. In 1833 Mr Hampson dropped dead in the street and Mr Hadfield hanged himself.[40]

\* \* \*

In the days following the disturbances at the Sanctuary in February 1831 there was a 'mighty sharpening of razors and scissors' in Ashton and many 'new faces' were seen about the streets.[41] The *Manchester Guardian* of 13 March 1831 quotes a delightful verse which appeared in a barber's shop window at Ashton-under-Lyne in the wake of the disturbances of 27 February. The enterprising barber had penned the following ditty:

UPSHOT OF THE SOUTHCOTTIANS, OR MODERN ISRAELITES,
ALIAS WROE IN THE SUDS

> In ancient times, as I've been taught,
> Long beards an ornament were thought;
> But now, that fashion's quite abolish'd,
> Step in, and have your faces polish'd;
> With steady hand and razor keen,
> Your face from whiskers I'll shave clean.

Five weeks after the disorder in Ashton-under-Lyne on 27 February, Wroe was back in the Lancashire town again. There was great excitement in Ashton on Easter Sunday, 3 April 1831, when the Prophet visited the town for what was to be the last time for almost eight years. Wroe arrived in the area on horseback at about 2 p.m., accompanied by a companion. Travelling via the backstreets,

108

the pair tried to arrive unnoticed at the Sanctuary, where Wroe intended to preach a sermon. News of his arrival quickly spread and soon the scene was set for a repeat of the disturbances of five weeks earlier. This time, however, members of the congregation managed to lock the doors of the building and secure them against the mob outside. Much fighting took place in the street. Stones and mud were thrown, and the crowd again smashed the windows above the entrance doors, which were the only ones that could be reached from the front of the building. On this occasion the entire congregation evacuated the Sanctuary via the passageway that led to a member's house in Park Parade.[42] Here Wroe was thought to have remained until 5 a.m. the following morning, when he made his escape through the centre of the town.

Some of the remaining faithful also left Ashton early that day, symbolically making their way to the gatehouse on the Mossely Road, where Wroe's trial had taken place, which until 2004 was the Odd Whim public house. They took with them the society's printing press and types, valued at £50, carried in a cart drawn by four beautiful black horses with uncut manes and tails, which were the property of John Stanley. The company repeated the Lord's Prayer in Hebrew as they marched through the streets, chanting and singing accompanied by their band of musicians. The sun rose as they arrived at the gatehouse, and the party rested as the carts were reloaded before departing.

Wroe left Ashton accompanied by William Tillotson in the early morning. As they walked away from the town, however, the pair noticed that they were being followed by four or five people, including two of Wroe's most bitter opponents, Masterman and Spencer. The men caught up with Wroe, and Spencer and Masterman seized him by the collar. Although the men had turned against Wroe, they were not disillusioned with millennial religion, but had transferred their allegiance to John 'Zion' Ward.[43] Masterman demanded to know if Wroe had received a letter from him, in which he was ordered to appear before Ward, who Masterman referred to as Shiloh. Ward was another millennial leader, who, like Wroe, the old guard of the Southcottians (such as Mr Foley) had refused to recognise. Wroe said he'd returned the letter unopened, which angered one of the others, who told Masterman to 'knock his head off'. At this point the men saw the group of Christian Israelites travelling with the printing press coming towards them. Wroe, relieved on realising that his enemies were outnumbered, stood on a pile of stones and began to preach. Masterman, Spencer and their cohorts turned round and walked back to Ashton.

When the people of Ashton awoke, they were angry that the Prophet had slipped through their grasp. They nevertheless took out their fury against Wroe, by incorporating him into a curious local custom that traditionally took place in the town on Easter Monday. The custom was the ceremony of 'riding the black lad', when the effigy of the Black Knight in armour is placed on horseback and paraded in procession through the town, dismounted and hung at the cross in the old marketplace. On Easter Monday 1831, the effigy paraded through the streets of Ashton, and finally shot at in the market, was that of John Wroe.

By the time of the Easter Monday festivities in Ashton, Wroe was well on his way back to Yorkshire. The company took a route via Huddersfield, resting at Wakefield on Monday night, Barnsley on Tuesday and finally Sheffield on the Wednesday. The musicians played at every town and village through which the party passed. Occasionally Wroe would preach to those present, warning of the millennium. The party consisted of about forty people, male and female. As well as the cart carrying the printing press, Wroe travelled in a splendid car drawn by a mule, while two luggage carts made up the rear of the procession. *The Times* comments that while the 'seducer Wroe' travelled in luxury, the bearded brethren and sisters had to walk.[44] At least the weather for the journey is described in *Divine Communications* as being 'as fine as possible for the purpose'.

Wroe's comfortable life at Ashton-under-Lyne had also come to an end. Just a couple of days earlier when Mrs Wroe had returned to the sumptuous house at Shepley, she found the building had been ransacked. Samuel Walker had searched the house, opening all drawers, cupboards and boxes, breaking into anything which was locked. Valuables were removed, including silver plate which had belonged to Wroe's father. The silver was later returned, but the Wroes could not take it back because it was against their laws to receive goods that had been stolen.[45] During the burglary, the leaders of the Christian Israelite Society at Ashton had deliberately waylaid Mrs Wroe to prevent her from disturbing Walker.

Walker and Masterman's new mentor, John 'Zion' Ward had two chapels in London and a following in the Midlands and the Bristol area. No doubt he had encouraged the two men in the vociferousness of their pursuit of Wroe. On hearing of the Prophet's downfall he had hurried to the Lancashire town, eager to steal Wroe's crown. His attempt to usurp Wroe's followers in Ashton was, however without success and within a month he had returned to London.

\* \* \*

Although Wroe had escaped Ashton without injury, he was far from safe in Yorkshire, in particular in his native Bradford. The following Sunday, 10 April 1831, witnessed a riot against the Prophet in that town that was even more severe than the disturbances that had occurred at the Ashton Sanctuary in February. Wroe left Wakefield for Bradford at 11.20 that morning accompanied by James Rephah Shand, a shoemaker from Kirkgate, Wakefield. Wroe and Shand arrived at Bradford three hours later and made their way to the Christian Israelites' meeting room, where a congregation was waiting.

Shand entered the room and started reading part of the service, but he was immediately interrupted by boisterous members of the congregation. 'We don't want you, we want Wroe!' they shouted, and many demanded 'an explanation of the seven virgins'.[46] Wroe spoke to the gathering for between fifteen and twenty minutes, but this did not pacify some elements in the crowd. Again they demanded to know about the virgins' allegations, and when Wroe failed to respond they began to smash up the furnishings. Shand halted the service, while one or two of Wroe's friends ran from the room to get the help of local constables Joshua Pollard and Joseph Smith.

Pollard was scathing when approached, mocking their requests, saying, 'Do you think we will protect such a villain as he? Why does he come here to make such a disturbance? Bring him out to the people, and they will be satisfied!' The constables did cooperate, however, and eventually managed to clear the meeting room of all but Wroe and his close colleagues, who locked themselves inside (the meeting room at Bradford lacking handy escape tunnels such as those built behind the Sanctuary at Ashton-under-Lyne). The mob outside were not pacified for long. Within half an hour they had succeeded in breaking down the door (still in its frame). They rushed into the room and grabbed Wroe, dragging him outside by the hair of his head and beard, pulling out his beard by the handful.[47] At this point one of the constables gave a signal to the crowd, saying, 'Go it, lads!' and the Prophet was thrown down steps from the third storey to the ground floor, where he was trampled underfoot. Baring-Gould argues that the anger of the crowd had been stirred not only by the virgins' allegations, but also by the death of another infant, named Wood, whom he had allegedly circumcised.[48] No mention can be found relating to this death in the newspaper reports of the riots.

Elements among the crowd were intent on causing Wroe serious harm. Some cried 'murder him'; even Constable Pollard was hostile and, along with his fellow constables, allegedly drunk. 'Throw him into the beck!' cried Pollard. 'If he cannot divide the water, let him sink or swim!' The Bradford beck was by this period in the town's history so badly polluted that Wroe would probably have been poisoned before he drowned. The mob instead dragged Wroe along the street, but as they passed the door of Mr Bilton's shop, a quick-thinking young man somehow managed to make a grab for the Prophet and pull him inside the shop door, closing it behind him.[49]

Panes of glass were broken in Mr Bilton's windows, but Wroe remained in the shop until about 10 o'clock, by which time Bilton and others had managed to persuade the constables to take Wroe to a safer place. They took him to The New Inn, escorting him through the dense crowds.[50] The constables brought him some women's clothes so that he could escape through the crowd undetected in the dark, intending to take him to a bed in the vagrants' office. Wroe would have nothing of their scheme: 'Have you brought me here to make sport of me? Has not the mob done enough?' Instead he waited until 11.30, when he left The New Inn accompanied by his sister and niece. Wroe had been so severely assaulted that three of his ribs were broken, and the bleeding from his mouth and ears offered more ominous signs of internal injuries.

Wroe left Bradford in the early hours of the following morning and arrived at Wakefield at 3.15 in the afternoon. He stayed at Wakefield for a couple of weeks to recover, before travelling on to Sheffield for a month and then on to a visit to Devonport, where the Christian Israelites had a keen following.

Wroe clearly regarded this day as the most terrible of his controversial religious career, far worse than the incident at the Sanctuary at Ashton-under-Lyne, as on this occasion he had been unable to evade the crowd and had suffered a serious physical assault. Yet despite his close brush with a more dreadful fate, Wroe and his remaining supporters were reported by the press as rejoicing, because their Prophet had been 'thought worthy to suffer persecution for righteousness' sake'.[51] Another reason for the satisfaction of Wroe's followers was that the riot had been predicted. At Street House, Bradford (in the farmhouse where Wroe's apprentice Martha Whiteley later worked and where the virgin Sarah Pile had acted as his scribe), Wroe had prophesied that 'There will be a greater tumult at Bradford than there was on the day when I was stoned before [after the fourteen days in 1824], and I shall be left for dead.'[52] He made further reference to the imminent event on the day he was pursued by Spencer and Masterman as he and William Tillotson left Ashton. On the morning of the event itself he reportedly told William Whiteley at his home in Ings Lane [Road], Wakefield that this was the day that he would 'be trodden under the foot of man'.[53] Even when the Prophet was in the locked meeting room with his close Christian Israelite friends, he turned to James Shand and said, 'James, they will break the door open: this is the time that I am to be delivered into their hands, which I saw seven years since, that they should take me and trample me under their feet.'

Wroe's original success at Ashton-under-Lyne had come about as the direct result of the sexual impropriety of a leading Southcottian in the town. Surely the irony of the circumstances surrounding Wroe's fall was not lost on his former followers there. It was some years before Wroe visited Ashton again, and following the disturbances in Bradford his occupancy of the Tong Street farmhouse came to an end because of the local population's hostility towards him. Prophet Wroe may have 'officially' lived in Lancashire (at Ashton-under-Lyne and Park Bridge) for a mere six years out of his forty-three-year religious career, and even during that time he was away on many visits as well as residing at his farmhouse at Street House. He is, nevertheless, forever connected with Ashton, the scene of his most ambitious architectural millennial scheme (the 'New Jerusalem') and also of his spectacular fall in the wake of the virgins' allegations.

*7*

# Return of the Native

A fter what was in effect temporary banishment from Ashton-under-Lyne, Wroe decided to settle back on his native side of the Pennines. Bradford was fraught with danger and Wroe had experienced hostility on several occasions, on two of which he almost lost his life. Instead, in the wake of the disturbances at Ashton and Bradford, he decided to live in the comparatively safe county town of the old West Riding – Wakefield. Wroe had lived at Sandal Magna, a parish two miles south of the town, in late 1830, where his youngest daughter Sarai was born. Wroe first took tenancy of a house in Park Street, off Kirkgate, Wakefield in 1831, before moving soon afterwards to Thompson's Yard, Westgate. Here he set up his organisation's printing press, and the Christian Israelites had their chapel nearby. An 1837 edition of *White's Trade Directory* lists Wroe as a printer and binder, so presumably this trade supplemented his income. Interestingly, twenty years later, in November 1857, Thompson's Yard was the birthplace of the novelist George Gissing.

Although the number of Christian Israelites in Wakefield was far less than in Ashton-under-Lyne, their appearance made them conspicuous about the town. In his *Home Tour through the Manufacturing Districts of England*, Sir George Head wrote of a coach journey from Leeds to Wakefield in the Summer of 1835.[1] Head travelled on top of the coach with a father and daughter whom he took to be Southcottians, although they were almost certainly followers of John Wroe. He described the couple as 'A strange looking pair . . . dressed, though probably according to regulations, as I considered in a very extraordinary way'. The father was, according to Sir George, aged about 40:

115

of a light dapper figure, carefully set off to the best advantage, and most remarkable as to the Vandyke-cut of his unshorn beard; in order to trim which to the present style of exquisite perfection, the scissors had evidently been put in requisition. His broad low-crowned beaver hat was of a reddish brown, and his gaberdine and Wellington boots fitted him so neatly, that without changing his costume he might have danced a quadrille without inconvenience.

As for his daughter, the:

florid, healthy girl of 18 wore, though in the middle of the day, a Parisian straw bonnet, decked with huge curling full dress bunch of white ostrich feathers, a blue cloth habit, the back seams of which were ornamented with a wide military border, the latter made of parallel stripes of orange coloured silk twist, and a petticoat plaited with broad plaits, disposed about the hips with great care, and laid one over the other with exceeding regularity – nay, as it were, with such geometrical precision, that as nature had been bountiful in those latitudes, they exactly resembled the meridian lines of a terrestrial globe.

From at least July 1837, if not before, Wroe moved to Brandy Carr House, an elegant sandstone farmhouse on high ground overlooking the industrial hamlet of Wrenthorpe, about two miles north of Wakefield. The farmhouse stands in Jerry Clay Lane, then a quiet country lane, which had been constructed as a result of the 1793 Inclosure Awards, when the open lands of the ancient Wakefield Outwood were parcelled into fields and allotted to private owners. Its name came from one of these local owners, Jeremiah Clay, but such was the notoriety of Wroe's residence in the neighbourhood that on the 1851 census returns the lane is recorded not as Jerry Clay Lane but as Prophet Wroe's Lane.[2] Even today, when this house is near the very edge of the green belt, it is still not difficult to imagine the Prophet wandering along the nearby footpaths, crossing the gurgling becks and climbing the steep hills seeking inspiration.

As with Dukinfield, Wrenthorpe was part of a large and ancient parish with less than ideal conditions for worship, which had only been relieved by the construction of two Commissioners' churches at Stanley and Alverthorpe in the mid-1820s. A church was not built at Wrenthorpe itself until 1874. Spiritually, Wrenthorpe itself was a sensible place for Wroe to live, as the area had had strong Nonconformist and Southcottian traditions. Documents in the Joanna Southcott Collection at the University of Texas show a sizeable Southcottian following in Wrenthorpe (or Potovens, as it was then known) in the late 1810s, with seventy-six registered followers there.

The populace of Wrenthorpe was unconventional, if not unruly. In a letter to his parishioners dated October 1877, Wrenthorpe's second vicar, the Revd Francis Dudley reminded his flock that 'only forty years ago no decent person could pass through the village without insult'. Poverty was rife in the area. Ordnance Survey maps of the mid-nineteenth century illustrate a crammed central section of Wrenthorpe comprising a haphazard crush of higgledy-piggledy terraces, and back-to-back and blind-back cottages. The four main occupations of the locals were coal-mining, rope-making, woollen manufacture and agricultural/horticultural labouring. Their poverty and struggle to finance the construction of their parish church are permanently commemorated by an inscription carved in stone on the west wall of St Anne's Parish Church, beneath the rose window. It reads, 'Let no man despise our poverty for we have done what we could, but rather let him amend our work and always pray for us.'

Brandy Carr House is the only property for which it has been possible to find John Wroe's name recorded on the census returns. The census of 6 June 1841 in Alverthorpe-with-Thornes township records Wroe (described as a 'preacher'), his wife and three of their children.[3] Other occupants of Brandy Carr House on census night were three apprentices and one servant, as well as three members of the Deane family from Gravesend.

It was while they were living at Brandy Carr House that a disturbing incident took place involving the Wroe family and their servants. Between midnight and 1.00 a.m. on the morning of Thursday 4 August 1842 six burglars broke into the house. One cut a pane of glass out of a downstairs window and then let the others in through the front door. Prophet Wroe was away from home that night, sleeping at his property in Thompson's Yard, Wakefield. The only people in Brandy Carr House were Mrs Wroe, Susanna Wroe and a female servant, Sarah Hartley. Wroe's son Benjamin and a servant were sleeping in a nearby outhouse. The women were woken by the noise of the burglars – who had blackened faces and wore miners' working clothes – climbing the stairs, three carrying candles, two armed with pistols and one with a gun. They screamed at the shock, which was fortunately enough noise to wake up Benjamin and his servant. Benjamin entered the house as the six burglars were coming down the stairs. He threatened to shoot the men, but his gun was not loaded and while he loaded it they fled, escaping with a gold watch and chain. Young Wroe fired after them with no effect.[4] Burglaries were common in Wrenthorpe at that time: earlier that same week Wroe had had one of his sheep rustled from a field at Brandy Carr.

On Monday 8 August, three men appeared at Wakefield Court-house, charged with their part in the burglary. They were Benjamin Pickersgill a coal leader and beerhouse keeper of Bragg Lane End, Wrenthorpe, his son John, and James Ramsden, a miner from Lawns near Carr Gate. John Clark and William Iveson had also been apprehended, but were then discharged. The court was crowded to excess during the case, and hundreds massed outside. The three men were committed for trial at the York Assizes. None of the prisoners were known thieves and all three had proclaimed their innocence in court. John Pickersgill declared, 'All I wish to say is, I leave it all to the mercy of the Lord, I'll leave it with Him, He knows all.'

At the ensuing York Assizes the men were sentenced to trans-portation to Australia for ten years. In August 1844, however, James Hudson, a convicted criminal under sentence following a burglary at Gildersome near Leeds, made a voluntary confession to the Governor at York Castle that he and five others had carried out the burglary at Brandy Carr House.[5] Ramsden and the Pickersgills were innocent men. This confession was compounded by other declara-tions, including a statement from the female servant at the farm-

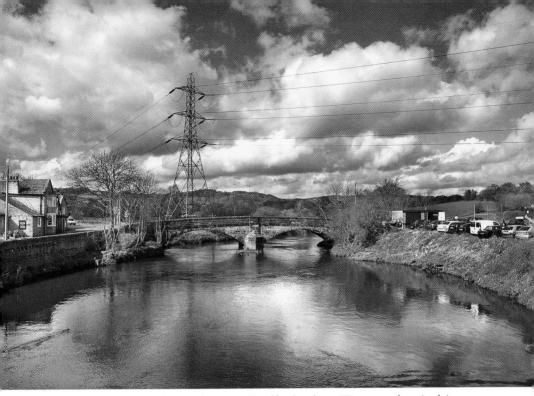

The River Aire at Apperley Bridge near Bradford, where Wroe was baptised in 1824. *(Bradford Telegraph and Argus)*

Watercolour by C.H. Mitchell: 'Ashton-under-Lyne, view from Dukinfield, 1852'. The stone Doric pillar fronted mansion was originally built for Prophet Wroe. *(Astley Cheetham Art Collection, Tameside MBC Museums & Galleries)*

Moss Lodge, Ashton-under-Lyne, during demolition *c.* 1992. Note the resemblance between Moss Lodge and the Odd Whim. *(Tameside Local Studies and Archives Centre)*

The Odd Whim, Ashton-under-Lyne, *c.* 1970 when it was called the Stamford Park Hotel. Wroe's trial took place in this building over six days in October 1830. *(Tameside Local Studies and Archives Centre)*

Brandy Carr House, Jerry Clay Lane, Wrenthorpe, *c.* 1968. This was the scene of the dramatic burglary at the Wroes' in August 1842. *(Jenny and Keith Orrell)*

The Christian Israelite Sanctuary at Fitzroy, Melbourne, Australia. *(Sandra Hargreaves)*

The City Police Station and Town Hall, Melbourne, Australia from an engraving by S.T. Gill which first appeared in *Victoria Illustrated* (Melbourne: Sands & Kenny, 1857), *(Rare Books Collection, State Library of Victoria)*

Melbourne House, Wrenthorpe. *(Kingston Communications)*

The elaborate staircase in Melbourne House, *c.* 1900. *(The John Goodchild Collection)*

Melbourne House, Wrenthorpe in the 1950s. *(Joyce Bramley and www.twixtaireandcalder.org.uk)*

The site of Wroe's grave, Melbourne General Cemetery, Australia. *(Sandra Hargreaves)*

Jezreel's Tower, New Brompton, Chatham, Kent, *c.* 1900, showing the crossed swords symbol associated with John Wroe. *(From an original photograph at Gillingham Library)*

The Christian Israelites' printing-press building, Richmond Street, Ashton-under-Lyne.

*Above:* George Wroe at Melbourne House Farm, Wrenthorpe in the 1920s. *(Bernard Arundel)*

*Left:* Lieutenant 271922 Benjamin Wroe, 7th Battalion, Green Howards (Yorkshire Regiment), *c.* 1943. *(Old Silcoatians' Association)*

*Below:* The grotto in the grounds of Melbourne House *(Brian Collinson)*

house, who acknowledged she did not know any of the burglars, but had made her previous statements under compulsion. It turned out that two of the real offenders had actually been apprehended and discharged.

The *Wakefield Journal and West Riding Herald* expressed the naive hope that 'our Magistrates will take measures by which these innocent men will be restored to their homes and their families again made happy'.[6] An application for release of the three convicts failed to have immediate success, and they were eventually sent home some five years later. Local historian, solicitor William Stott Banks, writing in his *Walks About Wakefield* (1871), described what happened to the families of the three innocent men. 'The consequences were disastrous to them – the mother of one had worn herself out with grief and wandering; the wife of another had gone wrong; the wife of the third had died, and his house had been broken up and his goods sold.'[7]

Other than the controversy caused by the burglary at the Wroes, the years at Wakefield and Brandy Carr in the 1830s and 40s were comparatively calm, as shown by the entries in *Divine Communications*. Any antics as such were considerably more constrained. Gone were the fourteen days of wandering, the eating of butter, milk and honey, and the baptisms. In their place were more conventional and sedate activities, such as a complete reading of the Bible:[8]

At the beginning of December 1832, John Wroe said he had received a command from the Lord that six men should read over the Bible before him, and that the Lord had promised to put his Spirit upon him, and by his Spirit pick out such and such passages, and gather his children out of all nations where they were driven, of which passages the fragments stood typical, spoken of by Jesus.

And they began reading and writing out verses which they were ordered on Monday 3rd instant, at ten minutes before two in the afternoon, and continued day and night till it was ended, which was on Thursday, the 6th at four o'clock in the morning, which was sixty-two hours, wherein John Wroe neither ate bread nor drank water, and there were never less than three men in his company during the time, who bear witness of the above.

After this some of them being asleep, John Wroe said those that are asleep, let them sleep on, for as ye see it now, so shall the end be, rushing to and fro.

They then took refreshments, and sung a hymn, and John Wroe said the angels were rejoicing at what had taken place.

In the wake of the disturbances at Ashton and Bradford, Wroe contented himself with more foreign travel, his preaching, and answering questions from believers, as well as carefully recording his prophecies and visions. Most of these are contained in *Divine Communications* and are extremely verbose and difficult to understand. *The Life of John Wroe, with Divine Communications revealed to him* was published in three volumes running to over 1,600 pages, and covers his many travels and preaching as well as the 'divine communications'. Entries range from a few lines to several pages and in the traditions of the prophets of the Old Testament they were transcribed by a member of the sect. For typical instance, the half-page entry of 6 March 1831, which starts, 'The Spirit of the Lord is upon me, to cause the things to be written', was transcribed 'from the mouth of John Wroe by Robert Blackwell'.[9] William Tillotson was the most prolific of all Wroe's scribes, but also suffered the unfortunate fate of being the subject of one of Wroe's prophecies. At the Christian Israelites' Meeting Room at Wakefield, on 28 August 1846, Wroe declared that 'There are things that in secret lie hid, like an adder in the grass, for a while: so it is with William Tillotson, he will soon be taken away by death like unto his brother; and though I shall see him cut off before my face, yet he will die in the faith.' William Tillotson did indeed die on 2 December of that year, at 4.55 a.m.

The following, as a random example of an entry in *Divine Communications*, is Wroe's interpretation of a dream from Ephraim Lovering of Ashton-under-Lyne, interpreted by Wroe in about May 1849:[10]

One night I dreamt I was on a little island, very small and round, sloping down to the water's edge. I found myself sliding in the water. I was sitting with a fishing line between my legs; there was nothing I could snatch hold of; it was green; there was nobody with me but my son Edwin, and he was asleep; the water was smooth; there was a roll or swell rolling towards me; I kept calling, but I could not awake him – at last I gave a scream, and he caught hold of me, and I awoke.

Wroe prefaced his chilling and ominous reply with the words, 'if the Lord be pleased to answer through his servant, John Wroe, I shall be thankful for the interpretation'. He continued:

Answer. It is thy son Edwin who is trying to snatch thee from the land of the living, by thee getting hold of his words to entangle thee, that thou might fall from thy faith, and thy mortal body die, and thou shalt die, [a footnote here points out that this 'took place on the 20th of 1st month 1855'] but yet if thou continue in thy faith it shall live.

The *Divine Communications* books cover the years up to 1852 and are useful in providing information on Wroe's whereabouts on particular dates. His activities can be followed further by tracking local newspaper reports. Interestingly, Wroe notes days and months numerically, such as '1st day of the 10th month', instead of using their names. It is important to note the minor alterations in the different editions of *Divine Communications*. Later editions include footnotes to indicate how some of the prophecies have been fulfilled since the first edition was published. Although usually written in the first person, an 1851 edition of *Divine Communications* is written in the third person and includes an Introductory Address, which considers the suffering of the biblical prophets.[11] It is also divided differently, with sections including visions, travels, persecution, divine communications and doctrinal instructions.

The very first prophecy recorded by Wroe in *Divine Communications* predicts changes in transportation.[12] The prophecy was transcribed by a near neighbour, William Muff of Little Horton, Bradford, on 26 December 1819:

> John Wroe has declared at various times . . . that he saw shipping in the sea, and in the rivers, go without sails, contrary to the wind . . . that he saw carriages in the high roads, with men, women, and children in them; and they went without horses; he even saw them pass by his own house, and he saw them plow [*sic*] and harrow in the fields without horses, and carriages go on railroads without horses . . . he said, as it was said to him it would surely come to pass in many nations.

Such prophecies about the various anxieties of the new industrial age and the concerns of the expanding populations of the industrial towns gave the Society of Christian Israelites a contemporary relevance. Wroe's prophecies of a political nature ranged from prediction of election results to the outcome of that Bradford wool-combers' strike in 1825.[13] Were these predictions deliberately aimed to appeal to the concerns of people in expanding industrial towns who were experiencing rapid socio-economic change?

A close analysis of the prophecies within *Divine Communications* concerning Wroe's own life and times reveals a number of areas upon which he made pronouncements. Wroe has things to say about the new forms of machinery and transport of the Industrial Age; about industrial relations and politics; about 'plague'; and about freak weather; and about matters of a more personal nature.

INDUSTRIALISATION

A large proportion of the prophecies relate to the introduction of new transport and machinery, and the techniques of industrial production. Railways feature prominently, which is not unexpected in the age of 'railway mania'. The following (given at Wakefield in July 1833) is typical of one of his railway prophecies: 'Thus saith the Lord: They shall take breakfast in Edinburgh in the morning, and on the same evening worship in the sanctuary in London which is upwards of three hundred and ninety miles.'[14]

As was common with later editions of the books, there is even a helpful footnote to explain fulfilment, which reads 'that part of the prophecy relating to the journey from Edinburgh to London is now accomplished, through the facility afforded by the railways'.

Wroe continued to issue prophecies about the railways even in the 1840s and 50s, by which time it must have been obvious to the majority of the population that most towns and many villages would be provided with a railway station. However, in December 1843, on the first of his five visits to Australia, he ventures an even more bold prophecy, the prediction of air travel.

Later in his career, Wroe mocks Britain's showcase as the 'Workshop of the World' when he takes a swipe at the Great Exhibition of 1851. The following entry was written at the Ashton-under-Lyne Sanctuary on 15 August.[15]

Now, many have been up to see the idols at London, which have eyes, but see not; ears, but hear not; legs but walk not. And some members of this society, who have pawned their clothes to go up thither to see the works of men, are not here.

Have not those who are seeking the salvation of the soul been up to see them? Is there anything there which has not been seen before?

If all that some men had seen before were gathered into one compass, would there not have been as great a variety?

There is a model of a coal pit gone out of Wakefield, and many who went from there did not know it when they had seen it.

I may have been tempted to go, but I overcame that temptation.

Those who have been, who are seeking the salvation of the soul, will have it separated from the body, and from their spirits till the first or final resurrection.

But should you who are seeking the life of the body go to look at pictures and likenesses – pictures that are the exact likenesses of human life? Is it not like the worship of images? Must they not be in their hearts?

POLITICS

The prophecy on the outcome of the wool-combers' strike contained in Chapter 4 is by far the best example of Wroe's pronouncements on industrial unrest, but there are other instances of prophecies relating to contemporary political events. Wroe predicted the passing of the 1832 Reform Bill,[16] but the most notable of these political prophecies is Wroe's correspondence with Lord Morpeth, a candidate in the election in 1835 at Wakefield of a knight of the shire for the West Riding of Yorkshire.[17] Wroe claimed to have received a vision that 'there were two colours before me, but victory was given to the yellow, let the man be whom he may', and assumes this to mean a victory of the Whig candidate over the Conservative. Wroe sent Morpeth his prediction and assured him he would not need his vote because he would win so convincingly. Lord Morpeth went on to win with a majority of 2,807. Over a decade earlier, as has already been mentioned, Wroe had attempted to jump on another more significant political bandwagon, the Queen Caroline Case.[18]

PLAGUE AND DISASTERS

In the great tradition of the prophets of the Old Testament, Wroe also predicts catastrophic disasters about to beset the population. These included forecasts of freak weather and, particularly, outbreaks of 'plague', which he usually defines as cholera. Indeed, the gatehouse of the 'New Jerusalem' of Ashton-under-Lyne, where Wroe's trial had been held in 1830, became a cholera hospital in the early 1830s, and many of the victims were buried in the grounds.[19]

Again, later editions of *Divine Communications* provide helpful footnotes as to how various prophecies were fulfilled. For instance, on Sunday 21 April 1833 Wroe preached at the Christian Israelites' Chapel at George's Street, Leeds.[20] Again he warned of the plague: 'Ye think ye have done with the cholera, but I tell you no! For the destroying angel will go from nation to nation, and the plague will return to this land England.' The footnote points out that 'cholera returned to England in the same year, and prevailed greatly in London, as well as the country'.

Closely linked to prophecies of plague and disease are prophecies predicting freak weather or bumper harvests. One of the most extraordinary of these predictions relates to Wroe's banishment from Ashton-under-Lyne following the riots in April 1831. It was many years before he returned. *Divine Communications* tells us that 'He frequently declared he should not re-enter that place until those who had risen up against the word of the Lord were dead, and when he did so not a dog would move its tongue against him.'[21] The book tells us that Wroe returned to Ashton the day after a 'memorable hurricane', which had occurred on Sunday 6 January 1839:

> On the morning of Monday he went into the town in the midst of falling slates, &c., and although if he had done so some years ago, he would have been almost immediately murdered, and ill-treated, he was now allowed to do so peaceably, and although well known to some of those who saw him, yet he was not treated with one disrespectful word.[22]

There are several contemporary accounts of the severity of that night's storm. One such example, Henry Clarkson's *Memories of Merry Wakefield*, first published in 1887, tells of the 'terrible damage . . . done all over the country'.[23]

PROPHECIES OF A PERSONAL NATURE

The final set of predictions relate to named individuals and unpleasant fates that will occur to them. Again, these are usually backed up by footnotes in the later editions of Wroe's books. The most notable of these personal predictions refers to Wroe's brother-in-law, Joseph Appleby of Farnley Mills near Leeds, whose demise Wroe predicted in the spring of 1820.[24] This was one of the predictions which led to his notoriety and assisted in his quest for leadership of the Southcottians. A year later Wroe started work for his cousin, another John Wroe, in Bradford. A quarrel with his cousin's son is recorded in *Divine Communications*:[25]

'Take notice of this young man [his cousin's son], he will never either take any more work in, or pay any more wages.' The young man began to be ill immediately after, and continued for about nine months, and then died, and he never took any more work in from the day that the words were spoken to him. Many are witnesses to the truth of this.

Followers who had crossed Wroe received the same treatment, particularly those who had assisted in his fall from power at Ashton. Think of the fate which befell Samuel Walker, the chief instigator of Wroe's trial at Ashton, and the publishers of the *Voice of the People*, who had dared to print the majority of the virgins' allegations in an edition of their paper.

\* \* \*

Of all the notes and observations recorded among the many prophecies in *Divine Communications*, the following four incidents have been chosen, as representing the most bizarre. Two are observations witnessed by believers; one is a prediction about lunacy, the other a report of a healing carried out by Wroe. Each is transcribed in full.

*Divine Communications*, volume 1, p. 236:

On the 7th of 10th month, 1824, at a quarter before five o'clock in the evening, Mary Brown, John Brunton, junior, and James Clayton, junior, all of Bradford, saw a very particular sight, and many who are not believers saw it at the same time. They saw the sun in the full size, and it appeared red as blood, though the day very dark and dull; and they saw as if a hand cut the sun in two, and then cut it across several different ways; and wherever the hand cut it appeared a dark stroke, as if really cut through, and then it disappeared all at once. John Brunton, junior thinks the appearance lasted about a quarter of an hour.

*Divine Communications*, volume 1, p. 217:

Wonderful noises heard by David Hainsworth.

In the year 1820 I was living at a place called Adwalton, in the county of York, five miles from Bradford. I think in the month of May . . . There burst forth a loud thunderclap over our heads, then a wonderful sound like hounds; then there mixed with them different sounds, like bulls, lions, tigers, men, women, and music; all this was strong, deep, and powerful, and it was very near. This continued six or eight minutes, and then began to move southward. We thought we heard them miles as they passed away, with the most dreadful howlings, groans, and shrieks, which they passed away at a great distance, and ended with a clap of thunder. This I heard, but understood not.

*Divine Communications*, volume 3, pp. 56–7:

Ashton, 22nd of 11th month, 1846.

John Wroe called a meeting of the friends at half past six o'clock in the evening, when he spoke nearly as follows:

As years increase, so will lunatics increase: for within ten years of this date men will go to the market, and they will go home lunatics; they will meet each other, and knock their heads together like drunken men: the land will be full of asylums.

Within three years of the date of this there will be great dearth in the land, first among the cattle, and then among the people.

A footnote to this communication states that:

'Statistics show that the number of lunatics in this country is now, relatively to the population, nearly double what it was in 1844. Similar results appear on the face of the registration statistics in France.' *Manchester Examiner*, 10th of 2nd month, 1869.

The following incident has to be the strangest in the entire book. It concerns healing, which was a characteristic of Wroe's ministry, and comes from *Divine Communications*, volume 1, pp. 632–3:

In the year 1830, a girl named Ann Holgate, daughter of Joseph Holgate, wool-sorter, of Union Street, Bradford, was afflicted with a strange malady; she was frequently seized with apparent madness. According to her own account she saw living beings in the form of men coming towards her, which appeared to her to get smaller and smaller in size as they got nearer to her, till they entered her mouth, and went down her throat, at which time she appeared to be choking. During her agonies she was dumb, and appeared anxious to bite anything she could get hold of, and made a hideous noise, and leapt off the bed on which she was laid like a frog. She was in this state about four months, and continually got worse. She at various times said John Wroe would be made an instrument to heal her, which her father told to John, but he said it had not been revealed to him that he would have the power of healing.

On the 17th of the 6th month, 1830, hearing that John Wroe was at James Laycock's, adjoining the meeting house at Bradford, she urged her father to go there with her. Her father accordingly went with her, and left her at the outside of the door, and told John Wroe. He said to him, 'Where is thy daughter?' He answered, 'At the door'. John said, 'Tell her to go into the meeting room', which she did, and John followed. She sat down upon a form, round which she twisted herself, and also rolled on the floor like a ball.

John Wroe said three distinct times, 'In the name of Jesus, the son of the living God, I command thee, thou foul spirit, to come out of her, and enter no more.' And at each of the three times speaking she said something like a frog came out of her mouth, which turned into the form and size of a man, whose flesh was black, and they all three (spirits) stood together in the room, apparently gnashing at John Wroe with their teeth.

John Wroe and Joseph Holgate, with his daughter and the others, then left the meeting house. And from that time she has never been attacked with anything of the kind.

Witness Joseph Holgate, aforesaid, William Muff of Little Horton, and others.

By the early 1850s, the Wroes were residing at the select Georgian square, St John's in Wakefield, a premier address in the nineteenth-century town. These fine red-brick townhouses look out over the classical St John's Church, which was consecrated in 1795. In the 1851 census returns, we find Mrs Wroe and her daughter Sarai living there. John Wroe was by now, however, spending more and more time away, particularly abroad. Mrs Wroe died on 16 May 1853. Her age was registered as 74. Her death occurred a few weeks after her husband had left Wakefield on his second visit to America. Marriage to the Prophet cannot have been easy, but this feisty Yorkshire woman fought hard. This was best demonstrated during Wroe's trial in 1830 when she had threatened to stab one of the witnesses and was restrained with some difficulty and removed from the court room. Mary Wroe was buried in the churchyard in St John's Square on 18 May. The burial register is signed by the well-known local vicar and artist, the Revd Thomas Kilby.

# 8

## Preaching to all Nations

Early in his religious career, Wroe had embarked on two tours of Europe, both in 1823, visiting France, Germany, Italy, Gibraltar and Spain. It was during his time in Gibraltar in June of that year, he received a divine communication that 'seven nations shall receive thee and seven times thou shalt return unto thine nation'. A footnote explains how this actually happened. He returned from Spain and France in 1823, 'from Australia in 1844 and again in 1851; from America and Australia, making one journey of it, in 1854; from America in 1859; and from Australia in 1860, thus making seven returnings to England'. However, incredibly, the footnote's compiler (probably Joseph Corry) overlooks the fact that Wroe first visited America in 1840, when the 57-year-old left Bristol on the ship *Trenton*, bound for New York.

The sect was extremely proactive throughout Wroe's lifetime, with missionaries being sent all over the world. Two nations were particularly receptive to the Christian Israelite message – America and Australia. The Christian Israelite religion was first taken to America as early as 1823 by two preachers sent across the Atlantic by Wroe. He proclaimed their mission on 11 April, and the two men set out on their voyage in November of that year. Their names were William Midgeley, of Thorpe near Huddersfield, and Robert Harling, of Thornhill near Wakefield – contrary to the announcement, which named William Muff, not William Midgeley, as one of the preachers.[1] The outward voyage was far from successful, as the men explained to a committee of the Church at Ashton-under-Lyne in May 1824, when they were questioned about the reasons for their premature return.[2] As *Divine Communications* records, the committee was not so much concerned with the men's missionary achievements in America, but rather with the inquest into Harling's disorderly behaviour.

According to the account in *Divine Communications*, the men's ship encountered a severe storm some 700 miles off the Irish coast, and was damaged. It was forced to turn around and dock at Cork in southern Ireland, where the vessel and its passengers and crew remained for about two months while the ship was repaired.[3] It was here that 'Satan . . . got advantage of Robert Harling', in that he started drinking. On the voyage to New York he got drunk on two occasions, but claimed he had been drinking spirits to keep his body warm on board ship.

Nine days after the men arrived in New York, they preached in a large schoolroom which belonged to a Mr Fitz, a printer who published the *Gospel Herald*. The publication included pieces on the doctrines of the various Christian denominations who had preached in the room. This was, however, the only success achieved by the Christian Israelite delegation in New York. Harling's behaviour was, according to Midgeley, 'too glaring', so that he was starting to prejudice 'the minds of the people against what they had to hold forth, which destroyed a great deal of their usefulness'. Midgeley therefore resolved that they should both return home.

The men boarded a vessel for England, but during the return voyage Harling's alcoholism got even worse. Harling agreed to share his gallon of rum with three steerage passengers who were temporarily unable to get access to their five gallons, as luggage had been placed on top of it in the hold. After eight or nine days Harling's rum was exhausted. Once the three steerage passengers had opened their cask, Harling had free access to it at any time. The temptation was too great for Harling: as he took regular draughts of it during the day and often got up during the night to get a drink.

About a week before the ship arrived home, two passengers came to tell Midgeley that they thought Harling was dying, he lay 'nearly on his back, with his eyes fixed, dead drunk'. Six of the steerage passengers took matters into their own hands and decided to make a public example of Harling, trying him in a mock trial. One passenger acted as judge, the other five as jury. Their verdict was that

131

Harling was to sit on the capstan and drink three glasses of salt water, acknowledging in front of all the crew that he 'was not fit for a minister of the gospel, nor a member of any religious society unless there was a thorough change in his conduct'. Yet despite the humiliation, Harling continued to steal, pilfering brandy from another passenger's chest. There were clues to Harling's unreliability in a previous missionary tour he had undertaken, accompanying Wroe on his visit to Gibraltar, then deciding to return to England as soon as they arrived.

A year later two further preachers travelled to America, where they met with even less success. David Hainsworth and Samuel Entwistle returned 'without commencing their work. On arriving, Entwistle gave himself up to the ways of the world, and Hainsworth to despair.' It is interesting to note that this David Hainsworth was the individual who had heard the 'wonderful noises' at Adwalton in 1820.

Despite these very early difficulties, the Society of Christian Israelites was soon established in New York. The Church was successful enough for Wroe to want more direct involvement with his followers in the United States, and in June 1840 he embarked on his first visit to America, which lasted for three months. Two further visits followed, as well as five to Australia. The popularity of the Christian Israelites in the United States, and in Sydney and Melbourne as well as the gold-mining boom towns in Australia, can be attributed to a number of factors. Firstly, as with the new industrial towns in England, there was the lack of the influence of the Established Church. The Eastern Seaboard of America saw a period of rapid industrialisation in the mid-nineteenth century which was accompanied by social expansion and change plus the absorption of 'alien' cultures.[4] The foreign press were less critical of the sect, as Wroe's history was largely unknown. In some cases, the press was even sympathetic.

An article published in the *New York Daily Times* of 25 March 1854 portrays the sect in a favourable light.[5] The article was one of a series which chronicled religious sects within the United States, giving details of their history, doctrines, usages, numbers and wealth. It describes the Christian Israelite Society, 'which though not numerous in this country, has yet within its pale many intelligent and zealous disciples, distinguished in many cases by their religious enthusiasm as well as personal eccentricity, and largely characterised by the Christian beneficence'. The article also maps the extent of the spread of the Christian Israelite Church, stating that there were 50 societies in England, and a few in Wales and Scotland. There were also congregations at Cape Town, at the Cape of Good Hope and particularly in Australia. The largest congregations in the United States were to be found in Massachusetts, Rhode Island and New York. There were also congregations in Boston, Columbus (Ohio) and East Orange (New Jersey).[6]

Wroe's third and final visit to America took place in 1859, when he visited New York, Newark, Drummondville, Niagara Falls and Boston. The 'religious notices' column of the *New York Tribune* of 4 June made the announcement that 'John Wroe from England is to preach tomorrow (Sunday) afternoon at 3 o'clock at Mozart Hall, No. 633 Broadway'.[7] The event was watched by Daniel Milton, who noted Wroe's closing announcement, 'I have preached my last sermon in England, and now I have preached my last in America, and from here I shall go to Australia.'[8]

Apart from Daniel Milton, two of the Church's strongest adherents in New York were John and Margaret Bishop, who were preaching in the city as well as other parts of America and Canada from 1841. The couple frequently travelled with Wroe and spent much time in Britain. On the Wednesday after the formal opening of Wroe's country home, Melbourne House, in 1857, Margaret preached in the grounds of the mansion to a congregation, composed mainly of workmen and their families. She was described by the *Leeds Times* as being 'a fat, comfortable-looking female of about 40.'[9]

The positive response received by the Christian Israelites in parts of America was small when compared to their reception in Australia, where it was the only unorthodox sect to make any real impact. Here its followers became informally known as 'the Beardies'. The creed was first brought to Australia by Charles Robertson and Charles Wilson in 1839. Robertson had acted as a scribe for Wroe in

Bradford; his name first appears in *Divine Communications* in October 1832. He was one of the most zealous and productive of all the Christian Israelite preachers and worked with such success that the religion soon spread to Port Philip and Van Diemen's Land (Tasmania). Indeed, the following built up by Robertson was so enthusiastic that coercive action was considered.[10]

The enthusiasm of the new Australian Christian Israelite followers is demonstrated by a book of *Extracts of Letters from Australian Believers*, which was published by Wroe at Wakefield in 1841. Unfortunately, it has not been possible to locate a copy of this volume. The popularity of the sect in Australia was so great that in the mid-1840s the Society's printing press was moved from Wakefield to Gravesend in Kent, close to ships departing for the Southern Ocean, to supply the Australians' seemingly insatiable demand for Christian Israelite religious literature.

An early contemporary account of the Christian Israelites in Australia appears in a rare book, *Australia and the East*, by John Hood. Its author left Plymouth on 11 June 1843 on board the *Lady Kennaway*. He relates the journey, his experiences in Australia and the return trip via India. In Australia Hood met Charles Robertson on the mail coach at a settlement between Bathurst and Sydney, possibly Blackheath. As both men were from Scotland they soon got into a conversation. Robertson was from Aberdeenshire and told Hood that he was 'preaching the gospel to the brethren throughout the world.' Hood wrote:

He seemed at least 70 years old, but was hale, and had a fine full keen grey eye, and a very reverend aspect. He was in Edinburgh, he said, a few years ago, and I have no doubt it was there I had seen him. His beard reached to his girdle. He said something about the lost tribes, but I could not discover his particular tenets. The brethren were few, he said, in Australia, but he had been refreshing them in Bathurst. He was a person of humble sphere of life, and left us at an ale-house, whose landlord, half-seas over, received him familiarly as an old acquaintance, yet as a person whom he was proud to have within his gates. He was not a Jew, nor a Calvinist, nor an Episcopalian: but as to what he was, he left me in utter ignorance. The poor old man seemed to look upon me as the last link with his country, and seemed unwilling to leave me, returning twice from the house to speak another word and have another shake of my hand; at last he said feelingly, 'If you should ever happen to see any one that asks you if you saw me, say the old man is alive, and is still preaching the truth to the brethren.'

Wroe, much encouraged by the enthusiasm Robertson received, first visited Australia in 1843, leaving Liverpool in April on the 300-ton ship *Francis*. He arrived at Port Philip on 17 August, a date which, along with the dates of Wroe's travels during his first visit to Australia, can be gleaned from shipping intelligence in the local press and the pages of *Divine Communications*. A passenger list in the *Sydney Morning Herald* of 25 September 1843 includes Wroe, who arrived in Sydney on the 24th after a thirteen-day journey from Port Phillip. On the following day Wroe spoke at John Beaumont's house in Castlereagh Street, Sydney on the subject of Proverbs 6: 20: 'My son, keep thy father's commandment, and forsake not this law of thy mother.'

Wroe stayed in New South Wales for over four months, until the end of January 1844. He spent much of October at the nearby district of Penrith but did not travel far out of Sydney during this first Australian visit. We know that by this time 'the Beardies' had established a meeting room at Pitt Street, Sydney. It was here, in December 1843, that he made a particularly bold technological prediction: 'I tell you a thing before it come to pass: that you shall see the aerial carriage alight on this land before ye hear of its coming.'[11]

This prediction might sound extremely original, especially the use of the term 'aerial carriage'. A search of contemporary Australian newspapers by chance throws up the use of this phrase several months earlier. An August edition of the *Port Phillip Herald*, carries a passenger list of arrivals on the ship *Francis* from Liverpool on 17 August 1843.[12] Among the passengers is a John Wroe, described as a 'Jewish rabbi'. The same newspaper carries an article about the

'Aerial Steam Carriage'. A new company called the Aerial Transit Co. had been founded in London, and its proprietors really believed they were close to discovering the secret of flight. A further article was published on 25 August and there was doubtless some excitement about the subject. Perhaps this is what prompted Wroe's prediction on the 12 December in Sydney, for the predictions of flight in the newspaper articles are far bolder than Wroe's pronouncement. The aerial carriage would, according to the *Port Phillip Herald*, travel at 130 miles an hour, carrying both passengers and goods at a reasonable rate. The paper even states that the company would be able 'to carry passengers from London to Paris at 10 shillings each, and make a handsome profit'.[13]

A four-line notice in the columns of the *Sydney Morning Herald* of 27 January 1844 announces that 'John Wroe will preach next Sunday on the Racecourse at 8.30 a.m. from the 3rd Chapter 12th verse of 1st Corinthians.' At the Christian Israelites' meeting room at Pitt Street, Sydney on 2 February 1844, Wroe spoke of the plague, as he had done many times before in England. 'I tell you respecting the cholera,' exclaimed Wroe, 'that it shall visit many places within nine years, and every land that it has not gone through, it will go through.' The 1884 edition of *Divine Communications* contains a useful footnote amounting to three and a half pages of locations where there were outbreaks, giving examples from the years 1848 to 1854 inclusive.

The cholera proclamation would have been Wroe's parting shot – as he boarded a ship for England the following day – were it not for one final theatrical declaration. Following Wroe's baptisms at Park Bridge, Lancashire in 1823 and Apperley Bridge, Yorkshire in 1824, the Prophet had declared that 'by Him that liveth for evermore, there shall be time no longer'.[14] Living an aeon before the age of the mass media, Wroe was able to repeat without compunction publicity stunts he had carried out in England, and this declaration was again proclaimed in Australia, as Wroe stood 'at the government jetty at Sydney with one foot on the land, the other over the water'.[15] Wroe concluded that he had now finished what he had to do in Australia.

Wroe left Sydney for London on the *Ocean* on 28 January. The ship arrived in June. His safe arrival in England was confirmed by a strange notice in the *Sydney Morning Herald*, from 'a friend', dated 28 December 1844. The notice states:

> From the many falsified predictions respecting the destruction of the Messenger of God, or the Ambassador of the Nations (John Wroe), I have to announce his safe arrival in London, in June last per barque *Ocean*, from Sydney, and [he] is in excellent health.

Wroe's first visit to Australia was an enormous success, almost as if in fulfilment of a communication given to him at Park Bridge near Ashton on 10 March 1829. This stated that 'Thou shalt be hated in this land, England, and I will hide thee from them; but in other nations I will show thee openly.'[16] While in Australia, Wroe noted in his journal entry of 30 January 1844, 'If I had displeasure in England, it is not so here.'[17]

In Australia the sect's members, as with those in Manchester in the 1820s, were frequently mistaken for Jews. In his book *The Jews in Victoria in the Nineteenth Century*, Lazarus Morris Goldman tells of a meeting in Sydney in about 1844, addressed by Robertson, which turned into a sectarian riot:

> A man named Robertson, wearing the beard of a Patriarch and known locally as 'Beardie', attempted to draw the Jews away from their faith. He described himself as an Israelitish missionary and a disciple of Joanne Southcott. On one occasion, on a Sunday afternoon, he mounted a chair and addressed a crowd of 300 who had collected at the eastern corner of the Market Square. A Jew who was present asked him a question he could not answer, and upon a spectator objecting to the speaker being interrupted, an altercation broke out amongst the onlookers. Soon a cry went up, 'The sons of King William are not to be imposed upon!' and back came the opponents battle cry, 'Now is the time, down with the Orangemen.' Within a few seconds Protestants and Catholics were at each other's throats, and in the riot seven to eight persons were seriously injured.[18]

By the time Wroe visited Australia for a second time, in 1850, the Church had further expanded and was well established. In 1846 and 1847, Charles Robertson and John Cartwright had established bodies of believers in Geelong and Melbourne. This time Wroe's visit and in particular his predictions received much coverage in the Australian press. Wroe arrived on board the ship *Digby*, where two of his fellow passengers were Roman Catholic priests. Despite their differing religious opinions, 'the greatest cordiality and good feeling existed between them'. An article in the *Melbourne Argus*, covering the start of Wroe's visit, begins as follows:[19]

A hig'er honor has been confirmed on Victoria than any other British colony can boast of, viz, the visit of a real prophet – John Wroe, the founder of the sect known as 'the Israelites' who arrived by the *Digby* last Friday, having in one of those visions by which the spirit is pleased to hold communication with him been directed to undertake a mission to Victoria, Van Diemen's Land, Sydney and a particular part of China, at which latter place he is to remain until further ordered how and where to direct his steps. The prophet states that the Australian Colonies will occupy a distinguished position in opening up the way for the gathering of 'the elect' on the advent of the Millennium, and that in this great work the Colony of Victoria will be beyond all the others.

This Australian article may read as though it was written in a tongue-in-cheek fashion, but it is cited in the footnotes of later editions of *Divine Communications*.[20] Furthermore, it is referred to in an oral testimony given by the last Christian Israelite with original Ashton-under-Lyne connections, Elsie Wood. She was keen to include an extract from this article as part of her testimony.

According to the article in the *Argus*, on the Sunday afternoon Wroe was to have occupied Mr Cartwright's preaching ground near the Melbourne courthouse, but rain prevented him from carrying out this arrangement. However, he preached twice in the Tabernacle at Collingwood to congregations described as 'select and attentive'. The Tabernacle had been completed earlier in the year and the first service was held there on 8 May. Edmund Finn, in his *Chronicles of Early Melbourne 1835–52*,[21] gives a brief account of Wroe at the time of his preaching in this chapel:

> Wroe himself exhibited, for that beardless time, what was considered a frightfully disfiguring hirsute crop, which fell in plentiful coils from his face down over his breast. He passed himself off as a bearded prophet, but his foretellings were not as realistic as his hair. He pretended he had confidential communings with a Holy Spirit, who deputed him to declare that the future of Melbourne would be of the brightest description, only that the early coming of the millennium would spoil everything.

Later during his second tour, Wroe travelled to Little Scotland, or Geelong. In a letter to his wife of December 1850, he wrote that there were 'more spectators than there were at the Governor's arrival at Melbourne'. Here he was met by a large body of friends, and at the place where he stood up 'there were hundreds who could not get in'.

Attempts to establish Christian Israelite churches in other countries were not always successful. The mission to China in 1851 was particularly tragic. In a letter dated 12 December 1850, Australian believer Joseph Donnolan wrote of his joy – 'I have arrived from Van Diemen's Land to this colony, and I have seen most of the bodies of Israel's hosts: surely they are the Lord's pleasant plants! O Israel, happy are they! For the things that are pleasing to God are made known unto them' – and his hope of accompanying Charles Robertson on a voyage to China.

The two men left Australia for China in April 1851. Wroe proclaimed that 'there was an army of angels sent to prepare the way before me, and that army is now in China preparing the way before these men'. We do not know what happened to these men, other than that Joseph Donnolan died in China in 1851 and Charles Robertson died on the return voyage to Sydney, in late 1851 or early the following year.

By the time of Wroe's third visit to Australia, in 1853, the Christian Israelites were firmly established. He arrived in Melbourne on 10 November, after a 116-day voyage from New York on the American ship the *Sea Ranger*. John Wroe, then aged 71, is listed as a cabin passenger. The *Melbourne Argus* of 12 November records a vote of thanks to the Master of the *Sea Ranger*, Captain Lothrop, signed by Wroe and seventeen other cabin passengers.

The year had been a successful one for the Christian Israelites in Melbourne. Their Sanctuary at Fitzroy Street (on the corner of Napier Street), Collingwood (now Fitzroy), was registered as a place of worship with the Acting Registrar General in early August 1853. The original Sanctuary building was taken down and replaced just eight years later, in 1861, with the present structure, which is the Christian Israelites' Australian headquarters. Constructed of bluestone, the building, like the old Christian Israelite Sanctuary at Ashton-under-Lyne, has no windows, its interior being illuminated by enormous glass roof lights.

An account of part of Wroe's 1853–4 visit to Australia has recently been uncovered in the diaries of Thomas Field, who moved his wife Annie and their young children from Cape Town to Australia in 1853. The family were Christian Israelites and underwent the practice of 'naming' their children (in place of baptism, which was used as a rite of forgiveness). The diaries record the birth of the Fields' son Moses on 11 March 1853 at Hunt Street, Cape Town. Moses was 'named' and circumcised by Wroe at Adelaide on 29 December of that year, the day after Annie and her seven children had arrived in Australia. Unfortunately, Moses died on 14th May 1854.

Australia's remoteness, coupled with the freak weather in parts of the country, meant that Wroe's oratory, along with the predictions and prophecies he had been making since the 1820s struck a chord with the local population. In a letter to Wroe dated 1852, Australian evangelist John Cartwright speaks of seventy-four lives lost in the township of Gundagai, 244 miles from Sydney, where all but four houses were swept away by flood, after the river had risen by 44 feet.[22] A similar fate had also befallen Wagga Wagga. Cartwright also writes of his personal experience:

On the coast of Moreton Bay, it has become an awful scene with wrecks. I am told there are about thirty vessels wrecked in this year, 1852, but I will now state no hearsay. On Tuesday, the 15th of 6th month, as we were coming to Sydney, and off Smoky Cape, we were driven back about twenty miles into Trial Bay; five more vessels put in also. One vessel called the *Rose of Eden* had on board a crew of a vessel which was wrecked on Bellinger Bar, not far from Trial Bay; another vessel is a wreck on the same Bar. Four of these vessels in Trial Bay were bound for Sydney. On Friday evening, the 18th, the *Rose of Eden* made a start, and on Saturday morning, the 19th, the other three started; also the one I was in. We soon came in company with the *Rose of Eden*, and the five of us were in company until Tuesday the 21st, when about twelve o'clock at noon (we were about thirty miles from land) the sky became dark, and the wind blew a hurricane from the eastward; it also came on to rain very heavy. The vessel was laid to, to keep off land, and about half past two o'clock on Wednesday, I awoke in my berth; I did not know we were in any danger, and I believe not one on board apprehended any, but something aroused me to pray, but yet I had no fear. I prayed as I did when thee and me were going to Hobart Town, and when I had done, the mate called out for the captain. We were then amongst the breakers and the rocks. All on board got up; they asked me to get up, but I said, If I was to perish, I might as well do so where I was. One of the passengers wanted to go on deck, and was prepared to go overboard if she struck, but they kept down the hatch. I heard the mate say to the captain, 'What are you going to do?' The captain ordered the helm to be put down, but the vessel would not move, then he said, 'Bring the helm hard up,' and just as they thought she was going to strike, and be dashed to pieces, the wind changed, and blew us off land for four hours; then when it became daylight, the wind changed again, and we got into Broken Bay, nineteen miles from Sydney Heads; we had to lay there until Thursday forenoon, then we left and arrived in Sydney on Thursday evening.

The bowsprit was carried away, the mizen mast sprung, and mizen sail torn away, and all the four vessels that were in company with us were lost. The *Rose of Eden*, which had the crew of one of the wrecks on Bellinger Bar, became a total wreck about three miles from Broken Bay, and all hands perished. The news is frightful, for there are many more vessels which have been damaged.

Australia may have delivered Wroe's most loyal supporters since his patriarchy at Ashton-under-Lyne, but it was also the home of some of his fiercest and most vocal critics. The most severe criticism came from Protestants, including David Blair (1820–99), a writer for the *Christian Times*, John Davis a working-class Presbyterian, and former members of the sect.[23] Davis published a pamphlet in 1850, *The Wroeite's Faith, Observations on the Garden of Eden. To which is added, Irreconcilable Contradictions in John Wroe's Writings*, which scripturally challenges the writings of John Wroe.

The fiercest and most remarkable of Wroe's Australian critics, however, was Allan Stewart, a young man who had himself been a Christian Israelite for six years, before he embarked on his tireless crusade against them. Shortly after Wroe's death in 1863, he published at least two pamphlets bearing the title *The Abominations of the Wroeites (or Christian Israelites) Fully and Completely Exposed*. Stewart's grievance stemmed from his interpretation of Wroe's prophecy, believing in the 'restoration of the children of Israel within 40 years of AD 1822'. In 1863, it had come as a 'terrible shock' to Stewart's 'former unreasoning belief' to find that 'the prophecy had most indisputably failed'. As Stewart wrote, 'my eyes were opened to my folly and I made wise resolution of quitting the society'. Stewart explained how he had come to join the Society of Christian Israelites:

Being apprenticed to a carpenter and thrown into the company of wild young men, I grew more careless, and the good impressions which I had received wore away, but still I was a sober, steady youth, though neglectful of religious observations.

Rambling about on Sundays I now met some of Wroe's preachers, listened to their sermons and read their tracts, which gradually worked upon my mind till I really thought I had met with the best and purest people on earth, who could most assuredly show me the way to heaven. I joined their society, was circumcised and devoted myself to their cause.

Never was there a more enthusiastic convert than I; for I thought no labor too arduous, no sacrifice too great, if I could thereby promote the interests of that church which I now considered so pure and holy.

Nothing could induce me to think evil of the leaders of the body – no argument could shake my confidence in them, and I became their willing slave. My parents entreated and threatened, my friends laughed at me, but all in vain; for I was fully persuaded that I had found the truth, and was prepared to suffer any persecution which the avowal of my principles might bring upon me.

Stewart had met Wroe in Melbourne in 1859, on the Prophet's fourth visit to Australia. Wroe requested that Stewart should preach a trial sermon to him, so that he could judge whether the young man had the 'gifts for the work'. After hearing Stewart, Wroe sent him out to preach the Wroeite doctrines, comforting him with the prophecy that he 'should have thousands of Jews and Gentiles to contend against – but the Lord would prosper him'. Stewart started out to the town of Ballerat without a penny in his pocket. He preached there, but without success, so continued on to Geelong. He then sold all his possessions and went to Adelaide, where he remained for three months, before returning to Melbourne. Stewart attributed his failure to a 'complete glut of preachers in the market'.

Stewart claimed that Christian Israelite meetings were conducted in Quaker style when strangers attended. Their meetings were very different, however, when no strangers were present. His pamphlet also talks about the rites of the Christian Israelites, including explaining the rites and processes whereby he became a full member of the Church:

143

As a first step, I had to write out my confession of all my sins against their laws, which I enclosed in an envelope, addressed to the Female Trustee . . . Then I underwent the unpleasant rite of circumcision, in which I was told I should be divinely supported; but I found it was a terrible operation which cost me three weeks of agony before I recovered from it.

As if the revelations contained in Stewart's pamphlet were not damning enough, to coincide with its publication he addressed a number of public meetings, denouncing the Christian Israelites. At one such meeting he boldly divulged the whole of the Christian Israelites' cleansing rite, the description of which was considered so depraved that 'all youths and females' were excluded from the hall. After Geelong he arranged a meeting in St George's Hall, Melbourne in early June 1863, where as many as 2,000 were present. Such was the audience's interest in the proceedings that the meeting resumed again at a later date.

According to Stewart, his meeting at Geelong had created 'considerable excitement in "the camp of Israel" '. He met with much criticism from Non-Christian Israelites who considered the sect peaceable and harmless. The young man wallows in the attention his first pamphlet received:

Upon two occasions when about to disclose some of their horrible and revolting monstrosities, one of them (whose name shall be secret) came to me with knitted brow and lips compressed and his teeth clenched like the jaws of an iron vice and blazing with a fury dreadful to behold, placed himself in an attitude as if about to commit the deed, and clenching his hand as if he had already grasped the weapon, he hissed forth, 'Divulge if you dare – if you do I'll stab you to the heart.'[25]

A man who attended the St George's meeting in Melbourne wrote of his disgust to the columns of the *Melbourne Age* newspaper. His displeasure, however, was not at the revelations revealed by Stewart, but at Stewart himself, whom he believed was merely seeking notoriety. He berates Stewart's lecture, writing that 'the worst sensation drama could afford nothing half so prurient as the filthy details revealed at last night's meeting.'[26] Was the anonymous correspondent, who refers to himself as 'an outsider' and signs his letter as an 'Observer', really a 'Beardie' who was seeking to discredit Stewart? The newspaper agreed and castigated the chairman of Stewart's meeting, Dr Milton, in its editorial three days later.[27] The *Age* claimed that 'if John Wroe, the defunct prophet, failed to attain much celebrity while in the flesh, he has left a legacy which John L. Milton knows how to turn a profitable account'.

Despite criticism from the mainstream churches and Stewart's denunciations, the popularity of the sect spread throughout the 1850s. By the end of the decade there were fifteen groups in New South Wales, three in Victoria, two in Van Diemen's Land (Tasmania), and two in South Australia.[28] In August 1859, Wroe made his fourth voyage to Australia, visiting Collingwood, Geelong, Hobart Town and Sydney. In November he also preached in the goldfields of Ballerat, this being at the time of the gold rush. In February of the following year he made his return journey to England. He was to visit Australia for one last time in 1862–3.

Just as the millennial churches and sects had succeeded in England during the 1810s and 20s in parts of the country experiencing rapid socio-economic change and an inadequate response from the Established Church, the Australian gold rush of the 1850s presented the Christian Israelites with an unexpected opportunity to gain support. This time rapid socio-economic change was 'wrought by the gold rushes in Victoria, when class distinctions were almost obliterated by recently independent diggers'.[29] The new Christian Israelite Church offered order, stability and hope, as opposed to the existing churches, which were initially overwhelmed by the population explosion of immigrants to the gold-rush areas.

Contrary to expectations, the sect did not die out with Wroe in Australia. One possible explanation of this is that the Australian papers were less critical of the Christian Israelites than the press of the mother country. The most favourable article appears in the local newspaper, the *Dunolly and Betbetshire Express* in the issue dated

3 March 1891, as part of a series entitled 'Some of the Brighter Sides of Melbourne Life'. Dunolly is a town about 60km to the west of Bendigo, Victoria, and was a gold-rush town from 1857. The article opens with the statement, 'I suppose that no body of Christians have been more misunderstood and more misrepresented than the denomination known as the Christian Israelites.' It continues, by explaining the history of the Church, the background of John Wroe and, importantly, the difference between the Christian Israelites and their forerunners, the followers of Joanna Southcott. It also outlines the Church's service and doctrines, mentioning *Divine Communications* and explaining their rejection of all pictures, images and profuse ornamentation. The article was printed again in the *Express* of 22 November of the following year, this time with an introduction of:

It is the common fortune of all people who advocate and defend principles and opinions not clearly understood, or who adopt manners and customs which to the uninitiated appear strangely eccentric, to be made the subject of misrepresentation, ridicule, and too often scorn. The Society of Christian Israelites have been singularly unfortunate in this respect, and sneers and jeers of the most bitter kind have been levelled at them.

The article was, indeed, so popular with the Christian Israelites that the Church subsequently printed copies of it themselves for distribution. How could they not want to publish it when it contains lines such as:

It has not been my good fortune to see John Wroe, but in conversation with those who knew him intimately I am assured that he was a good man, full of the Scriptures, a man who lived a pure life, and one whom to know was to love and admire for his manifold virtues and excellent qualities.

It certainly explains an unexpected boon enjoyed by the sect in the early 1890s, after the death of Mr John Perry, an 'old and energetic' member of the Society of Christian Israelites, was reported in early 1891. Following his death the *Collingwood Observer* had reprinted most of the original article. This led to an animated controversy lasting several weeks, which attracted considerable attention. This helped enormously in removing 'much of the prejudice and misunderstanding' which had hung over the sect. At that time the Society reportedly had between 200 and 300 adherents in Victoria. The *Express* called them 'a people zealous of good works'.

Writing in the *Imperial Review* in the mid-1890s, James Francis Hogan, the MP for the Mid division of Tipperary, Ireland, makes a tantalising reference to the 'peculiar suicide' of a leading member of the Christian Israelite Church.[30] Hogan, had emigrated to Australia as a child and was brought up in the district of Geelong, which was once known as Little Scotland. On his last visit to Australia he had come across the 'ruined and desolate church of the Beardies' on a site behind the Culloden Castle Hotel. He writes of an August heatwave in England, which was too hot for one Christian Israelite to bear. The man cut his hair, but later took his own life in remorse.

Just as the Christian Israelites were to have vociferous challengers for leadership in England in the wake of Wroe's death, in Australia they were also confronted by competition from a new millennial figure, James Fisher, otherwise known as the 'Nunawading Messiah'. He was born at Bristol in 1832 and worked as a sailor, but deserted the brig *Esperanza* in 1852 for the Australian goldfields.[31] His bizarre conversion to millenarianism came about according to a revelation he received, reported in the *Age* newspaper:

Joanna Southcote [*sic*] had a son when everybody thought she did not have any. This son was carried up into heaven. Fisher was told that the spirit of the son, that was Messiah, had descended from heaven upon some cabbages in his garden. He was to eat the cabbages and then he would have the spirit.

When the vast majority of the Beardies disclaimed him, Fisher established his 'Church of the First Born' which he led for almost fifty years.[32] The sect started at Nunawading, Victoria, a place then completely in the bush, though only eight miles from Melbourne, and continued later at Wickepin in Western Australia. Scandalous revelations were made about Fisher – most seriously, allegations of polygamy.

Membership of the Christian Israelite Society declined rapidly in England during the years following Wroe's death; but it is in Australia, where the Christian Israelite church has achieved its most enduring appeal. At the end of the twentieth century, the sect founded by Wroe could list on its website churches at Melbourne, Sydney, Singleton, Terrigal, Windsor, Brisbane and Kempsey in Australia, as well as Indianapolis in America. The church at Singleton, for instance, celebrated its 125th anniversary in 1987. Although Singleton was not one of the many places Wroe visited while on his travels, the building is one of the longest-standing Christian Israelite churches in the country, having been originally founded in 1862.[33] Early preachers included Isaac Easterbrook, Joseph Holgate and John Cartwright. The congregation's new Sanctuary was constructed in 1934. Unlike the Ashton-under-Lyne Sanctuary and the Sanctuary at Fitzroy, the building has stained-glass windows. A booklet outlining the history of the Sanctuary at Singleton, published in 1986, shows the enduring importance of music to the Christian Israelites. Musical organisations at Singleton include a brass band, a choir and an orchestra.

The Christian Israelite Church's quarterly magazine, *Latter Rain*, keeps the Old World in touch with events in the Australian Church as copies are regularly sent to the local-studies libraries at Wakefield and Ashton-under-Lyne. In 1989, Australian pastor David Knight embarked on a tour of places associated with the Church in England and the United States, including Bradford, Wakefield, Ashton-under-Lyne and New York, depositing Christian Israelite literature in libraries and records offices in each location. During his tour Pastor Knight also visited the place in England which had the closest association with Australian believers; for it was Wroe's Australian faithful who contributed the lion's share to building the Prophet's mansion, Melbourne House, at Wrenthorpe near Wakefield.

## 9

# Prophet Wroe's Mansion

The Christian Israelite Church survives into the twenty-first century, with churches in Australia and one at Indianapolis in the United States. Wroe's most lasting legacy in England, however, is a large country house three miles north of Wakefield, less than half a mile from junction 41 of the M1. The circumstance by which it came to be built is, like so many other aspects of Wroe's life, most extraordinary. In 1854, Wroe announced that he had received a command from heaven to build a temple, which was to be dedicated to the Lord, belonging to the members of the 'House of Israel' gathered out of all nations. Although the building is officially called Melbourne House, to this day locals still know it by its more informal name of 'Prophet Wroe's Mansion'.

A large area of land near Foster Ford at Brandy Carr, Wrenthorpe was purchased from Peter Heywood esquire, together with a neighbouring farm of just under 100 acres. By strange coincidence, the site chosen on the Bradford Road at Wrenthorpe was close to East Ardsley, an area associated with another Yorkshireman who had suffered for his faith. Ardsley was the birthplace of James Nayler, who fought for parliament during the Civil War, became a Quaker, but was punished for his so-called blasphemous preaching.[1]

The design of Wroe's new building was not to be drawn by an architect: instead it was to be built 'as the Spirit directed'. That was his original intention, at least, though eventually an architect had to be engaged, a Mr Thorp of Wakefield, a man who, according to Baring-Gould, was 'worried out of all endurance' by Wroe.[2] The costly building was called Melbourne House and designed to resemble the old town hall at Melbourne, which Wroe would have

149

seen in 1854 on his third visit to Australia. There was a definite resemblance between the Melbourne Town Hall, and Prophet Wroe's Mansion on the other side of the world.

The old Melbourne Town Hall had been designed by ex-convict architect James Blackburn, who had been appointed City Surveyor in October 1849. Blackburn reported to the council on 29 August the following year.[3] His drawings detailed a completed two-storey structure which was cleverly 'contrived so as to admit of being erected piecemeal at five or six different periods'. The ground floor contained a 'great hall' for public gatherings, measuring 60ft by 40ft, and 30ft high. Off the great hall were a council chamber and library, as well as offices, and a strongroom for the storage of documents. Blackburn's proposals cost an initial £2,100. Excavations for the basement and foundations had been completed by March 1851, but building work was delayed by the gold rush and was not completed until 1853.

The bluestone building had a short life of a mere fourteen years. It was demolished in 1867, ten years after the completion of Prophet Wroe's Mansion. The new (and current) Melbourne Town Hall was built to the designs of Messrs Reed & Barnes, its foundation stone being laid in November 1867 by the Duke of Edinburgh. The demolition of the old building after such a short existence may sound wasteful, but it reflected the vast expansion in municipal affairs in Melbourne caused by the gold rush. Fortunes were being made in many areas of Australia. Citizens of cities such as Melbourne were keen to catch up with their European home towns, and the grandest, most imposing buildings began to appear.

The financing of the construction of Melbourne House proved the most controversial of the financial scandals involving the Prophet. Money was successfully obtained by Wroe in 1856, when he revealed that the Lord had declared to him that every member of the Society should wear a gold ring, to the value of £1 3s 6d to be purchased from the Prophet. By the following year 6,000 rings were said to have been sold – 700 to Society members in Ireland and probably most of the remainder to Australian and American believers. Astonishingly, only one member of the Society decided to have their ring tested for purity, and discovered it to be made of a base metal not worth even 8½ per cent of the price at which it was sold. Wroe threw the blame on the goldsmith and ordered that no more be issued.

The case of the gold rings can be verified, but another report relating to the financing of Melbourne House is without foundation. This further controversy came about when Wroe was granted the use of a fund supposedly called the Flying Roll money. This capital had allegedly been collected by all sealed members of the Southcottian Society following the death of Joanna Southcott. Each had contributed according to their ability or income. The purpose of the fund was to publish the *Eternal Gospel*, proclaiming the millennium in all parts of the world. Publication had been scheduled for 1854, forty years after Joanna's death. The total sum available in the Flying Roll fund was said to amount to over £2,000. The Flying Roll story is clearly false, as the majority of Southcottians who became followers of Wroe had been followers of George Turner. Wroe was distinct from the old Southcottians and not recognised as their leader. It therefore seems impossible that they would have handed over their publishing funds to contribute towards the construction of his residence.

Money for the project did come from the congregations of the Christian Israelite Sanctuaries. The contribution of every member was to be recorded secretly. Even the poorest were expected to contribute at least 10 per cent of their earnings. Any possible attempt at cheating was suppressed, as members were required to keep records of their earnings to prove they had paid their tithe. Any additional donations were to be sent to John Wroe at Wrenthorpe. During the following two years post-office orders flooded in from all over the world, particularly Australia, and it was said locally that Wroe cashed more orders than all of Wakefield's tradesmen put together.

Not surprisingly, such vigorous fund-raising activities caused resentment in some of the Christian Israelite congregations. Thomas Fielden resigned from his church in the Lancashire town of Bacup, disgusted at the fund-raising for Melbourne House. His disagreement stemmed from the inspection of Church accounts. Fielden published his grievances in a pamphlet with the lengthy title, *An Exposition of the Fallacies & Absurdities of the deluded Church, generally known as Christian Israelites or 'Joannas' with a number of Prophecies taken from Prophet John Wroe's Writing, Proving him to be one of the Greatest Impostors of Modern Times. Written by one of its own members.* The pamphlet tells the history of Wroe's fund-raising for Melbourne House and explains how nearly twenty members of the Rossendale congregation either resigned or were excluded from the Church because of their unwillingness to show their accounts to Wroe's appointee, John Gill.

Fielden's pamphlet throws light on further evidence of the astounding credulity of some of Wroe's Christian Israelite followers. It contains the distressing revelation that some members of the Church in Lancashire gave all their possessions to the funding of Melbourne House and ended up in the workhouse.[4] It cites the case of Henry Robertshaw, a member of the congregation at Newchurch, Lancashire, who appealed to his local Board of Guardians for relief on the parish. Board member and magistrate Mr Munn had formerly employed Robertshaw as a servant, during which time he was paid a wage of approximately 15 shillings per week. Munn asked what had happened to the money he had earned, to which Robertshaw reluctantly replied that he had 'given it for the spread of the gospel'. Fielden comments with disdain:

If Mr Munn would like to see what the money is laid out in, he has nothing to do but take a trip to Yorkshire and call upon a country place which goes by the name of Wrenthorpe, and there inquire for Melbourn[e] House, and no doubt he will be conducted to a stately built mansion compared to which his own house would be but a poor specimen.

Not only were several Church members in Lancashire far from happy about the fund-raising procedure for Melbourne House, there was even discontent in Australia. In his first pamphlet, *The Abominations of the Wroeites*, former Australian believer Allan Stewart had stated that as soon as the revelation to build the mansion was made known, 'the saints emptied their pockets at his feet'. Stewart estimates the cost of the building project to have amounted to upwards of £15,000. He mocks the pride of the Church members in Victoria, Australia, who, because of their generous contributions, had the mansion named Melbourne House in their honour.

If these financial allegations were not shocking enough, new sexual revelations surfaced in the pamphlets of both Fielden and Stewart. Thomas Fielden explained the cleansing process carried out by the women of the church:[5] 'The woman takes the man by his privates . . . she holds him by one hand and gives him the stripes by the other'. The stripes were made by dipping a piece of lint in water and striking the man with it. 'With a piece of chalk in his hand he counts the stripes as he receives them at the hands of the female; for every twenty stripes he makes a mark on a board provided for that purpose, and when he has got fifty chalks he is then made whole.' Fielden states that Isaiah 47: 2 – 'Take the millstones and grind meal: uncover thy locks, make bare the leg, uncover the thigh, pass over the rivers' – was used as justification for this ritual. The following verse (Isaiah 47: 3), with its references to 'nakedness shall be uncovered', 'shame' and 'vengeance' is probably more apt.[6]

The startling and seemingly absurd revelations contained in Fielden's pamphlet, published in the early 1860s, could have been dismissed by the Christian Israelites as the writings of a turncoat, was it not for the existence of Allan Stewart's pamphlet. The Australian follower's allegations were published in Melbourne in 1863, shortly after Wroe's death. His revelations are strikingly similar to Fielden's assertions, if not even more vulgar. In the antipodean version of the cleansing process, Stewart was told to remove all his clothing except for his shirt. This time the woman handed him a piece of paper and a pin and asked him 'to stick the pin in the paper every time she paused, until she had made the requisite number of pauses'. Stewart described the remainder of the humiliating procedure:

She then dipped her hand in a basin of water, which action she repeated twice during the process. In her left hand she held my private parts, while with her right she manipulated my posteriors, pausing at intervals, at each of which I thrust the pin into the paper and repeated the following words after her – 'In the name of the man Christ Jesus have I received this cleansing as a purgation from my sins.' I do not remember the number of pauses she made; but when she had completed the operation, she directed me to confess my transgressions, which I accordingly did. I dressed myself and came away.

Stewart underwent the cleansing rite on two separate occasions, first in Hobart, and then at the Fitzroy Sanctuary. The second process was almost identical to the first and took place in a cellar room lined with green baize. However, in this instance, 'instead of the pin and paper, brass buttons were used, one of which I was directed to drop every time the female cleanser made one of her pauses'. Keen to publish the testimony of another former Christian Israelite who had undergone the cleansing rite, Stewart also included in his pamphlet an affidavit from John L. Milton MD, dated 11 June 1863:

I do solemnly aver that about seven years ago Alexander Payne voluntarily came to me and defined the ceremony known among the Wroeites as the 'cleansing process', and I do affirm that his description of the process, manipulations &c., were in exact accordance with the statements that have been repeatedly made by Mr Allan Stewart.

Mr Payne stated that the female cleanser and he were alone together in a private place belonging to their Sanctuary, and after putting to him some questions, he was requested to denude the lower part of his body, and bow down his head upon a table, whilst she threw his shirt over his back, laying bare his posteriors, and then began to manipulate his private parts till he was afraid he would not be able to contain his . . . [The '. . .' was inserted by Stewart.]

He shortly afterwards left them in disgust.

Revelations such as these relating to sect initiation caused shock, outrage and ridicule among polite nineteenth-century society, not least because Stewart's allegations were subsequently published in the *Melbourne Argus* and relayed at public meetings at which he denounced the sect. Credence must be given to these two sets of allegations, as they come from former Christian Israelites from opposite ends of the globe. Clearly, Fielden and Stewart could not have been in contact with one another. The shocking sexual nature of Stewart's allegations was regarded as so obscene by the Australian authorities that a few days after publication police searched the printing works and seized 2,000 copies of the eight-page pamphlet.[7] Stewart subsequently published a second pamphlet, this time sixteen pages in length, challenging the Wroeites on doctrine, but with no further mention of the cleansing ritual.

Melbourne House was completed in early 1857. The mansion, built of stone from Harehills, Leeds, occupies a high position at Brandy Carr. Its frontage faces towards Wrenthorpe and Wakefield with views of the cathedral – Yorkshire's tallest spire. The building work had been a lengthy process, for as Wroe realised how quickly funds were accumulating, he had much of the work done two or three times over. The north-east wing of the building was taken down so that the property could be enlarged. Once the glazier (a Mr Slater) had completed his tasks, Wroe decided that he wanted every pane removed and replaced with good plate glass. Many workers were still engaged in completion work at the mansion in the days after it had officially opened. Estimates as to the final cost of Melbourne House vary widely, from figures in excess of £9,000 to even as much as £15,000.

The women members of the Society of Christian Israelites furnished the mansion for Wroe. As with the funding of the building project, their efforts were surrounded in secrecy. Married women were forbidden to tell their husbands how much they contributed. Many pledged amounts that they could not afford. Baring-Gould tells of women having to sell goods and borrow cash in order to keep up the payments to the end of 1856.[8] Economies were made through dietary constraints, including vegetarianism.

Wroe had the mansion's interior decorated with beautiful woodwork, much of the raw material for which was imported from Australia especially for this purpose. The large reception rooms were hung with silk tapestries and, throughout the house, fine timbers were used in the doors, door frames and panelling. A fine staircase, constructed of mahogany and cedar, runs behind the mansion's façade. Its banister rails are made alternately of maple and ebony. Halfway up the staircase is a handsome grandfather clock, standing over 14 feet high. It contrasts with another unusual timepiece at the mansion, the sundial in the shape of a pineapple above the central portico on top of the mansion's façade.

One of the best contemporary descriptions of the interior of the mansion is given in a lengthy article in the *Wakefield Express* written in July 1879,[9] a little over twenty years after its formal opening:

Nothing meaner than cedar, mahogany, maple, box-wood, and black ebony have been used in the making of the doors, furniture, floors and fittings, and everything is genuine to the last degree. The cedar was brought from Lebanon during the Crimean War. The principal rooms would vie in appearance with those of any gentleman's villa for miles around, while their appointments are far more genuine and substantial. Some of the walls are hung with crimson and other coloured cloth of the finest texture, with borderings and tracery in gold.

With regard to the exterior of the mansion, the grounds, surrounded by high stone walls, were planted with rhododendrons, cyclamens and other flowering plants. A major feature of the beautiful gardens was a large rockery made up from the stone left over after the boundary walls were constructed. The *Express* continued:

Within the boundary walls there is about two acres of ornamental garden ground, kept in first-class style. The hothouses and con-servatories are quite a feature, and for completeness of arrangement and quality of fruit and flowers they are surpassed by few in the neighbourhood of Wakefield.

There were originally four lodges outside the grounds of the mansion. One had to be demolished when the Bradford Road was altered; another (which guarded what was then the principal entrance at the substantial main gates) was restored and extended in 1993.

Melbourne House was formally opened at daybreak, precisely 3.53 a.m. on Whit Sunday (31 May) 1857. The ceremony was attended by between 250 and 300 Christian Israelite delegates from all over the world, particularly from America, Canada and Australia, gathered to hear the words of their Prophet. The assembled gathering wore white robes and processed around the grounds before entering the mansion, the women behind the men. They were followed by the Prophet, then aged 75, described as having a 'long beard and unshorn hair' and wearing a 'low-crowned hat and long brown coat'. The remainder of their service took place behind closed doors, well away from the prying eyes of the press, but the singing could be heard to continue until about 5 o'clock.

The media took great delight in its mocking coverage of the proceedings. The *Leeds Times* in particular used the mansion's opening as an opportunity to carry two highly critical articles on Wroe and his followers. Its first lengthy article was a précis of the career of Joanna Southcott and an overview of how Wroe's mansion came to be built. It comments on his early deeds as a successor to Joanna, including his baptism at Apperley Bridge, as well as his prophecies. While reading the critique of Southcott's career, the eye is drawn to an apocalyptical story at the top of a neighbouring column, headed 'Will the Comet Strike us?'

The *Leeds Times* alleges that Wroe 'confidently predicted' while speaking at the Queen Street Chapel, Leeds, that within a few years it would be possible to travel to America by railway. 'The thing would be easily accomplished.' According to the *Times*, 'the rails would be joined together as two tea-cups might be, and we should travel the great Atlantic pathway without wetting our feet'.

A reporter on the *Times* did, however, manage to achieve quite a scoop, by securing an interview with Wroe.[10] He visited the mansion on the afternoon of Wednesday 3 June and was directed to one of the lodges. Here he met Prophet Wroe, apparently asleep, lying on the kitchen table with his head on a pillow. The reporter was far from surprised, as he had heard of Wroe, in his hours of trial, 'sitting with his head in the oven, and lamenting his sins literally in the ashes'. Wroe rolled off the table to the floor. He adopted a somewhat truculent tone at first, saying he had nothing to tell the press. Eventually he became more communicative, saying that although he was now aged 75 he intended to go on another voyage to Australia. The sea air always did him good. As for his mission, he said it was still unfinished. According to the *Times*, he had to 'go into the world again before his labours would be over'.

Prophet Wroe complained to the reporter about the disorderly behaviour of local residents at Wrenthorpe during the construction of Melbourne House. Local children had stolen many items from the building site. Their parents were 'nearly as bad'. When he complained to his neighbours about the thefts, he was merely laughed and scoffed at. But none of this mattered now, as the mansion was at last complete. Sunday's opening ceremony had passed off without the slightest disturbance.

The following week's *Leeds Times* contained a short, critical letter from two elders of the Society of Christian Israelites, Benjamin Eddowes, Wroe's secretary, and John Laden Bishop, a preacher from the United States. They took issue with several points raised in the article, including the apparent claim to walk on water made before Wroe's baptism and the prediction of the railway to America. The most important inaccuracy they pointed out, however, was the purpose for which Melbourne House had been built. In their letter, which the *Times* has headed 'John Wroe and the Wrenthorpe "Temple"', the men clearly state that the mansion was not intended to be a place of worship, but a private residence, 'John Wroe's private property'. Eddowes and Bishop are quite correct on this point. The mansion was never used as a temple – either during the Prophet's remaining lifetime, or in the years following his death. Nor was the property ever the seat of an alternative community, institution or any sort of commune as can be proved by contemporary newspaper reports, census returns and forty years of close observations made on the property by the obsessive Daniel Milton. Melbourne House was built purely for residential purposes, of similar proportions to the contemporary dwelling of a coal-mine or woollen-mill owner. It did not even contain a private chapel or sanctuary.

A subsequent article published in the *Leeds Times* of 20 June outlined Wroe's career in the 1820s at Ashton-under-Lyne. Not surprisingly, it reminds readers of the disturbances in the wake of the virgins' allegations. It also quotes several of Wroe's prophecies from *Divine Communications*, which are simply rejected as 'rubbish'. Four prominent members of the Church in New York took objection and wrote a strong letter of protest to the editor of the *Times*, dismissing the articles as 'calumny and unmitigated flagrant falsehoods'. They compared the articles in the *Times* with a favourable piece about the Church in an 1854 edition of the *New York Daily Times*. The letter, dated 25 September 1857, was never printed in the Leeds paper, so the Christian Israelites published it themselves at their Gravesend headquarters during the following year. The American signatories to the letter were Frederick Thomas, Thomas Gwynne, Julius Wiele and Daniel Milton.

The letter emphasises the fact that John Wroe had lived for the past 27 years as a citizen of the Wakefield area, a 'free man' who had now 'established a permanency of character, not an erratic one'. It also gives the Christian Israelites' explanation of the events that had indirectly brought him to Wakefield, the virgins' allegations of 1830. Blame is placed with John 'Zion' Ward, who had declared he was Shiloh and exerted influence over Wroe's persecutors Walker and Masterman at Ashton-under-Lyne. The two men were treasurers of both the Society of Christian Israelites and the Christian Israelites' co-operative 'Shop Company'. The letter alleges that they tried to defame Wroe by charging him instead of the Society's treasury, so that Wroe was pursued as a debtor. When this tactic did not succeed, the two men prepared their document of virgins' scandals to release to the press.

\* \* \*

Despite the comfort of Melbourne House, John Wroe was not able to enjoy an entirely peaceful semi-retirement. It was the unexpected arrival of the above-named 'Judge' Daniel Milton that was to cause Wroe the greatest irritation at Wrenthorpe during the final years of his life. Milton challenged both Wroe's right to lead the Society of Christian Israelites and his ownership of Melbourne House, which Milton believed really was a temple, a holy place, not the country residence of a wealthy Victorian gentleman.[12]

Daniel Milton was born in October 1821 at Portsmouth, New Hampshire. His real name was Daniel Trickey and for many years he worked as a shipwright in New York. In his early 20s, Daniel became interested in the Millerite Church, a body which had been founded by William Miller, who had predicted the return of Christ in 1843. Throughout 1842, Milton travelled all over New England expounding this Second Coming of Christ. As with Turner's Shiloh prediction, however, Christ did not appear and Milton was one of many disappointed who sought spiritual fulfilment elsewhere. Daniel converted to another millennial Church, the Society of Christian Israelites.

Milton's rise to power within the American body of the Christian Israelites was rapid, and he soon became a leading figure. In 1849 he was elected Judge of the Christian Israelite Church in New York, and he continued to make use of the title for the rest of his long life. In January 1845 he had married a Scottish member of the sect, Barbara Kemp Williamson from Edinburgh, and the couple had three sons and five daughters. Milton's business prospered and in 1851 the Judge was instrumental in the establishment of the first Christian Israelite Sanctuary in America, at number 108 First Street, New York. He was made president and first trustee of the Church on 12 November of that year.[13]

Daniel lived in Brooklyn in the 1850s and it was here in 1854 that he met Wroe on the second of his three visits to America. Milton showed the Prophet around the house he was building for himself, after which Wroe told him, 'Daniel, you will one day have another house built for you.' At the time Milton did not understand what Wroe meant by that strange prediction, but he began to interpret the meaning later that year, when Prophet Wroe announced he had received a command from the Lord to build a 'Temple'.

The co-writing of the *Leeds Times* letter appears to have been one of the last acts Milton performed as a leader of the Society of Christian Israelites in America. For at about this time the bizarre obsession lodged in his mind that not only had Melbourne House been built for him according to his interpretation of Wroe's words, but also that he, Daniel Milton, was the Promised Shiloh, the spiritual child of Joanna Southcott. As he explained in an interview towards the end of his life, 'I am the child that was born at first as a spirit; and on 12th October 1821, I was born into the world in an ordinary way.' Church members immediately turned against him and his family left him, but Milton was resolved in his belief. Milton was not the first person to proclaim he was Shiloh, John 'Zion' Ward had declared himself Shiloh almost thirty years earlier, in 1828.

Milton was convinced that Wroe's mission would end in November 1859 (forty years after his first vision). He proclaimed his own mission in the *New York Sun* of 31 July 1858, and made his way to England the following year to claim Melbourne House as his rightful inheritance. By the time he reached Wakefield in February 1860, Milton had just a farthing left in his pocket. He made his way to Melbourne House and confronted Wroe, quoting the Prophet's own words at him and stressing that Wroe's ministry was over. Wroe refused, of course, and after many arguments a perplexed and crestfallen Milton headed back to America.

Milton returned during the following year to stake his claim once again to the mansion. Disturbances were frequent, and Milton attempted to gain the support of believers and the public by staging a series of open-air meetings. These took place on Sunday afternoons and brought crowds of thousands of spectators, who witnessed the Judge preaching from an open cart. Daniel was soon in trouble, however, for blocking the highway of Brandy Carr Road. Unperturbed, he hired a nearby field from Jane Ramsden, but the crowd of between six and seven thousand people who attended on 14 April again blocked the highway and Milton was taken to court by Wroe's lawyer, Wakefield solicitor Robert Barratt.

Milton's quarrel was not only with Prophet Wroe, but also with fellow American John Laden Bishop. Bishop and his wife Margaret were Wroeite preachers who had accompanied the Prophet on some of his travels and were responsible for converting Milton to the Christian Israelite faith. Margaret Bishop was originally married to John Williamson, both of whom were active Christian Israelites in Britain in the late 1820s and early '30s. She was also the mother of Milton's wife, Barbara. When Milton joined the Society of Christian Israelites he was circumcised by his future step father-in-law, John Laden Bishop at New York in September 1844. The Bishops preached at the Market Cross in Wakefield following the opening of Melbourne House and are often referred to in Wroe's books.

The cause of the altercation, according to Milton, was that John Bishop had turned the New York congregation (including Milton's wife and children) against him. Milton frequently recounts a particular dispute with Bishop in the grounds of Melbourne House in May 1861. The police escorted Bishop back into what Milton called the 'holy place' (the mansion), but Milton had another confrontation with Bishop later and 'broke his power by seizing hold of his long black beard'. Constable William Ramsden intervened and asked Bishop why he was keeping Milton's wife and children from him.

Another way in which Milton vented his grievances against Wroe was in the printing of handbills stating his claims. In August 1861 Milton again appeared in court at the Wakefield Petty Sessions, charged with doing wilful damage to the property of John Wroe – pasting handbills onto the high stone boundary walls of the mansion grounds. Wroe had warned Milton not to stick bills on his property and had gone to the trouble of carving the notice 'stick no bills on these premises' into one of the stones on the wall near the main gate. The notice can still be read. On 16 August Milton was caught billposting and was challenged by a visitor to Melbourne House, who pointed out Wroe's notice. Daniel continued sticking up his bills, saying the notice did not apply to him. The damage amounted to 6*d*, which Milton was ordered to pay, plus 14*s* 6*d* expenses. Milton was threatened with fourteen days' imprisonment, but on this occasion the fine was paid. Soon afterwards, a frustrated Judge Milton again returned to the United States.

August 1861 had proved to be something of a fraught month for Wroe; besides the episode of Milton's bill posting, opponents of the Prophet managed to get their hands on some gunpower, which was placed in one of the lodges at Melbourne House and set alight. The explosion blew the roof off the lodge.

Milton was not the only person who crossed the Prophet during his residency at Melbourne House. A strange incident apparently involving Wroe and a local villager was related to Dr J. Walker by an old nurse in a cottage at Bragg Lane End, Wrenthorpe in 1887.[14] She had been one of Wroe's followers until one particular afternoon when the Prophet called on her, saying, 'Mary Smith, the Lord appeared to me in a vision in the night and said: "John, thou must go to Mary Smith and tell her that I command her to give up her best cow to thee as a trial of faith."' 'The Lord's will be done!' replied Mary, sorrowfully. 'Prophet, if the Lord appeared to thee and wanted my best cow, thee must take her.' As Wroe departed with the cow, a sudden thought struck Mary and she beckoned him back, asking at what time the Lord appeared. 'About a quarter before two this morning,' answered Wroe. 'Well,' said Mary, 'the Lord appeared to me in a vision at a quarter to three o'clock and said: "Mary Smith, the Prophet will come to thee and claim thy best cow in my name to try thy faith and courage, but if thou grant my request there is no need for him to take thy cow as thy faith has been proved."' The Prophet departed once more, but this time without the cow and looking very much downcast. Walker states that Mary left the Christian Israelites soon afterwards.

This story would appear to be original, were it not for a newspaper article published some thirteen years earlier in the *Wakefield Free Press* of 28 February 1874.[15] This states that 'he sometimes took fancies for articles belonging to his disciples and that when he did so he occasionally had a "revelation" from the angel of the

Lord, telling him that such articles were to be given up to him'. It quotes the example of the 'shrewd Yorkshire woman' and the cow, but then goes on to state that similar stories are commonplace in the neighbourhood of the mansion and probably not true.

Baring-Gould tells of another story. While residing at Melbourne House, Wroe bought a fine mule with a long flowing tail, a basket carriage and a handsome silver harness. One day he drove to Sandal, just south of Wakefield, leaving his carriage and mule outside the house where he had business. On leaving the house, he became enraged, discovering that some local wag had shaved the mule's tail. He never visited Sandal again.[16]

A house built for such an unusual individual is bound to have gathered myths and stories associated with its rich history. Perhaps surprisingly, many of the stories concerning the mansion in the years following Wroe's death do have some foundation in fact. There is no truth, however, in the crazy tale that the Prophet was forced to flee Melbourne House for Australia when he left for the final time, leaving via a secret passage from the mansion to the now-demolished (north-west) lodge. On the contrary, with Milton back in the United States, everything seemed set fair. In the summer of 1862, the octogenarian Wroe left Melbourne House bound for Australia on another mission. Although the Prophet thoroughly intended to return to Wrenthorpe during the following year, this was to be his final voyage.

Melbourne House at Wrenthorpe and the part that remains of the Odd Whim building at Ashton-under-Lyne are the only surviving buildings of several that were once built for Prophet Wroe. The mansion was to remain largely unaltered for over a hundred years. Its significance to the Christian Israelite Church is still evident, as it heads a page on their website. Writing over a century ago in his book *Round the Home of a Yorkshire Parson*, the Vicar of Filey, Canon A.N. Cooper, commented that in Melbourne House, where 'one finds a handsome country house is the temporal reward of a man of the poorest attainments, of the craziest creed . . . surely we may cease to wonder at anything'. In short, 'Wrenthorpe witnesses to the gullibility of a past generation'.

# 10

# Death and its Aftermath

John Wroe visited Australia for the fifth and what was to be the final time in 1862, arriving at Melbourne on the *Shalimar* on 15 November after a three-month journey. During the voyage, he fell on the deck of the ship and dislocated his shoulder, which never properly mended. He died suddenly at the Christian Israelites' Sanctuary, Fitzroy, Melbourne on 5 February 1863. On the day of his death he had returned from a walk, sat down on a chair, then suddenly fell forward to the floor, dropping dead on the spot. Wroe had been on a fund-raising mission, but as soon as his death was rumoured, the Melbourne members of the Church demanded their donations be returned. Wroe's secretary, Benjamin Eddowes, was threatened and obliged to surrender some of the cash. Eddowes managed to hide in a blacksmith's shop before finding a ship on which to sail back to England, still over £600 to the good.

The death certificate was registered at Melbourne the day after his death. He is described as 'John Wroe, Gentleman', and his age is incorrectly stated as 81. The causes of death are given as 'old age' and 'bronchitis', certified by T.N. Fitzgerald, who had last seen the Prophet a few weeks before he died. Wroe was buried on 7 February at the Melbourne General Cemetery. The burial records show that he was interred there under the name of 'John Rowe'. He is buried in part of the cemetery designated for 'other denominations', including Chinese people who died in Melbourne, together with the more unusual sects. Methodists, Wesleyans and the other conventional Nonconformists have their own sections of the cemetery.

Unlike Joanna Southcott before him, John Wroe's grave is not marked by a headstone and the absence of a report on the funeral in the local press echoes the criticism of the Christian Israelites vented by Allan Stewart in his second *Abominations* pamphlet. Stewart stated that membership of the sect was in decline and believed that the sect would die out. 'And when at last they fall, no dirge will be wailed o'er their grave: no funeral oration will be preached o'er their decease; they will die, and they will make no sign.' Surely there is a strange analogy between the death of Wroe and Stewart's predicted end of the sect as a whole.

There is scant coverage of the death in the Australian papers, other than the *Melbourne Weekly Review*, which uses Wroe's demise to print a deeply critical article about him:

It will probably be a piece of perfectly novel intelligence to the bulk of our readers to learn that the wretched old man who thus obscurely ended his career, was up till the very last looked upon by his deluded followers as an inspired personage . . . able to bestow immortal life on all who believed in him . . . The miserable maniac who died the other day at the 'Synagogue' in Fitzroy, steadily declared all his life that neither himself nor his followers could ever taste death, but that both they and he would be translated to Heaven as Elijah was! Indeed John Wroe's latest 'revelation', delivered only a few days before his death, was that he should return to England within a few months. He had actually taken his passage by one of the Liverpool liners, in fulfilment of this prophecy, when the inevitable hand of death fell upon him . . . His duped followers, it is averred, are at this hour looking for his resurrection and reappearance amongst them.

It was several weeks before word of Wroe's death reached England. The news was first reported in the Wakefield press in the Friday 29 May edition of the *Wakefield Journal and Examiner*. Two further papers, the *Wakefield Express* and the *Wakefield Free Press*, covered the story in their editions of the following day. All three newspapers quote the *Melbourne Weekly Review* as their source.

Any such rumours were firmly denied by the servants at Melbourne House, who confidently stated that Wroe was to return home aboard the *Great Britain* steam vessel. Indeed it was many years before Wroe's deluded followers would admit he was dead. Some said Wroe would never die, and indeed he had predicted his own return. Speaking in Wakefield on 28 August 1846,[1] Wroe had said, 'In the name of God, I tell you a thing before it comes to pass: I shall be taken away from you one year, two years, yea, three years; and some shall say that I am dead, and behold, I shall spring up amongst you.'

Others, however, were in no doubt over his death and were only too keen to gloat at victory over an old adversary. The 18 June edition of the journal *Notes and Queries*, contains an obituary of Wroe penned by one of his harshest Australian critics, David Blair of the *Christian Times*. Like Stewart, Blair wrongly concluded that the Christian Israelite sect would soon die out. Of Wroe, he wrote:

He founded a sect which numbered adherents in all parts of the world; and which held, as its cardinal article of faith, the divine inspiration and absolute authority of its founder. His followers here in Melbourne looked confidently for his resurrection, but they have probably abandoned that hope now. The sect called themselves 'Christian Israelites,' but were popularly known (from wearing the hair uncut and unshaven) as 'Beardies.' They were zealous and incessant street-preachers of an incoherent and unintelligible doctrine; apparently compounded of Judaism, Christianity and the principles of the Adamites of Munster. From inquiries made here, I am led to infer that John Wroe was unmistakably a lunatic of a common and harmless type; but nevertheless he was constantly attended by a secretary, who took down everything which fell from his lips; and those notes were sacredly preserved as divine communications . . . Although the sect was strong enough to have its own prophet, its own liturgy, code of laws, church constitution, and special literature. It has survived the death of its founder; but seems, from all I can learn, to be now dying out. This is an additional reason for leaving some mention of it on the pages of contemporary history.

As there was such controversy during the lifetime of the Prophet, it is not unexpected to find bitter controversy in the aftermath of his death. John Wroe's will was proved on 7 March 1864. It had been drawn up by his solicitor, Robert Barratt, on 1 August 1862, only three weeks before Wroe had left England for Australia, on 21 August, on his final voyage and less than six months before his sudden death. The twelve-page document offers a fascinating insight into the wealth of Prophet Wroe, who owned land and property near Wakefield (at Wrenthorpe, Carr Gate, Snow Hill and Alverthorpe) as well as a few houses at Bowling, Bradford. Despite Wroe's laws on abstinence from spirits, we learn from the will that the Prophet not only bequeathed his 'wines and liquors', but that he had actually owned a public house. This was The Malt Shovel at nearby Carr Gate, which still is the nearest pub to the mansion, although the building Wroe would have known was demolished in 1937.

James Wroe inherited the majority of his grandfather's estate, including the 'Mansion House called Melbourne House with the greenhouses, hothouse gardens, grounds, outhouses, stables and buildings belonging thereto'. He was also left land at Brandy Carr, Carr Gate and Bragg Lane End, plus several cottages at Carr Gate. James was the first son of Prophet Wroe's third eldest son, Benjamin Appleby Wroe of Gravesend. Records at the West Riding Registry of Deeds show that Benjamin had himself started acquiring property at Wrenthorpe in the early 1850s when he purchased houses and land at Bragg Lane End in 1852.[2] Benjamin had married Mary Ann Deane at St James's Church, Clerkenwell in May 1848. She was the daughter of William Deane a butcher at Gravesend. The couple had four children in the Kent town before the untimely death of Benjamin in 1860. His widow had then married Ashton-under-Lyne grocer William Farrand on 30 December 1863 at Gravesend Parish Church. They moved to Ashton, re-establishing the Church's headquarters in that Lancashire town. Mary Ann's mother at Gravesend temporarily took on the role of recognised head of the Society of Christian Israelites in the wake of Wroe's death.[3]

The remainder of Wroe's family were well provided for. His only surviving son, Joseph, was left land and coal-extraction rights at

Willow Lane Close, Flanshaw near Wakefield as well as land at Bragg Lane End, Wrenthorpe, along with The Malt Shovel plus land and cottages at Carr Gate. Prophet Wroe's eldest daughter, Susanna Wilson, was also bequeathed houses at Bragg Lane End, together with cottages at Snow Hill near Wrenthorpe and Swain Green Houses at Bowling, Bradford. Sarai, Wroe's youngest daughter inherited houses in Alverthorpe, the neighbouring village to Wrenthorpe, where she lived with her husband, joiner Joseph Teale. Baring-Gould calculated that the property left to Wroe's children at the time produced an annual income of £60 for Joseph and £50 each for Susanna and Sarai.

Wroe's three trustees and executors were prominent members of the Christian Israelite Church: John Snell, a cloth dresser of near Sheepscar Bar, Leeds, Joseph Corry, a grocer of Ashton-under-Lyne, and John Gill, also a grocer, of Newchurch, Lancashire. Although these men had the honour of being trustees, they were left nothing by Prophet Wroe. The controversy of the will is mocked by contemporary local historians such as Baring-Gould and Walker. Baring-Gould believed that Wroe had deviously conveyed his estate to his descendants, despite giving assurances to Church members that the mansion and land would be left to the Christian Israelite Society. He had, according to Baring-Gould, drawn up a will in the presence of several pillars of the Church. It was subsequently superseded.

When the news of Wroe's death reached America, the irrepressible Daniel Milton decided that the time was ripe for him to return to England, with a fresh determination to gain possession of Melbourne House. In late November 1863 Milton gave a sermon from outside the front door of the mansion – an event which had been announced on placards posted throughout Wakefield. On 4 February of the following year he actually managed to enter the building and claimed the mansion as what he called 'Church property', holding it against a siege. Inside he met a young Irish servant, Abby Eccles, who told him she believed Wroe would return to Melbourne House when he had been dead for twelve months and that she was keeping the property ready for him. Milton held the mansion for almost a month, but was forced out on 1 March by a group led by the Deputy Chief Constable of the West Riding Constabulary and Wroe's lawyer. Wroe's will was proved less than a week later and denounced by Judge Milton as 'a villainous Church-swindling instrument'. Not surprisingly, there is no mention of Milton in the entire document.

Despite being ejected from the mansion and excluded from the will, the American's delusions and obsession over the stately property continued for four decades. Battling against extreme poverty in later life, Daniel Milton lived an odd existence, spending the little money he could earn on printing religious pamphlets airing his grievances against the leadership of the Society of Christian Israelites. Wearing his Quaker-like clothes, he would carry a stepladder from his humble cottage along the Bradford Road to look over the high boundary walls of Melbourne House, the property he still believed was his by right. He was a well-known figure in late-nineteenth-century Wakefield, where he would preach 'Israelitish drivel' in the marketplace. His hopeless quest to gain possession of Prophet Wroe's Mansion may have ended unfulfilled, but the story of his futile struggle is nevertheless fascinating.

By the 1870s, Daniel had settled into an odd pattern of travel between England and America in his attempts to assert his claim to Melbourne House and gain leadership of the Society of Christian Israelites. He survived by undertaking various jobs, such as carpentry, painting, whitewashing and making items on his joiner's bench. He lived in a cottage at Woolstone Nook, which neighboured the grounds of the mansion. When this cottage was demolished, he moved to another at Wilson Hill on the northern side of the Bradford Road. This row of houses survives and has been converted into the Poplars Guest House. Here he was happy (according to one contemporary account), as many of his neighbours were Christian Israelites too. In fact the terrace was known locally as 'Joanna Row'.

Milton appears to have lived in at the very least two other properties, both in a row of late Victorian red-brick houses known as Springfield View at Bragg Lane End.[4] This terrace is situated in a part of Wrenthorpe known as Robin Hood, because it is believed to be the site, where, centuries earlier, Robin Hood had feuded with George-a-Green, the Merry Pinder of Wakefield.[5] Milton's feuds with the Wroes and prominent Christian Israelite Church members, however, usually took the form of printed literature. When funds permitted, he issued pamphlets from what he called the *Hebrew Press* at Wrenthorpe. When in America he issued similar pamphlets from the *Hebrew Press* at an address in New York. In April 1876, his Wrenthorpe office was raided by the police and the printing press thrown out onto the street.

Milton's publications had titles such as *The Millennial Educator*, *The Believer's Manifesto* and *The Perfect Gospel Advocate*. Indeed, in the 1881 census returns Milton appears to make a particularly bold claim, even for him. Then aged 59, he described himself as the 'Editor and Publisher of the *Eternal Gospel*'. This however turns out to be the title of yet another of Milton's publications. In 1891 he describes his occupation as 'Christian Israelite Minister', and in 1901, most modestly of all, as 'printer and publisher'. A typical edition of one of Milton's *Church Circulars* from 1876 begins as follows:

Dispute and Adventures
With
Hireling Priests! Wicked Professors! Lying Lawyers!
Violent Policemen! Oppressive Magistrates!
Dabblers in the Affairs of the Christian Israelite
Church and Melbourne House Estates.

Judge Milton, of Melbourne House, Wrenthorpe, near Wakefield, England, has had eighteen years contention in America and England, with the above named characters – during which time he has been deprived of the company of his wife and has been imprisoned twelve times, crossed the Atlantic Ocean fifteen times and travelled at his own expense in the defence of the Church more than sixty thousand miles.

There is also evidence that he tried to join a Shaker community in America. A surviving letter from John Whiteley, a leading light of the Shaker community of Shirley Village, Massachusetts, rejects Milton's unconventional approach to lead the sect, which he made on a visit to the States in 1893.[6] Milton seems to have barged into Whiteley's shop, claiming that the Lord had sent him to take over the management of the Shaker community. Whiteley's reply was swift and had shades of the 'shrewd Yorkshirewoman and the cow', namely that the Lord had said nothing to him on the subject. The library of the Shaker Community at Sabbathday Lake Village, Maine has a collection of material relating to Daniel Milton, as part of its Radical Christian Collection. The late Brother Ted Johnson carried out research on Milton and connected him with at least three Shaker communities: Mount Lebanon, Canterbury and Shirley.

Judge Milton took delight in any misfortune that befell the Wroe family and is said to have kept a list of all the deaths that occurred on the Wroe estate after Milton's rejection by Prophet Wroe. It is very reminiscent of the footnotes in Wroe's books, relating to the fates that befell named individuals who had crossed him. There were constant skirmishes between Milton and members of the Wroe family as well as workers on the estate. Prophet Wroe's eldest son, Joseph, lived at Carr Gate, on what is now the Old Bradford Road. He threatened Milton several times and on one occasion got a gang of men from the pub to drive him away from the gates of Melbourne House. The Judge was frequently pelted with stones and clods of earth and had buckets of 'dirty water' thrown over him. Only days before the Judge's death one of the Wroes turned a hose on Milton as he walked by the gates of the mansion.

In an article in *Yorkshire Life* magazine in January 1967, Prophet Wroe's great-granddaughter, Miss Marion Wroe, talked about her notorious ancestor and life at Melbourne House in the late nineteenth century. She remembered Milton as a man with flowing snow-white hair and recalled how he would follow her father James as he collected his weekly rent from his numerous tenants. Milton would wave his stick shouting, 'Do not pay this man. He's an impostor!'

Like Prophet Wroe before him, the more Judge Milton was persecuted, the more this determined his resolve. The sacrifices he made for his deluded belief were immense: his wife and family, his business and his comfortable home in the United States; and all because he believed he was the promised Shiloh and harboured the futile hope of one day possessing of Wroe's mansion. Again like Wroe, Milton was of the strange belief that he would never die.

Three letters survive written by Milton to George Horridge, a Wakefield printer and the publisher of the *Wakefield Almanack*.[7] The first, dated 17 September 1872, arranges for his goods to be shipped back to Portsmouth, New Hampshire and tells how he had spent the summer working at his brother's farm to pay off all his debts. The other two letters are from ten years later and mention Melbourne House. Writing from Ayres, Massachusetts on 28 January 1882, Milton states that he has been anxious to obtain a photograph or engraving of the mansion, but has failed, and concludes it was 'not for me to get one, as it will only be a shadow, and what do I want of a shadow when I get in Melbourne House and have the substance'.

In the letter, Milton's bitterness towards his in-laws, the Bishops resurfaces. When John Bishop had died in 1866, Milton's wife paid for both his funeral expenses and a burial plot. The Judge writes of visiting the graves in New York of his eldest daughter who had recently died and four other children who had presumably died in infancy.

There are now five of our children . . . in Cypress Hills Cemetery with their Christian Names only on their gravestones. No one would know but they were all John Bishop's children, as he lies buried in the midst of them, and on his stone is pronounced a tender parent, when he never begot a child in his life.

Any poignancy however, soon gives way to the usual ranting, for within a sentence we read:

But she [Milton's wife] will see better days with me in Melbourne House. If the Ashton Tribe discard James Wroe's right to the property, what position are they in? Will they not be brought face to face with me? Remember I told thee they would come at the Last and bow at my feet. What they have caused me to suffer knows no one but myself.

The local media were fascinated with Milton's character, and several articles were written about the Judge, dubbed the 'Prophet of Potovens' by one paper.[8] In interviews Milton's religious frenzy continues undimmed, as he repeatedly insists that he is the 'Promised Shiloh', 'Joanna Southcott's spiritual son', who was (according to Milton) 'foretold by Jacob'.

As well as his religious beliefs, the press also gave coverage to Milton's unconventional lifestyle, in particular his vegetarian diet. Daniel had given up eating meat as a young man and from that age to his death he was also a non-smoker and drank nothing but cold water. In his latter years this meagre diet became essential because of his poverty, and it was said locally that he survived on swede and cabbage. In an interview in the *Manchester Guardian* of 22 December 1899, he tells of a typical day's meals: 'For breakfast I generally have boiled beans and toast. For dinner I have pea-flour – you can make a pint of excellent soup with two tablespoons of pea-flour, and it improves it to add some breadcrumbs. My third and last meal is supper – sometimes bread and water, sometimes pea-flour.'

The articles also describe his meagre living room with its bare stone floor, old-fashioned hand-printer, boxes of type, bundles of literature and heaps of books. There were no blinds or curtains at the windows of his cottage. Instead the Judge pinned old newspapers to the window frames to keep out both the draught and the inquisitive eyes of passers-by. Above the mantelpiece the following was printed in large letters:

Jesus and Joanna
My two witnesses
Shiloh

Because of his belief that he was Shiloh, Milton was also convinced that he was the rightful custodian of Joanna Southcott's box. He hounded the then owner, John Jowett of Apple Hall, in the Barkerend Road area of Bradford, in another of his futile quests.[9] Milton's behaviour led all subsequent owners of the box to keeping knowledge of its whereabouts a closely guarded secret.

In the 1890s, Milton decided to stay in England, as old age, bouts of ill health and perpetual poverty had somewhat curtailed his travel. The output of religious pamphlets continued when funds permitted. In his printed appeals he rails against his many oppressors: magistrates, solicitors, the police, the Home Secretary, all of whom failed to help his cause. He even criticises the newly formed Stanley Urban District Council for charging rates to a poor old man. One of Milton's appeals, published in the local press in late 1890s, begins with the wonderful lines, 'Sir, it is no disgrace to be poor, but it is very inconvenient.'

Milton found himself in the news again at the turn of the twentieth century, following eviction from his cottage for rent arrears. The octogenarian spent a night sleeping by the side of the Bradford Road guarding his possessions and was forced to sell many items, including his carpenter's tools, to find rent for a neighbouring cottage.

Judge Milton vigorously pursued his claims to Melbourne House right up until the very week of his death. On Monday 14 December 1903, a delighted Milton managed to get hold of a key to one of the lodges of Melbourne House. A local policeman, Constable Lindley, was called and eventually persuaded Milton to give it back. Constable Lindley heard Milton the following evening as he walked along the Bradford Road past the Judge's cottage. He said he often heard the Judge talking and singing at night.

On the Wednesday of that week a neighbour, Mrs Elizabeth Ball, grew worried, as she had not seen Milton around that day. She peeped through a gap in the newspapers covering the windows and saw Daniel lying on the floor at the bottom of the stairs leading to the kitchen. She sought assistance to break into his cottage, where 'Shiloh' was found lying unconscious, his head cut and bruised. Milton never regained consciousness and died the following day. At the inquest into his death, held at The Wheel, Bragg Lane End on Saturday 19 December, a verdict of accidental death was returned.

Milton appears to have been respected by local villagers in Wrenthorpe. Perhaps this was because of the unease they felt about the Wroes. Their respect for the aged, almost patriarchal figure was, however, not as great as their pity. One account of Milton's death states that 'the villagers are touched with sadness that so sturdy and kindly a creature should have lived and died in such a pitiable cause.'[10] Milton's funeral took place on Monday 21 December 1903. About a dozen people attended, and local villagers contributed £2 towards the costs. The coffin was interred at Alverthorpe church-yard, which was also to be the final resting place of several of Prophet Wroe's descendants, including grandson James, who, fol-lowing Milton's death, lived on peacefully at Melbourne House for a further fifteen years.

One achievement attained by Daniel Milton, but not John Wroe was that Milton had a street named after him. In the 1850s when Milton was a successful businessman in New York, a new street, Milton Street at Greenpoint, Brooklyn was given his name. The street, 'M Street' was opened in 1852 and re-named in 1855.

In the years after Wroe's death, while Melbourne House was still occupied by his descendants, many local stories emerged about how his followers believed he would one day return to Wrenthorpe. His room at the mansion was always kept warm, and food was provided for him. It was said that his favourite cup and saucer were clean and ready for immediate use, and even his slippers were placed by his bedside awaiting his return.

These stories have wrongly been dismissed as just local gossip, for there is plenty of evidence to suggest they really were true. The article on Melbourne House in the *Wakefield Express* of 5 July 1879 mentions that the blinds at the mansion were mostly kept drawn to save the expensive wall hangings from the damage of strong sunlight. This 'no doubt often conveyed the impression that the mansion is not tenanted. Though there is now no master in posses-sion, yet servants live at the place to keep it in order, and occasion-ally members of the Church come on visits from various parts.' The mansion was still virtually empty a decade later, in February 1889, when a reporter for a Yorkshire newspaper, who was recording the local wildlife in his column 'Miscellaneous Rural Notes',[11] wrote the following:

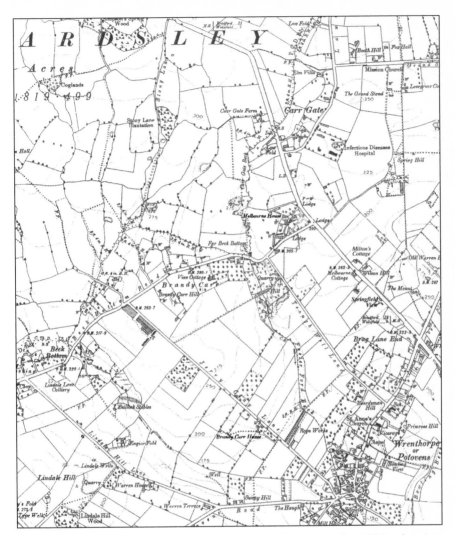

Old large scale Ordnance Survey map of Brandy Carr in the 1890s showing properties connected with John Wroe and Daniel Milton.

The sole occupants of the Mansion, which is very large, are a housekeeper and one servant, but women from the lodges are employed regularly to assist in house-work, and all the furniture, floors, staircases, and internal fittings are kept in good order and scrupulously clean. There is a meeting-room or chapel here in which the members meet on Sundays and Fridays. They are,

177

however, few in number, except at Whitsuntide, when there is a general muster from all parts of the country.

Daniel Milton too provides plenty of evidence that the mansion was left virtually empty for about twenty years following the Prophet's demise. He reported his conversation with servant Abby Eccles inside Melbourne House in February 1864. Seventeen years later he quizzed the census enumerator after the 1881 census returns had been recorded. At the mansion, the enumerator had asked for the 'Master of the House', but the two servant women there told him that 'there was none'. He then asked who paid the rent, but according to Milton the two women just looked at each other before Abby Eccles, the servant still working at the mansion, said that he had better write down the name of the other servant, Mary Burnley. James Wroe and his young family lived at the neighbouring Melbourne House Farm, which had until the 1870s been tenanted by John Buckley. James was a dairy farmer.

Of all the stories about Melbourne House being kept ready awaiting the Prophet's return, one of the most delightful can be found in the late-nineteenth-century press-cuttings books kept at Wakefield Local Studies Library.[12] The writer had heard that on the anniversary of Wroe's death the servants at Melbourne House placed his shirt in front of the fire to air. Some years after his demise, on the night of the anniversary, the shirt was duly hung over a chair near the fire. It caught alight and was burnt to rags. It was said that 'Prophet Wroe had called for his shirt'.

# 11

## *The Demise of the Christian Israelites in England*

Following the scandal of the case of the seven virgins at Ashton-under-Lyne in 1830–1, Christian Israelites in the town faced a combination of ridicule and outrage. Wroe, however, continued to enjoy support from the rump of his remaining supporters – the most notable outside of Ashton were many of the Christian Israelites at Chatham and Gillingham in Kent. The Chatham millennial group later formed a new Church called the New House of Israel, and briefly achieved their own prominence and notoriety in the 1880s under the leadership of the charismatic James White. At Ashton, the Christian Israelites clung on determinedly, but could never regain the momentum their sect had enjoyed in the 1820s. The Christian Israelite legacy remained in the town for many decades, particularly in the form of the so-called 'Johanna Shops'.[1] It was not until as recently as 1979 that the organisation's printing press in Richmond Street closed down.

Of Wroe's one-time influential supporters in Ashton-under-Lyne – the three wealthy families, Lees, Stanley and Swire who once bankrolled his schemes – all remained in the town and prospered. Members of these families enjoyed civic status within Ashton and neighbouring Stalybridge as councillors and mayors. Samuel Swire and the Lees family broke away from the Christian Israelite Church.[2] The Lees went back to the Church of England. William Lees (Wroe's faithful companion during his tour of Europe) and his wife Cordelia had all their five sons baptised at Ashton Parish Church: Edward on 5 June 1831, John Pipler on 18 November 1832, Thomas on 1 April 1835 (the same day as Sarah Lees Hague),

179

George on 30 July 1837 and Alfred on 12 January 1840.³ Henry Lees was a local churchwarden.

John Stanley, on the other hand, remained faithful to the Society of Christian Israelites right up to his death in 1855. Politically a Conservative, Stanley became a councillor in 1849 when Ashton-under-Lyne was made a borough council. He was also the chairman of a sub-committee of the Board of Poor Law Guardians, devising methods of forming a 'fit for work' programme for the able poor. Such moves made him extremely unpopular with the people, causing the threat of riots that necessitated bringing in troops from the nearby Ladysmith Barracks, which in 1845 had been built a little way up the road from the Odd Whim. Stanley's son, John Stanley junior, also at one time became a high priest of the Church, but was persuaded to leave by James Smith. He lived for a time at the Taunton Lodge gatehouse, but left the area in 1845 and moved to Pembrey House at Pembrey in Carmarthenshire, where he purchased the bankrupt Pembrey Iron and Coal Works.⁴

A long-standing misconception worth clearing up is that the remaining Christian Israelites in Ashton after the dramatic events of the spring of 1831 did not convert to another millennial group. They were still Christian Israelites and recognised John Wroe as their leader. Ashton-under-Lyne's mid-twentieth-century historian, magistrate Winifred Bowman desperately tried to separate Wroe from the 'Southcottians' in Ashton. She cautiously stated that later Johannas were 'a credit to their towns', as if she was attempting to airbrush the undesirable Wroe element from the history of her town.⁵ However, these worshippers were not Southcottians who had been temporarily hijacked by Wroe, as Bowman implies, but an Ashton congregation who continued to follow the Christian Israelite Wroeite faith for several decades after his death.

Another myth about John Wroe and Ashton following his supposed exile in 1831 is that he never returned to the town again. Although Wroe did not return to Ashton for almost eight years following his banishment in April 1831, there is plenty of evidence that he visited the town on many occasions between January 1839 and the early 1860s. He even preached at services and officiated at

The Christian Israelites' Sanctuary, Church Street, Ashton-under-Lyne. (Howcroft, *Tales of a Pennine People*, (Oldham: 1923), p. 77)

weddings held in the Sanctuary. Post-1837 marriages were allowed to take place in the Sanctuary under the direction of the local registrar and are described as 'civil marriages'. Weddings prior to that date had to be conducted in the parish church. Several pre-1837 Christian Israelite marriages took place at Manchester Parish Church (now Manchester Cathedral), where the parties were not known and consequently no questions were asked relating to church attendance or even more embarrassing matters.[6] The Christian Israelites carried out christenings on their own premises even before

1837. An index of births and christenings (the naming ceremony) at the New Jerusalemite or Christian Israelite Meeting House, Bowling Lane, Horton, Bradford, 1823–36 is preserved at The National Archive at Kew.[7] The Society of Christian Israelites made no record of baptisms, as that rite may be carried out on several occasions during the lifetime of a believer, as was the case with John Wroe.

In August 1841, Wroe conducted the marriage of Hannah Lovering, a dressmaker from Portland Street, to Robert Smith Walker, a grocer of Welbeck Street. Walker's father was John, a farmer; Hannah's was Ephraim Lovering, a shipwright. The register, signed by Wroe, reveals that same scratchy, slightly shaky handwriting that is recorded in the notebook prescribing the jewellery to be worn by pregnant women, in which he signed his name as 'Yaakov Asriel'. Another Lovering marriage at the Ashton Sanctuary was that of Hannah's sister Emma. She married John Thompson on 29 September 1839. She was also a dressmaker from Portland Street. This time Aaron Woollacott signed the register, describing himself as 'Priest'. Hannah and Emma's brother Edwin was the subject of Ephraim's dream, interpreted by Wroe, which is described in Chapter 7. A Margaret Lovering, presumably Ephraim's wife, gave evidence in favour of the Prophet at his trial in October 1830.

The decline in Church membership continued throughout the 1830s and 40s. At the time of the controversial 1851 religious census, the number of Christian Israelites in Ashton was estimated at 185, probably about a third of the total of the faithful in the town in the 1820s, when the number of Christian Israelites was at the very least 500. William Cooke Taylor refers to the Christian Israelites at Ashton in his *Notes of a Tour in the Manufacturing Districts of Lancashire*, first published in 1841. He records that the town, 'Ashton, some years ago, was the great metropolis of the followers of Joanna Southcote [*sic*]'. Cooke Taylor notes that many of them, doubtless disillusioned, had been 'absorbed into the Mormonites, who are picking up fragments of all the broken sects in the North of England'.[8]

Comparison has been made between the Christian Israelites in the nineteenth century and members of the Church of Jesus Christ of

Latter-day Saints, with Wroe being described as 'a lesser Joseph Smith'.[9] Both men had attempts made on their lives, successful in the case of Smith, who was murdered; and there are, of course, obvious similarities between the New Jerusalem building project at Ashton-under-Lyne and the creation of Zion at Salt Lake City.

Despite the rapid fall in membership of the Church, congregants in Ashton received some consolation in the 1860s when the Christian Israelites re-established the town as their headquarters. This occurred after Benjamin Appleby Wroe's widow Mary Ann married Ashton grocer William Farrand at Gravesend Parish Church in 1863. The faithful still looked eagerly for the millennium. A mid-1870s article in the *Glasgow Weekly Mail*, reproduced in the *Wakefield Free Press*,[10] described the typical Christian Israelite service:

> They meet every Sunday and conduct religious services among themselves. They have no peculiar rites or ceremonies in their ordinary Sunday Services. They commence by singing, and then following the scriptures after which each person is left alone to offer silent prayer or meditate . . . There is no address or sermon except on special occasions.

A copy of the Christian Israelites' hymn-book is preserved at the British Library. Called *Song of Moses and the Lamb*, it was published in 1862 by William Deane of Stone Street, Gravesend. It contains 135 hymns, 87 of which were their own and 48 borrowed 'from the Wesleyan and other collections'. Some of these are familiar to us today, including 115: 'Through all the changing scenes of Life'; 123: 'Come Holy Ghost, our hearts inspire'; and 121: 'God moves in a mysterious way'. The first hymn in the book, one of theirs, points optimistically to the imminent event:

> Behold, the wonders now appear,
> Which in the Revelation stand;
> To show to man the end is near,
> And his redemption is at hand.

The Christian Israelites' love of music is shown by the book's index, which lists the hymns by long meters, common meters and various meters, yet there is no indication as to who actually wrote the words of these hymns. A second book contains the sheet music for thirteen tunes plus '12 chants for the Israelites'.[11] The article in the *Leeds Times* reporting a service held in the grounds of Melbourne House during the week following its formal opening records that the service concluded with the singing of the hymn 'Deliverer Quickly Come' to the tune of 'God Save the Queen'.[12]

As the number of the faithful continued to diminish, the Christian Israelites at Ashton-under-Lyne were forced to relinquish their costly Sanctuary, following which the once-lavish building endured a chequered history.[13] After the Christian Israelites the building was briefly rented by the United Methodists, but it proved too large and expensive. In 1879, it reopened as the Star Theatre of Variety. Its name was a throwback to the Christian Israelites, to the symbol of the Church, the Star of Judah, which was still carved in a huge stone slab at the front of the building. The theatre lasted for thirty years, when it was acquired by the Weisker Brothers, who turned it into Ashton's first cinema, renaming it the Picturedrome.[14] By the 1920s the cinema's name had become the Star Cinema, but although the building's interior had been gutted to fit a modern gallery, some of its strange millennial features could still be discerned. Its original eight long and slender cast-iron columns reached from floor to roof, forming an octagon.

The Star Cinema closed its doors for the final time on 28 March 1947. Public-safety fears had prompted the closure of the building as arrangements were deemed inadequate in the event of a fire. The final phase of the Sanctuary's life commenced shortly afterwards, when the building was acquired by the GPO for use as a sorting office. Sadly, it has since been demolished, and a modern sorting office stands in its place.

It was during reconstruction work on the site in December 1953 that workmen made an unusual discovery, which gives credence to a local Wroe legend. While excavating holes to accommodate two large petrol tanks, they came across what appeared to be the entrances to four tunnels. The vaulted entrances were of plain brick and high enough for a person to enter. Each entrance was separated from its neighbour by an 18-inch-thick wall and approached by a downward flight of steps. The tunnels were blocked by tons of rubble and the entrances sealed in concrete by the workmen.[15] It is feasible that these tunnels led to the cellars of houses in Park Parade, immediately behind the Sanctuary, one of which was lived in by the faithful John Stanley. This probably explains how Prophet Wroe made his miraculous escape from the riot in the Sanctuary in February 1831, and how the entire congregation were successfully dispersed during their afternoon service on Easter Sunday of that year.

Of the four gatehouses to the New Jerusalem, only a part of one now remains, the former Odd Whim pub building at Mossley Road, Ashton. This building was the most important of the four gate-houses, as it was the site of both Wroe's trial in October 1830 and the fracas that took place there in February of the following year. In 1837, the property was purchased by John Saxon, who opened it as a public house and appropriately named it the Odd Whim to commemorate the building's previous history. In 1897, its name was changed to the Stamford Park Hotel, and it was not until 1971 that the pub's original name was reinstated.[16]

For part of the period between its use by the Christian Israelites and its conversion into a pub, the building and its grounds were briefly put to a more macabre use. An infectious diseases hospital had opened in Scotland Street, Ashton-under-Lyne in 1830, but it was inadequate to cope with the scale of the cholera epidemic of 1832. Consequently, another building was needed and the former Christian Israelites gatehouse was chosen. The gardens of the Odd Whim were used as a burial ground for its victims.[17] Further down Mossley Road was another cholera burial ground for the forty-three victims of an outbreak of the disease in Ashton and Hurst in 1847. Their graves were marked by small one-foot high stones bearing the initials of the dead.[18] By the early years of the twentieth century there was nothing left to mark the graves of the victims, and the burial ground's boundary walls had been removed.

In the 1990s Tameside Metropolitan Borough Council erected a commemorative blue plaque at the Odd Whim pub in memory of Prophet Wroe. Its wording was, however, ambiguous if not misleading, as it implied Wroe was permanently banished from Ashton and left England to live in Australia.

The fact that the Odd Whim building, the venue of Wroe's 1830 trial, was used as a cholera hospital was pointed out by Wroe less than two years later. A footnote in an early edition of *Divine Communications* describes the epidemic as the fulfilment of a prediction he had made at Whitby a year after the trial. Preaching there on 30 October 1831, he proclaimed: 'O Ashton! Now is thy plague: what thou didst unto my servant whom I sent unto thee, the same shall they do one to another. It shall come to pass that they shall be weary of burying their dead in that place.'[19] Moreover, Wroe's footnote to the prophecy points out that: 'In summer 1832, it appeared at Ashton; and the very house where John Wroe's trial took place was taken for the cholera hospital; and the ground belonging to it was taken for a burying place for those who died of the disease.'

Although the Christian Israelite congregations at Ashton dwindled considerably following Wroe's fall from grace, certain members of the Church continued to have a highly visible presence in the town for many decades. The Christian Israelite grocers continued to prosper, and the local population continued to confuse the Christian Israelites with the Southcottians, still referring to their shops as 'Johanna Shops'.

William Farrand and John Stanley had two of the oldest 'Israelite shops' in Ashton, next door to each other in Stamford Street. Gay-Jeanne Oliver of Stalybridge has traced the location of these shops, while researching the family history of her late husband Mike. Mr Oliver's great-great-grandfather Robert Stanley was born in Cardiff in 1828, but came to Ashton at the age of 10 to work in the 'old Johanna Shop' of his uncle John Stanley. Robert was Mayor of Stalybridge in 1874–6. Mrs Oliver has traced the position of these shops from old trade directories, and although they have changed hands many times since the days of the Israelite traders, the buildings still stand. By strange coincidence, her husband Mike had actually started his first day of work in 1958 in the building that was once Stanley's shop.

Two of the three trustees mentioned in John Wroe's will were grocers: John Gill of Newchurch, Lancashire and Joseph Corry of Ashton. On the 1881 census we find Gill, aged 66, working as a grocer and shoe dealer in Kirkgate, Newchurch. Corry's shop was at 186, Stamford Street, Ashton. The 1881 census describes him as a 'grocer employing four men.' He died in April 1914, aged 85, the last surviving of Wroe's trustees and still publishing new editions of *Divine Communications* in the early years of the twentieth century.

Joseph Corry was almost certainly a son or nephew of horse dealer James Corry, a neighbour of John Stanley at Park Parade in the 1830s. James was a very good judge of 'horseflesh', making a trip to his native Ireland for this purpose each year and breaking them in himself. Could it have been James Corry who supplied Stanley with the four beautiful black horses used to remove Wroe's printing press from Ashton in April 1831?

Joseph Corry's niece Sarah married 'Prophet' Wroe's grandson, and principal heir, James at St Peter's Church, Ashton in 1875. James Wroe's younger brother, Joseph was also a grocer – a tea dealer in Briggate, Leeds. Born at Gravesend in 1855, he married Bessie Schofield at Leeds Parish Church in August 1881. Bessie was the daughter of an Ashton-under-Lyne cotton-factory manager. By the time of the 1901 census, Joseph had remarried and was working as a tobacconist at Sculcoates, Hull. He died in January 1904, leaving a widow, Florence, and their 31-month-old daughter Muriel Doris Wroe. Joseph and James Wroe had two sisters, Mary and Elizabeth Wroe, as well as a stepbrother, John Farrand. Mary married Samuel Crapon Brine, who was yet another grocer, a tea merchant in Enfield, Middlesex.

In a letter to the *Ashton-under-Lyne Reporter* in December 1954, Hugh Mottram of Penrhyn Bay, Llandudno recalled the Christian Israelite grocers that were still trading in Ashton at about the time of Queen Victoria's Golden Jubilee in 1887: Mr Corry, who kept the shop next to the Wesleyan Church, now occupied by the rubber company; Mr Jesse Farrow at the corner of Henry Square and Portland Street, now occupied by Messrs Lawton Bros; Mr Henry Farron [Farrand] kept a store at the other end (corner of Welbeck Street); Mr John Gill in Cavendish Street (corner of Moss Street) opposite what was then John Robinson's timber yard; Mr John Wood, Old Street, near The Pitt and Nelson Hotel.

Mr Mottram described them as 'good standing and upright men and women', and the shopkeepers prospered as they had the reputation of being fair and honest traders. All the traders mentioned by Mr Mottram had died by 1954, the last being master grocer Jesse Farrow, who would only have been in his mid-20s at the time of the 1887 Jubilee. Mr Farrow married Sarah Knott in 1891 and lived for many years in Hyde and then in Llandudno. Cross-referencing Mr Mottram's reminiscences with entries in contemporary trade directories, we find that John Gill is listed in Morris & Co's 1878 directory as a grocer, leather seller, strap manufacturer and boot and shoe dealer of 291 Stamford Street. John Gill junior is a tea dealer at 13 Henry Square. Henry Farrand was a grocer and corn dealer with a shop at 7, Henry Square and a home in Welbeck Street.

* * *

Just as successors including Wroe had come forward to challenge for leadership in the years following the demise of Joanna Southcott, in the years after Wroe's death new candidates hoped to gain leadership approval from the Society's trustees at Ashton-under-Lyne. Of these, Daniel Milton was the most spectacularly unsuccessful. Another contender who was rejected by the Ashton trustees was the enigmatic James White. Unlike Milton, however, White merely formed an evolved Church, initially with the support of followers at Chatham in Kent.

Private James Rowland White of the 2nd Battalion of the 16th Regiment of Foot called at the home of Mr and Mrs Head, the leaders of the Chatham body of Christian Israelites, on 13 October 1875, enquiring as to 'the way to salvation' and expressing his interest in becoming a member of the sect. White was handed a book written by Wroe and returned two days later, stating that he was perfectly satisfied, and signed the document to join the Society, which was known as the New House of Israel. White rapidly made a favourable impression on other members of the local Christian Israelites and increasingly regarded himself as Wroe's rightful successor. He had for some time been writing down his own ideas and beliefs, which, like Wroe before him, he claimed were divine communications.

On 24 December 1875, White made a precocious challenge for the leadership of the Chatham body, declaring he was a messenger of the Lord and inviting members of the Society to hear a reading of his messages on Christmas Day. White was dismissed from the Society on the 26th, but his challenge had caused the fracture of the Chatham group and he took seventeen followers with him. White's communications were the start of his book *The Flying Roll*, which included his claims to be Wroe's successor. Seeking recognition, he sent the document to the trustees of the Society of Christian Israelites at Ashton-under-Lyne. Just as those closely associated with Joanna Southcott, such as Jane Townley, had rejected Wroe's approaches, the trustees of the Christian Israelites at Ashton were horrified by what they read. Joseph Corry regarded White as a heretic and threw *The Flying Roll* onto the fire.

Rejection determined White's resolve to establish a new society, which he called the New and Latter House of Israel. In 1879 he published a volume containing many of his sermons, entitled *Extracts from the Flying Roll*, by which time he had assumed the name James Jershom Jezreel. Although his writings were largely based on those of Wroe, White had fresh missionary and evangelical zeal that the ageing Christian Israelite trustees at Ashton-under-Lyne lacked. He was particularly successful in recruiting Church members and raising funds.

In the early 1880s he decided to emulate Wroe's Melbourne House at Wrenthorpe by embarking on his own building project. He chose a prominent piece of land at Rainham Road, Gillingham, Kent, which was close to where Wroe had visited in 1823. The building, however, turned out not to be a mansion, but a tower.[20] Construction work on the tower commenced in 1885. It was originally planned to be the largest church in Britain, capable of accommodating more people than St Paul's. Cement carvings were prominently displayed on each of its four walls. The first symbolised the 'Flying Roll', which was represented by the scroll attached to a trumpet, above which was a grid divided into twelve squares, representing the twelve tribes of Israel. The second was the Prince of Wales feathers and the motto 'I serve'. The third carving was a depiction of Wroe's crossed swords, with the initials 'I.C.', for Joanna Southcott, either side. Above the swords was a crown, which supposedly represented Jezreel himself, showing continuity and superiority.[21]

Construction work on the tower was never completed. James White died prematurely on 2 March 1885. His wife, 'Queen Esther', aka Clarissa Rogers, carried on the fund-raising campaign, but she died just three years later, at the age of 28. To the Jezreelites' frustration, funds ran out before the roof could be added to the building. The substantial structure remained a prominent local feature for almost three-quarters of a century after building work had ceased. It was finally demolished in 1960–1, a process which took fourteen months and cost the life of one of the workmen.

The demise of the Jezreelites rekindled public interest in millennial religion in the press. The *Daily Telegraph*, of 26 August 1896 included a brief, but particularly critical account of some of Wroe's exploits, focusing on the virgins, the female Shiloh, the sale of gold rings and the contents of Wroe's will. Writing almost sixty years later, Harold Wood threw new light on the incident of the gold rings, criticising the *Telegraph* for never having the courage to print the Church's rebuttal of the accusations.[22] According to the elders of the Church, writing in 1896, a member of the Christian Israelites in Australia had been guilty of the deception at the time of the gold rush in the mid-1850s. The miscreant was strongly condemned by Wroe.

At the height of the sect's success, just before Jezreel's death, the Jezreelites had an estimated membership of approximately 1,400 'regularly affiliated' members.[23] By the time of the demise of his widow three years later, the membership had slumped to a mere 250. Nevertheless, in the thirty years following their deaths, new claimants arrived at Chatham, attempting to claim Jezreel's crown. These included American Daniel Milton, an early claimant, who was sent back to his poverty-stricken existence at Wrenthorpe.

A more successful candidate was another American, Michael Keyfor Mills, a businessman from Detroit. Such was his commitment to the cause that on hearing of the death of Queen Esther he sold his home and his business and donated all the proceeds to the tower-building project. Mills, known as 'Prince Michael', founded another local community, The New Eve, consisting mainly of some of his American disciples.[24] Several of Mills's pronouncements did not gain him popularity, in particular a notice he published following the sinking of the *Titanic*. Mills claimed that the sinking had been foretold by Jezreel 'in the *Flying Roll*, Series II page 222, which speaks of the horse and his rider (Christendom) being overthrown into the sea'. He further expounded that *Titanic* victims the journalist William Stead and Mr Astor supposedly symbolised respectively 'the Steed of Christendom' and its rider.

'Prince Michael' died on 8 January 1922, three days after his wife. The few remaining Jezreelite adherents received a visit from Mabel Barltrop, aka Octavia, who attempted to persuade them to join the Southcottian community which she had founded at Bedford. The horrors of the First World War had given millenarianism new momentum. Octavia had combined elements of the doctrines of her seven of her predecessors, from Richard Brothers to Helen Exeter. The latter was an elderly widow who had helped Barltrop overcome her illness, and whom the Bedford group regarded as the seventh Angel.

Two very different groups founded soon after the death of Jezreel were, firstly, the Outcasts of Israel, established by William Forsyth of Dewsbury; Forsyth published a book called *The Bible Triumphant by Israel's Hope under Israel's Standard*, in which he claimed that Jezreel and Esther would be resurrected.[25] Secondly, a former follower of Michael Keyfor Mills, the American Benjamin Purnell, founded The House of David community at Benton Harbor, Lake Michigan in 1903.

The credulous beliefs of many of the Jezreelite followers are dwarfed by an even stranger religious sect that had a following in Kent in the 1830s. John Tom, a Cornishman who styled himself 'Sir William Courtney, Knight of Malta' and made himself out to be the Messiah, is believed to have modelled himself on Wroe.[26] Tom enjoyed support among the Kentish peasantry, which led ultimately to an uprising of his supporters that was suppressed in the so-called Battle of Bossenden Wood that took place on a spring afternoon during the first year of Queen Victoria's reign. 'Mad Tom' and seven of his deluded followers were killed in the fighting or died shortly afterwards.

* * *

Howcroft's *Tales of a Pennine People*, published in 1923, gives a bleak account of the few remaining Christian Israelites in Ashton in the years following the Great War.[27] By that time the sect was 'at a very low ebb indeed . . . In Ashton, the New Jerusalem, it still lingers about a dozen strong.' Of those who remained, there were only one or two followers old enough to remember the Prophet:

> Fallen from their high estate when a walled city was dreamed of, when their numbers easily filled the beautiful Sanctuary with rapturous believers robed in white raiment . . . the Johannaites [*sic*] are now a mere handful of exemplary and unobtrusive men and women, bravely holding the faith against the contumely of an unfortunate past.

After leaving the Sanctuary in Church Street, the Christian Israelites went back to the premises at the corner of Oldham Road and Catherine Street, where Wroe had been circumcised in 1824. The handsome brick and stone Georgian building now comprised of a public house, gas company showrooms and offices. The Church now tenanted a room in the top storey of the building. Howcroft described the members of the congregation as:

Crowded now into a little ante-room some ten or twelve feet square, whose ceiling may be easily reached by hand, their last remnant holds its simple services. The room is so small that the little harmonium is crushed out into the passage. Yet everything is so orderly and clean, and between the services the chairs and pulpit are always covered with white sheets.

George Margrave was the last Christian Israelite to live in Ashton-under-Lyne. He had converted to the faith when in his late 30s and was ostracised by his wife and family. Aged 84, Margrave died at Lake Hospital in early 1936, the same year that the Church's world headquarters was transferred from Ashton-under-Lyne to Wrenthorpe.

Despite the extinction of Christian Israelites within Ashton-under-Lyne by the mid-1930s, the town still remained important for the Church, as it housed its printing press. In the late nineteenth century the Christian Israelites printed their books and pamphlets in a small wooden building in Cavendish Street, near The Buck and Hawthorn Hotel. In 1924, however, an elaborate new printing-press building was erected at Richmond Street, equipped with the very latest machinery. A printer and Church member from Detroit (Mr Gamble) came over to England to operate the press, from which publications were sent all over the world. Mr and Mrs Gamble lived in Kenyon Street, Ashton for a few years, but later returned to America, as the Lancashire climate did not suit them. Following their departure the printing press was run by the Wood family of Hazel Grove, Cheshire.

As Church membership had declined throughout the nineteenth century, the members of the Christian Israelites at Ashton-under-Lyne became an increasingly close-knit community. Members of the Corry, Deane, Farrand, Gill, and Stanley families intermarried, as did the last Christian Israelite family in England with close Wroe connections, the Woods. Elsie Wood was born on 21 October 1888 at Guide Lane, Audenshaw in an area which was generally known as Hooley Hill. She was the daughter of grocer William Deane Wood and Ellen Wood (née Corry). Miss Wood became a member of the Christian Israelite Church in about 1901, when she was 12 years of age. She was followed during the next eight years by her younger sister Nellie and four brothers George, Frank, Alfred and Harold. They were the great-nieces and -nephews of Ashton grocer and Wroe trustee Joseph Corry.

Harold Wood, yet another grocer, became a trustee of the Christian Israelite Church (the Society of Christian Israelites by now had changed its name). As one of the last remaining adherents of the Christian Israelite religion in the district, he frequently had to defend the Church against criticism and slurs. He was particularly keen to show that the Christian Israelites were distinct from the followers of Joanna Southcott, and he took offence to them being referred to as 'Southcottians' or 'Johannas'. He also had to state that they had no interest in Joanna's box and neither had they ever printed Jezreel's *The Flying Roll* (although the Jezreelites did briefly have a chapel in Ashton in the late 1880s). In 1953 Wood travelled nearly 7,000 miles in Australia, attending conferences, indoor and outdoor services, visiting churches and the homes of many Church members in New South Wales, Queensland and Victoria.

Following the death of Harold Wood at Manchester Royal Infirmary in February 1963, his elder sister Elsie became increasingly involved with the affairs of the Church. By the late 1970s she had outlived all her younger brothers and was in effect the last remaining Christian Israelite in England. In December 1979, Alice Lock of Tameside Local Studies and Archive Centre decided to record Miss Wood's recollections for posterity, as part of the archive's oral history collection.[28] She remembers that Miss Wood was particularly reluctant to record any of the interview to tape and throughout kept asking to have the tape recorder turned off.

A transcript of the interview survives in the archive of Tameside Local Studies and Archives Centre. Miss Wood commented in her interview that 'as each of these trustees passed on, others were appointed in their places. However, it is no surprise to our present followers, who are mainly situated abroad, especially in different regions of Australia, that the membership in the British Isles has continued to decrease.' She conveniently explained that this was because it had been 'revealed to John Wroe about the middle of the last century that Ashton in particular would become naked of followers even though it contained the leading branch of the Christian Israelite Church'.

Earlier that year, the 91-year-old Miss Wood had retired from her work of single-handedly operating the Christian Israelite Church's printing press at 72, Richmond Street, Ashton. Following its closure she deposited a substantial amount of Christian Israelite material at the Tameside Local Studies Library, Stalybridge. Here much of it remained for approximately fifteen years until, in 1994, Ashton and Stalybridge were visited by a delegation of elders from the Christian Israelite Church in Australia. The visitors removed some of the archival material donated by Miss Wood, including a blank naming register, claiming them as Church property. They then set out on a sightseeing tour of Tameside, looking at the places associated with the Christian Israelite Church. Apparently, they seemed rather unusual, walking along Church Street in their flowing robes, staring at the Royal Mail sorting office, where their opulent Sanctuary had once stood, and then continuing on their visit via the Asda superstore.

Miss Wood died at her home, Brentwood, in Offerton Road, Hazel Grove on 27 January 1980. From the surviving transcript and the letters of Harold Wood, the sister and brother come across as aggressively dogmatic. This can be partly explained by the family's particularly close connection with the Wroes. The 1891 census returns for Melbourne House, Wrenthorpe list three relatives visiting the mansion on census night. One of those listed is a 2-year-old girl, Elsie Wood, whose place of birth is given as Hooley Hill, Lancashire. Miss Wood was the niece of the Prophet's grandson, James Wroe.

# 12

## The Last of the Wroes

Prophet John Wroe was survived by three of his children: Joseph, Susanna and Sarai. Joseph lived at Carr Gate near Wrenthorpe, a couple of doors away from The Malt Shovel pub, which had been part of Wroe's estate. Joseph Wroe died in Leeds Infirmary on 9 February 1890, aged 74. His property was valued at a modest £37. His widow (second wife) Sarah lived with her nephew's family at Melbourne House until her death in 1905, aged 92. Prophet Wroe's daughters Susanna and Sarai were considerably wealthy. Susanna had married Francis Wilson of the nearby town of Ossett and lived at Ash Villa, St John's, Wakefield. She did not follow her father's creed, for in her will she left £500 to the Methodist Free Church Missionary Society and £50 to St John's Church (in which churchyard her mother was buried in 1853). She did, however, show evidence of inheriting her father's financial astuteness, as she owned shares in several local gas companies. Susanna died on 12 March 1895.

Neither Joseph nor Susanna Wroe was survived by any children, unlike Prophet Wroe's youngest daughter Sarai, who was born at Sandal near Wakefield in 1830. She married Joseph Teale, the son of a wheelwright and joiner, at Alverthorpe Parish Church in September 1851. Joseph and Sarai had three daughters and three sons. If the name of their eldest son, Ethelbert, sounds unusual, their youngest son, born in 1867, a little over four years after the Prophet had died, was given the name John Wroe, after his notorious grandfather. Their daughter, Mary Appleby, was named after the Prophet's wife.

Sarai Teale died on 9 April 1909 and is buried with her husband in Alverthorpe churchyard. The epitaph on their elaborate gravestone is

196

redolent of millennial foreboding: 'Be ye also ready: for in such an hour as ye think not the son of man cometh.' Sarai left an estate valued at just over £2,816, which included property and land in Alverthorpe and nearby Flanshaw. Sarai, like her sister Susanna, was also a beneficiary of the estate of Peter Wroe of Methley, near Castleford, who was the nephew of Prophet Wroe (the son of his despised younger brother Joseph). Sarai Teale's son, John Wroe Teale, also died on 9 April, a mere three years after his mother. He too is buried at Alverthorpe. His son, another John Wroe Teale, was born in August 1902. He died in September 1985 at his home in Peacock Avenue, Wakefield. As strange as this continued loyal use of the name of a notorious ancestor was in the Teale family, it was not as strange and certainly not as tragic as the fates that befell the Prophet's direct male descendants.

Prophet Wroe's principal heir, James Wroe, died on 21 March 1919, aged 67. He had been just 10 years old when his grandfather the Prophet left England on his final voyage to Australia. A badly weathered gravestone in Alverthorpe Churchyard marks the final resting place of James and his wife Sarah, who died on 10 May 1922, aged 74. The couple had at least six children, of whom John, the eldest son, took up residence at Melbourne House and the leadership of the Christian Israelites. The neighbouring farm was taken over by his younger brother George, who had served as horse vet during the First World War. George was a well-known local horse dealer, a trait which was perhaps inherited from his maternal ancestors, the Corrys.

The 1920s saw a period of stability on the Melbourne House estate. Farmer John Wroe was well known in the area. Remembered as 'burly and eccentric', he had a long flowing beard and wore his long hair piled up on his head beneath a peaked cap.[1] His brother George did not share the Christian Israelite persuasion for, as the photograph of him shows, he was clean-shaven. The gardens of the mansion were kept immaculate, and peacocks roamed the grounds. Occasionally, when the handsome entrance gates were opened, motorists stopped to admire the gardens.[2] Christian Israelites from all over the world visited the mansion several times a year. The visitors from Ashton were well known in the area, their long hair, beards and clothing making them particularly conspicuous.

John Wroe II's life came to a sudden and tragic end on a dark winter evening in January 1932. He had been crossing the busy Bradford Road near Melbourne House, to post a letter, when he was struck head-on by a delivery van. He was taken to the Clayton Hospital, Wakefield, but died at 6.15 p.m., shortly after admission.

The inquest into Wroe's death took place two days later, on Wednesday 20 January.[3] Harold Hodgson, a salesman from Bradford, had been driving a Newbould's Bread van home along the Bradford Road at approximately 5.30 p.m. on the Monday evening. His statement is quite farcical to modern ears. Hodgson had been following a car driven by a Miss Muriel Cooke-Yarborough along the Bradford Road, but overtook her because she was a woman driver. The dimmer switch of his headlights was not working, so, on seeing the light of an approaching car he turned his headlights off. Hodgson did not switch the headlights on again, as he 'felt sure the road was clear immediately in front'. He consequently had to swerve to avoid a cyclist and did not even see Mr Wroe, who was hit at full speed. 'I did not see the man until I struck him,' he told the coroner. A verdict of 'death by misadventure' was recorded.

Not surprisingly, the accident was talked of in Wrenthorpe and Carr Gate for many years after the gruesome event took place, where the driver was regarded with contempt and disgust. I have heard from contemporaries of John Wroe's son that Hodgson had been speeding and that Wroe was hard of hearing. Neither of these factors is mentioned in the report of the inquest.

The funeral of John Wroe II took place on Thursday 21 January 1932. The horse-drawn cortège passed through Wrenthorpe village centre on its way up Silcoates Hill to Alverthorpe churchyard. The funeral was conducted by the Vicar of Alverthorpe, the Revd Joseph Walker. A little over two years later, Mr Walker had another Wroe funeral to conduct, that of John's widow, Ethel Grace Wroe who died in July 1934, aged 47. Mrs I. Margrave of Hurst visited the Wroes at Melbourne House in about 1926 with her husband and Christian Israelite father-in-law.[4] She recalled that unlike her husband, Mrs Wroe, was not a Christian Israelite, but a member of the Church of the Latter-Day Saints.

Less than two years after Mrs Ethel Wroe's death, the family put Melbourne House on the market, and a good deal of local excitement was created in September 1936 when it was realised that the mansion was to be purchased by the Christian Israelite Church to serve as its world headquarters.

John and Ethel Wroe's only son Benjamin was left an orphan at the age of barely 11. Ben Wroe was born at Belper, Derbyshire in early 1923 and was well remembered by people in Wrenthorpe, as from 1932 to 41 he attended Silcoates, the famous local public school. How could he not look conspicuous, walking through the village on his way to school in his green blazer, and particularly with his hair worn in two long plaits down his back? The length of Ben Wroe's hair caused problems for Sydney Moore, the school's long-serving headmaster. Mr Moore demanded he had it cut, though in the end a compromise was reached when Benjamin was permitted to hide his long hair under a hat.

It seems strange that a Christian Israelite was admitted to an independent school that had strong links with the Congregational Church. Harry Smith, the school's honorary archivist, speculates that Wroe was allowed to attend because of the death of his father, the close proximity of Melbourne House to Silcoates and the fact that the school was prepared to welcome both pupils and staff from other Nonconformist backgrounds.

Ben Wroe attended Silcoates at a time when long hair was equated with effeminacy and, according to his brief obituary in the school magazine that 'would have been enough to confer on most boys the label of "Sissie"; but that was a label Ben never got and anyone who thought him girlish had only to face him on the rugger field for an hour to arrive at a very different opinion'. Ben won the school's Second XV badge in the winter of 1940 and that of the First XV in the spring of the following year.

As well as his love of sport, Ben's strong beliefs and biblical knowledge are shown by the following discovery pointed out by Harry Smith. Some years ago a former pupil of Silcoates School was browsing through a second-hand bookshop when he came across a battered copy of the Authorised Version of the Bible, which he forwarded to the school. An inscription on the book's endplate identifies it as having been presented to Benjamin Wroe, winner of the Silcoates School Scripture Prize in 1934.

The years of John and George Wroe's residence at Melbourne House and Melbourne House Farm were remembered by the late Mrs Edith Hemingway, who tenanted the lodge at the junction of Bradford Road/ Brandy Carr Road for twenty-six years.[5] She particularly remembered the night of 14–15 March 1941. On that date, two 1,000-kilogram German parachute landmines exploded on agricultural land – rhubarb fields off Trough Well Lane, Wrenthorpe. The blast caused superficial damage to over 200 buildings in the area, including St Anne's Parish Church, Wrenthorpe Council School and Wrenthorpe Methodist Church. Melbourne House was another prominent local building affected by the blast.

Mrs Hemingway recalled walking through the grounds of the mansion on the foggy following morning to discover a great deal of damage had been done to Melbourne House. 'Every pane of glass was broken', and the front door had been blown open. Only a few days previously, soldiers resting at the mansion had left, saying jokingly that once they had gone Mrs Hemingway could expect bombs. Her home had sustained no damage and, within a couple of weeks, all of the mansion's broken glass had been replaced.

The village's safe deliverance from these bombs is commemorated on the Wrenthorpe War Memorial on the outside west wall of St Anne's Parish Church. On the same memorial stone are the names of those in the parish who paid the supreme sacrifice in the First and Second World Wars. Tragically, the final name listed, 'B. Wroe', is the previously mentioned Ben Wroe, John and Ethel Wroe's only son, the great-great-grandson of the Prophet.

Lieutenant 271922 Benjamin Wroe, 7th Battalion, Green Howards (Yorkshire Regiment) was killed in action on the afternoon of Monday 12 September 1944. He was 21. The Green Howards were in action to hold the recently taken bridgehead in the region of Het Punt on the Albert Canal. The fighting at that time was confused and ferocious, the German infantry backed up by paratroops and tanks desperately attempting to regain the canal crossings.[6]

Ben Wroe is buried at the Geel War Cemetery (CWGC reference IV.C.4.) along with seventeen other known servicemen from the 7th Battalion and thirty-four from the 6th. Ben Wroe's obituary in the Silcoates School magazine, *The Silcoatian*, probably written by Sydney Moore, pays tribute to Ben's time at Silcoates and acknowledges the young man's deep religious convictions: 'I do not know how the end came . . . But I know it would be a good end and a brave one, or rather, a fine beginning of a full life in which he had long been interested.'

Apart from the damage caused by the landmines, the mansion survived the war virtually unscathed. During the war years, it lost just one internal door, the one leading to the principal reception room on the left of the main entrance. As well as having soldiers billeted on the premises, part of the mansion was used as the regional headquarters of the National Fire Service.

On 1 June 1956, the trustees of the Christian Israelite Church put Melbourne House on the market with the Wakefield firm of auctioneers and estate agents Messrs Saville & Kilburn. The interior of the mansion had remained virtually unaltered since its official opening on Whit Sunday 1857 (ninety-nine years and one day earlier). Once again, the sale attracted a great amount of interest in the local press. The timing of the sale announcement was immaculate – just within a century of its opening, as if it had been ordained by some higher decree. During all this time few local people had seen inside the building.

The mansion was slow to sell, despite having a number of viable possible uses, including being offered to Stanley Urban District Council to be used as a venue for their council chamber. In November it was purchased by the Eventide Housing Association, to serve as a residential home for the elderly. At the time of the sale the old stories relating to the Prophet were trotted out in local newspapers with fresh gusto, yet without covering any new ground.

Again the silly myth surfaced about him having fled Melbourne House at the age of 80 to take refuge in Australia!

Peter Johnson, an excited reporter from the *Bradford Telegraph and Argus* actually managed 'to do what inquisitive sightseers have been trying to do for decades' – gain access to the mansion. Part of Johnson's article, which appeared in the *Telegraph and Argus* on 3 December is printed below:

Inside I met the elderly man who still lives in the kitchen portion of the mansion. His name? Wroe. [The man Johnson met was George Wroe, the great-grandson of Prophet Wroe and uncle of the late Ben Wroe]. People say he is a distant descendant of the 'Prophet'. 'There are a lot of people in England called Wroe,' said this Mr Wroe, noncommittally. 'And don't go writing any of those silly stories about the house. There's no truth in them.' If he were a distant relative of the 'Prophet', Mr Wroe did not inherit his ancestor's volubility, for this warning ended the interview. He refused to discuss the 'Prophet' or the legends that had grown up about him.

But, untrue stories or not, I found that the rumour about the mansion being maintained exactly as it was when Wroe lived there appeared to be borne out. The interior, sombrely decorated and a trifle gloomy, was neat and clean; the carpets in good condition and the beautiful mahogany balustrade – probably the finest feature in the house – brightly polished. I learned afterwards from a reluctant Mr Wroe that three women are employed by the trustees to keep the house in good condition.

Upstairs the bedrooms were in the same immaculate order, the beds neatly made and spread with plain coverlets – one trait of the Christian Israelite sect is the forbidding of embroidered flowers in the house. On an old-fashioned dressing table in one room stood a faded, yellowing photograph of a young woman of extraordinary beauty. A window overlooking the grounds had been propped open, ostensibly to allow ventilation, but . . . I hastened out before my imagination got the better of me.

Mr Wroe cut short the tour by announcing that he had some work to do and would have to lock up the mansion. He ushered me out of the huge oak door. The century-old veil of mystery had fallen back into place. Outside in the cobbled garrison-like courtyard it is easy to imagine that Whit Sunday almost exactly 100 years ago when 200 members of the sect, started by John Wroe, paraded before the 'Prophet'.

George Wroe remained at Melbourne House Farm until his death on 24 March 1957. His widow Margaret died at Brampton, Cumbria on 10 November 1992, aged 93. In her will, Mrs Wroe bequeathed the last parcels of land at Brandy Carr owned by a Wroe – a sixteen acre field off the Bradford Road and a nine-acre field known as Quarry Field at Trough Well Lane, Wrenthorpe.

Melbourne House Residential Home was officially opened on Saturday 26 September 1959 by Albert Roberts MP, whose Normanton constituency included the mansion. For the next thirty-five years, the property was to serve as a residential home for between twenty-five and thirty elderly ladies. The mansion was not treated kindly. The upstairs banister of the beautiful staircase had to be fully enclosed to comply with fire regulations in the 1960s. An unsympathetic lift shaft was added at the back of the mansion, and during the 1980s some of the upstairs rooms were subdivided. The property did not become a listed building until 1988.

The picturesque conservatory on the south side of the mansion was taken down in the early 1970s and replaced with an extension that was out of proportion and removed the symmetry from the frontage. One of the mansion's four gate lodges was demolished when the A650 Wrenthorpe bypass was constructed, although its destruction need not have happened.

Despite the alterations, I was immensely impressed when I first visited the mansion in August 1992, when I was putting the finishing touches to a book on the history of Wrenthorpe. The staircase was the most striking feature, but so were the huge windows and doorframes and panelling. Most of the woodwork was in immaculate condition, showing no signs of its 140-year age. The scale of the building was impressive, as was the discovery of some unlikely remaining features, such as the large lead-lined wooden water tank on the roof, approached by an internal staircase.

Much of the furniture in the reception rooms and hallway was original, and was sold with the mansion in the 1950s. At the time of the sale there were four four-poster beds, including the one in which the Prophet had slept. The Prophet's bed was removed, but another, together with two grandfather clocks (in addition to the spectacular timepiece on the staircase), remained at Melbourne House. A further four-poster bed from the house was donated to Wakefield Museum.[7] A tea service with a Hebrew inscription, a beautiful dinner service and several items of furniture also remained.

Melbourne House Christian Residential Home for the Elderly closed in May 1994, and the fourteen-bedroom mansion was put on the property market with a price tag of £350,000. Escalating costs such as high heating bills, coupled with constraints imposed by the mansion's listed-building status, prompted its sale. In the autumn of that year, it was sold to the Rushbond Group, a Leeds property developer, and was converted into offices.[8] The work, imaginative in its approach, included the demolition of the hideous early 70s extension, and the construction of new office accommodation in the form of a futuristic glass building was completed in June 1997. Amazingly, the grotto in the grounds of Melbourne House, where the Prophet spent many hours in meditation, survives. This unusual archway is situated in a sunken area of garden between the southern front corner of the mansion and the rear of the lodge closest to Melbourne House Farm.

The twenty-one items of furniture which had remained at the mansion for almost 140 years were sold at auction on 2 February 1995, fetching £20,000. Lots included a pair of mahogany hall stands, a mahogany bookcase cabinet, a mahogany extending dining table, a matched set of six mahogany hall chairs and a pair of mahogany pier tables. The top price was paid for a mahogany breakfront bookcase with four glazed doors, which fetched £4,200.[9] In addition to the sale of Wroe's furniture, another legacy of the Christian Israelites' close association with Melbourne House ended in the late 1990s, when Torch Telecom purchased land from them adjacent to Melbourne House. This transaction closed a chapter in the history of the Church as it was the last property the Christian Israelites owned in the UK.

The last Wroe to live in the vicinity of Melbourne House was Miss Marion Wroe, the elder sister of John Wroe II. She was born in 1877 and lived at the now-demolished lodge house until 1966, when the nuisance of increased traffic volumes along the Bradford Road forced her from her home.[10] Miss Wroe died on 14 December 1969 at the home of her niece, Phyllis Day, at Guiseley near Leeds. The 92-year-old was the last of Prophet Wroe's descendants to bear his name. Unlike her notorious ancestor, however, Miss Wroe was an Anglican and a member of the congregation of St Anne's Parish Church, Wrenthorpe for many years.

\* \* \*

Any hopes there may have been within the Church of creating a dynasty of Wroe leaders were cruelly dashed by the premature deaths of both John Wroe II and his son Ben. Nevertheless, the Christian Israelite Church in Australia has achieved a feat that few Churches or sects expounding a millennial creed have managed to match. It continues to exist. At the turn of the twenty-first century the Christian Israelites could boast seven churches in Australia (at Brisbane, Kempsey, Melbourne, Singleton, Sydney, Terrigal and Windsor) and one church at Indianapolis in the United States. The Christian Israelite Church was also at the forefront of new technology, having established its own internet website. The Church has recently tried to expand into Poland and Russia – two countries enduring tremendous socio-economic upheaval in their transition from state control to market economies.

# Genealogical Table

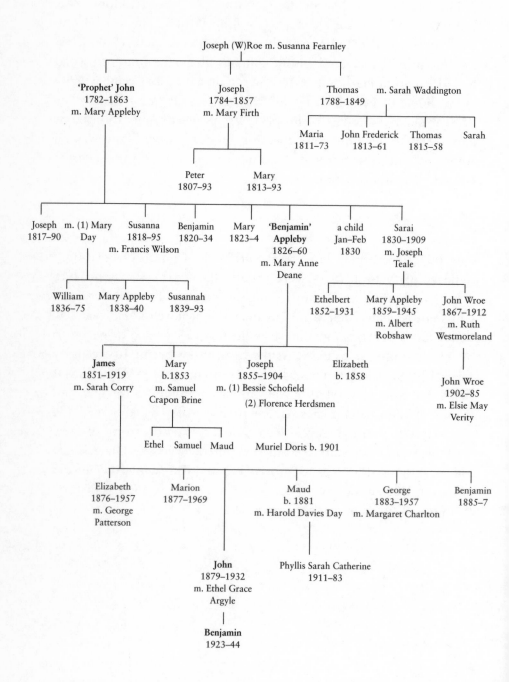

# APPENDIX 1

## *Allegations from The Voice of the People*

The disturbances against Wroe at the Sanctuary, Ashton-under-Lyne on Sunday 27 February 1831 generated a considerable amount of interest in the press, at a time when many papers were pushing for greater freedoms in the run up to the Great Reform Act. Only one newspaper, however, was bold enough to print the majority of the allegations levelled against Wroe. The Manchester paper, *The Voice of the People*, published these in its edition of 5 March.

### JOHN WROE, THE PROPHET OF TONGE, NEAR BRADFORD, YORKSHIRE

John Wroe assumed to be a prophet of the first order, and declared himself to be visited by the Spirit of a living God; and as a standard prophet for the whole earth; and as an instrument in the hands of God to warn, to seek, prepare and sort a people for the coming of the Lord God of Israel, in the name and person of Shiloh. He was received, believed, and obeyed as a prophet by the Israelites, without doubt or suspicion until about the 10th of October last, when, in consequence of some decrees of his own making, which were intended to conceal his diabolical acts of indecency, he was detected in his guilt.

In the course of a presumed visitation, he brought forth several commands, in the name of the God of Israel, of various dates, stating that he was to have seven young females, who should, on strict examination, be proved to be virgins; that they should wait upon, nourish, and comfort him, and be as wives unto him, except that he should not carnally know them; and to act as a kind of sign or type of the new kingdom of God; and as he overcome the lust of the flesh, so should the whole house of Israel overcome; and as it was with him, so it should be with the whole.

Out of the seven chosen virgins, two were from the west part of the

207

kingdom; one of them was called to live with him about two years ago, at that time making his residence at the New Buildings, Shepley, Cheshire, and also at Ashton. Shortly after the commencement of her service, he told her that she must sleep in the same bed with him, and that the Lord had commanded she should do so, in order to show his wisdom in man's fall and restoration; and they were to be a figure of it. He told her that all parts of their bodies were free to each other, except that he must not defile her body. This information, according to her own testimony, greatly distressed her. She knew not what to do, nor how to act. She feared to disobey the commands of God, particularly as he had told her some fatal judgement would befall her if she was disobedient; and that she would experience a like awful judgement if she mentioned it to any individual. She firmly believed him to be visited by the Lord, and, fearing to be cut short of his promises, reluctantly consented. His wife, be it understood, was at Bradford at the time.

In her evidence she declared that he came at night, and got into bed to her, and lay beside her; that he frequently kissed her, and required her to kiss him; he declared how great his love was for her, and that spiritual love far exceeded temporal; and such would be the love in the kingdom of heaven; and that his love for her by far exceeded the love which he had for his own wife. (It is then stated that he caused her to commit the most revolting and unnatural act of indecency which can be conceived, with the mention of which we will not defile our columns.) These acts, it appears, were committed frequently, even in the day-time, and became so common, that she had no doubt that it was right. He used to sleep with her during her illness, contrary to his own laws. She further stated that he had appointed her a husband, but of the young men belonging to the visitation; and that he should come forth and build a house or gate, such as are now built; and asked her if she should object to his coming and doing the same then. It so happened her time to serve in these ways was suspended, and a successor appointed, being chosen one of the seven, who had not the least suspicion that the same kind of conduct would be practised with her.

This young female came from the west part of the kingdom, was with him both at Street House, Bradford, and the New House, Shepley, Cheshire. According to her evidence it appears, that immediately after the commencement of her services he communicated to her the information that she must bed with him, assigning nearly the same reasons as the former and imposing upon her the same denunciation and restrictions. When she retired to rest, she found her bedroom door locked, which greatly increased her fears. She stated that she prayed the Lord would give his assistance to obey his divine will, as she believed it to be, and committed herself to his care. She also stated that she called out to know where she must sleep, as her bedroom door was fast, when he answered from below, the same bed that was for him was for her; that she slept in the same bed with him, and that he kissed and pressed her, declaring with great love for her, as he had done to the former one; that he strictly cautioned her against speaking to the former female, for she would do her no good, as she was a liar and very deceitful; that she fully believed and obeyed his word, and kept the former female at a distance, although they both met at one place of worship.

This second female he made the head of all the seven, and housekeeper to his wife, committing everything under his wife's inspection to her care. She also was in the habit of writing comments from his mouth, for which pretended purpose she used to sit up with him. She said that the whole of the family had retired to bed, except John Wroe and herself, who were in a room downstairs, when he stated that this female and himself must sit up to write a communication. They sat together in one chair for some time, gratifying his lustful inclinations, when they were suddenly surprised by the entrance of his wife into the room. Fortunately for him, there happened to be a clothes-horse with a quantity of linen upon it, which served as a screen between them and the door, otherwise his wife must have seen their very acts. At this moment, he said to the female, "Date it," thinking to deceive his wife by this means, as though he was giving a communication from God; to which his wife hastily replied, "Date it, is it!" and flew into a great passion, and severely abused him, for she considered him the worst of husbands; and that she was not jealous of him without sufficient cause, as he had been publicly charged, some time before, with having forced a child between twelve and thirteen years of age, for which disgraceful act he was brought before the magistrates of Bradford, when he absconded to Ashton. The former and the present circumstances appearing so much alike, operated very powerfully upon the feelings of his wife, and her passion grew so great, that it would have needed little more to have provoked her to kill him. The truth of this statement we have had from the wife herself.

John Wroe has declared before the whole congregation, in the sanctuary that these seven virgins would provoke his wife, and that she hated them in her heart; and he openly declared, in the sanctuary, before all then present, that the Lord had commanded him to take her out for a ride in the chaise, and make her promise never to upbraid him with his conduct towards these females; upon her refusal of which he was commanded to throw her headlong out of the gig, and break her neck. But prior to this last strange act, he ordered the gig to be got ready one night and sent forward to the turnpike gate, to wait there until he and two of the young females came, who were to bring their clothing with them. This caused a disturbance in the house, his wife endeavouring to prevent the gig from going, but to no purpose; he went forward, the females following at a little distance. The approached the gig, got in, and he drove off, as though he was going in the direction of Ashton. He had rode some distance, when the females became alarmed at the sudden strange appearances which were presented to them. To the view of one a large fire appeared before them, with naked men in a dancing or moving posture; to the view of the other a large piece of water, running with a rushing noise close by the road side. At this time he hastily said, 'We must turn round, and go back for the devil stands before us, to slay us.' He instantly returned home; and his acts of indecency with the female on this occasion exceeded that of the former. He used his expressions towards her in the most violent terms of lust. She openly stated that he used to suck on her breasts, and declared he could live on them. He caused her to inflict a peculiar punishment upon him, which he had appointed for disobedient and offending females, which is too gross to be mentioned.

The third of these seven females thus chosen, a fine girl, about 15 years of age, and the same that lived with him at the time as the one before-mentioned, came out of Yorkshire, and was to succeed the former of these females. Being of so tender an age, she became an easy prey to his acts of immorality, which even exceeded the two former. In her evidence, she declared nearly all the same facts as the other witnesses (except the female punishment, and the same charges to keep secrecy &c.) but that in the other respects he was continually practising them day and night, that he scarcely gave her time to perform her domestic duties; and when he came to the sanctuary, his appearance was so emaciated and pitiable, that he used to feign being ill, in consequence of having no rest during the night; and the girl herself looked ill. It appeared, from her testimony, that he had fallen a victim to the temptations which, according to his own public and private laws, would consign him to death and the grave. She also stated that he used to practice his filthy acts with her just prior to his going to the sanctuary, scarcely allowing her time to clean herself, to be in time for worship.

The means by which these immoralities and deceptions were discovered were as follows:- The prophet set off on a tour to London, and from thence to various places in Kent, and likewise to the west of England; but prior to his journey, he wanted to contrive to get the first of these three girls sent home. He was repeatedly railing against her to different persons and saying that she was a very bad girl. This kind of treatment, after all the former promises and pretensions, served only to stimulate her jealousy. She then told the persons who informed her what he had said, that if John Wroe did not let her alone, she would tell all that she knew about him. He still continued to slander her: the consequence was, she made a disclosure, although, he had previously told her that she should die if ever she mentioned any thing, as it was a covenant between God and herself. This information was given to the wife of the person appointed to travel with him to London, a hint of which was given to the husband previous to his departure. In the course of their journey, John Wroe made several observations respecting this female, and called her one of the greatest liars in the whole house of Israel; upon which the person travelling with him said, – "I think thou hast been more than usually fond of her. Didst thou never lie with her? She says thou hast." This he strongly denied, and gave the man orders to write home to his wife to dismiss her, whose servant she was at that time, and also for money to be paid out of the treasury for the purpose of conveying her home; but the wife disobeyed the command. She then communicated the information to the leading females of the society – and the girl underwent a very strict examination, and her depositions were taken in writing. Suspicion then fell upon the two other females, who were separately and strictly examined, when all their depositions were found to agree. This produced great uneasiness among some of the members of the society, and the meeting of the heads of it was called, when it was resolved that a communication should be sent to him, desiring him to return home, in order that he might answer to the charges laid against him. He was at Bristol when the letter reached him.

It appeared from his own testimony, that he was commanded by the Lord to embark for Ireland, which command he hesitated not to disobey, but returned back to Birmingham, and from thence to Sheffield instead of proceeding to Ashton, as an innocent man would have done. At Sheffield he selected a part of the jury who were to examine him, and endeavoured to impress them with the idea that it was a plot or conspiracy against him. From Sheffield he went further into Yorkshire, where the parents of this young female resided. The girl was much agitated at his appearance, as she had entirely concealed the above-mentioned facts from her mother. He told the mother, in the daughter's absence, that there were lies and wickedness going on at Ashton; and mentioned the name of the first female; and told her, if the people of Ashton sent for her daughter, that she must not let her go; for if she did something fatal would happen to her. The mother being still blind, and a firm believer, promised she should not go. With this assurance, he departed, being persuaded in his own mind he should overcome his opposers, without any great difficulty. He proceeded to Leeds, there selecting some jurymen. From thence he went to Wakefield, Bradford and Huddersfield, for the same purpose, and also to bring people who were blind to his craft to speak in his favour. He returned to Ashton on Sunday the 24th of October last, to the new house, Mossley Road, where the jury was met, for the purpose of examining him, when none were to be present that doubted his visitation, or believed the charges brought against him. Shortly after he entered the room, he began to address the jury of his own and his friends' choosing, for the purpose of prejudicing them against his accusers; but this was objected to, as being unjust. Shortly after, finding himself a little disappointed in his expectations, he rushed forward in a very hasty manner, and demanded the Bible, which was handed to him, and upon which he took a most solemn oath that he had not lain with any of the females, or defiled them, or known them man from woman.

This part of his conduct was a sufficient proof of his guilt to two of the jury, which led them to inquire into the cause of his making so circuitous a journey to come from Bristol to Ashton. They also asked one of the witnesses what questions he had put to her, and whether he had not been persuading her not to give evidence against him. His answer to these inquiries being rather contradictory to each other, rendered his innocence still more doubtful. Wroe's wife was present all the time, whose behaviour was very unbecoming; for previously before the return of her husband she was decidedly against him, and firmly believed the charges to be true; and had told the believers of several similar cases.

But the scene was now changed. She began to consider that the fat and luxurious living, the extravagant dresses and valuable jewellery, were at stake. Her behaviour then became violent in the extreme. She threatened to stab the second witness, and brought several persons forward to prove she had forsworn herself in other cases, in order, if possible, to destroy her evidence. But this scheme failed, although ten out of the twelve jurymen were his decided advocates. Great uproar then ensued, and the good lady was removed from the room.

On the following day he ordered two fresh jurymen to succeed the two former ones, and the business to commence at two o'clock and none to be admitted but the witnesses and himself. The two jurymen, however, were determined to resume their seats, and a scuffle ensued. Several of his friends stripped and attempted to turn one of the jurymen out of the room, but was prevented by the courage of the other. No business was done that day, and the prophet seemed much cast down on the failure of his schemes.

The examinations were still continued, and the prophet himself agreed that he would not appear before them until the whole of the witnesses were heard, which lasted about five days. At the conclusion of the examinations, he still protested his innocence, when ten out of the twelve jurymen were decidedly convinced of his guilt, and the other two, through blindness, still held him to be innocent.

Thus the business ended, no one taking upon them the office of judging or passing sentence upon him.

Many persons have since had their peculiar test of orthodoxy, their beards, removed, and the people seem at last to have recovered their usual good sense.

We are assured that this artful knave has, at his own disposal, immense sums of money. He had the entire control of the 'treasury of the Lord.'

# APPENDIX 2

## *John Wroe in Literature*

Two very different novels have been written – published almost 120 years apart – both of which in some way relate to Wroe's activities at Ashton-under-Lyne. *The Coming Man* by James Smith has already been referred to several times in this biographical history. It is largely a loosely veiled biography of its author, James Elishama Smith and can be taken as an important primary source of information as Smith was actually in Ashton at the time of many of the key events at Wroe's downfall. He was even on the initial jury at Wroe's trial at the Odd Whim building before being excluded. *The Coming Man* was completed in 1848 some nine years before Smith's death. It was published posthumously in 1873.

*Mr Wroe's Virgins* by Jane Rogers, on the other hand, is a wholly fictional account. Its author was aware of the case of Wroe's seven virgins and uses this as the starting point for her hugely entertaining story which explores the fictional experiences of four of the young women. The personality of the eponymous character has also been invented and he is cautiously referred to as 'Mr' in the title, not 'Prophet'. A popular BBC TV dramatisation based on Rogers' novel brought the name Wroe to public attention in 1993.

# APPENDIX 3

## *Saving the Odd Whim*

In early September 2003, the Tameside Reporter, the local paper for Ashton-under-Lyne reported plans to bulldoze the Odd Whim pub, the last remaining and most important of Wroe's four millennial gatehouse buildings in the town. Bondgate Developments Limited, a Stockport-based construction company was seeking planning permission to demolish the property and replace it and its grounds with 12 terraced houses.

Members of the Tameside Local History Forum and Ashton Civic Society were appalled at the proposals and mounted a strong campaign to get the building listed by the Department for Culture, Media and Sport. They stressed the historic importance of the building and managed to get Tameside Council to postpone their planning permission decision for a month.

At the speakers' panel meeting of Wednesday of 15th October, Alan Rose of the Tameside Local History Forum, put forward a robust argument for saving the building, asserting that the group had applied for spot listing of the building and that they expected a decision imminently. This last ditch bid was ruled out by the chairman of the meeting and the development was approved subject to a Section 106 agreement.

Fifteen minutes later, however, with the meeting still in progress, a fax arrived from English Heritage, saying that the property had been granted listed building status.

Copy of the Department for Culture, Media and Sport's Schedule, listing the Odd Whim as Grade II

MOSSLEY ROAD
Odd Whim

490629                                                              II

Public House, but built originally as a gatehouse to a Millenarian scheme centred around Ashton-under-Lyne by John Wroe. 1825 with later alterations.

**Exterior:** red brick, painted to front. Slate roof. Main front with projecting recent extension to ground floor. Right-hand part of building comprises a formerly symmetrical square house with a pyramidal roof: this is of two bays to the entrance front and of three bays (the outer ones blind) to the right-hand return. The ground floor extension obscures the former entrance, which comprised a pedimented Ionic doorcase set between large windows. Segmental window arches remain on the side and rear walls. The left-hand continuation of the building, with two windows at first floor level, is contemporary with the rest of the building and is not an extension.

**Interior:** not inspected, believed to be considerably altered.

**History:** this is the only building to survive associated with Millenarian visionary John Wroe (1782–1863). A successor to Joanna Southcott, Wroe founded a cult called the Christian Israelites which gained a considerable following in the 1820s: he prophecied that the sanctuary in which the godly would survive the Apocalypse should be built in Ashton-under-Lyne. In 1825 a grand sanctuary (now the site of the town's sorting office) and four gatehouses were built: this is the only building to survive from this unique instance of a built Millenarian scheme. Wroe's notorious behaviour led to his departure from Ashton in 1830 following an inquest held in this building, but his cult endured elsewhere, particularly in Australia. The building was subsequently used as a cholera hospital in 1832 (with associated burials believed to be in the vicinity) before becoming a public house in 1837, known as the Odd Whim. It changed its name to the Stamford Park Hotel in c1880. The ground floor front extension is of a late C20 date. Wroe was the subject of the 1991

216

novel by Jane Rogers, 'Mr Wroe's Virgins'. A metal plaque has been erected by the Tameside Metropolitan Borough.

**Assessment of importance:** the Odd Whim is listed for special historical interest rather than for architectural importance, having undergone adverse alterations to its fabric.

Nonetheless, it represents a unique survival of a building, erected as part of a Millenarian scheme and is a remarkable reflection of popular religion during an epoch of social, economic and political upheaval.

Dated: 15th October 2003

The Odd Whim closed for the final time on 30th May 2004 and in early August planning permission was granted to convert the property into two apartments, reinstating its original features. Somewhere along the line of this planning process, however, a horrendous blunder occurred as a large portion of the building was demolished. The Department for Culture, Media and Sport's Listed Building Schedule clearly states that:

The left-hand continuation of the building, with two windows at first floor level, is contemporary with the rest of the building and is not an extension.

The break in the brickwork (as shown in the plate section of this book) could indicate different building periods, but its comparison with Moss Lodge is clear from the photographs. It seems most likely that each of the four huge gatehouses would have been built to a similar design. Yet the people of Ashton-under-Lyne have ended up with a truncated building about half the size of what was listed and which probably should have been saved.

# Select Bibliography

PRIMARY SOURCES

THE BRITISH LIBRARY

Carlile, Richard, *The Republican*, vol. 11, no. 12 (7 Jan to 1 July 1825) pp. 353–63

Christian Israelite Church, New York, *Letter to the Editor of the Leeds Times on the Character of John Wroe* (Gravesend: Society of Christian Israelites, 1858)

Christian Israelite Society, *Song of Moses and the Lamb* (Gravesend: William Deane, 1862)

Davis, John, *The Wroeite's Faith, Observations on the Garden of Eden. To which is added, Irreconcilable Contradictions in John Wroe's Writings.* (Sydney: Robert Barr, 1850)

Fielden, Thomas, *An Exposition of the Fallacies and Absurdities of the deluded Church, generally known as Christian Israelites or 'Joannas' with a number of Prophecies taken from Prophet John Wroe's Writing, Proving him to be one of the Greatest Impostors of Modern Times. Written by one of its own members* (Rawtenstall: E. King, no date [c.1861])

Stewart, Allan, *The Abominations of the Wroeites (or Christian Israelites) Fully and Completely Exposed by Allan Stewart, for six years a member of their society* (Melbourne: Thomas Stubbs, no date [1863])

Wroe, John, *The Life and Journal of John Wroe, with Divine Communications Revealed to him being the Visitation of the Spirit of God to warn mankind that the Day of the Lord is at Hand, when the Kingdoms of this World will become the Kingdoms of God and of his Christ* (Ashton-under-Lyne: Trustees of Christian Israelites, 1900 [date of 1st edn unclear]) vol. 1

Wroe, John, *The Life and Journal of John Wroe* (Gravesend: Society of Christian Israelites, 1861) vol. 2

Wroe, John, *The Life and Journal of John Wroe* (Ashton-under-Lyne: Trustees of the Society Surnamed Israelites, 2nd edn, 1902 [date of first edition unclear]) vol. 3

THE NATIONAL ARCHIVES

Index of Births and christenings at the New Jerusalemite or Christian Israelite Meeting House, Bowling Lane, Horton, Bradford, 1823–36, ref. RG4 1711

BRADFORD CENTRAL LIBRARY

B920 WRO 'Prophet Wroe's Mansion' cuttings from local newspapers describing Melbourne House near Wakefield, the home of Prophet John Wroe

Simpson, John, *Journal of Dr. John Simpson of Bradford 1 January to 25 July 1825* (Bradford: Bradford Metropolitan Council Libraries Division, Local Studies Department, 1981)

THE STATE LIBRARY OF VICTORIA, MELBOURNE, AUSTRALIA

'Some of the Brighter Sides of Melbourne Life – The Christian Israelites' in *Dunolly and Betbetshire Express*, 3 March 1891

Hood, J., Australia and the East (London: 1843)

Stewart, Allan, *The Abominations of the Wroeites (or Christian Israelites) Fully and Completely Exposed* (Melbourne: Thomas Stubbs, no date [1863]), [a subsequent volume]

TAMESIDE LOCAL STUDIES AND ARCHIVE CENTRE, ASHTON-UNDER-LYNE

Carlile, Richard, 'Journal of Mr Carlile's Tour through the Country: Ashton-under-Lyne' in *The Lion* vol. 1, no. 3 (18 January 1828), pp. 78–9 and vol. 1, no. 4 (25 January 1828), pp. 97–104

Oral History Tape 49. An Interview with Miss Wood (aged 91), dated 7 December 1979, about the Christian Israelite Movement in Ashton.

NCI2. Notebook of one of Wroe's followers, probably Samuel Lees of Park Bridge. It details jewellery female members of the sect were to wear, and bears the signature of Wroe (in various alias names).

WAKEFIELD CENTRAL LIBRARY

*Newspaper cuttings*

Classified file 920 – John Wroe
Classified file 728.83 – Melbourne House
Late 19th–early 20th-century cuttings books. General information on the
    Christian Israelites: Cuttings vol. 87, p. 141. Details of 'Prophet Wroe's
    Mansion': vol. 88, p. 57. Account of 'Prophet' Wroe and Joanna
    Southcott: vol. 88, p. 210
Late 19th – early 20th-century cuttings books, brief information on Wroe –
    cuttings reference numbers: vol. 8, p. 59; vol. 18, p. 216; vol. 43, pp. 59,
    179, 209; vol. 87, p. 72; vol. 88, pp. 109, 114, 124–5, 198; vol. 89,
    pp. 7, 135
Milton, Daniel, *Abomination of Desolation, compiled from 12 Church
    Circulars by the Promised 'Shiloh'* (Wrenthorpe: Hebrew Press, 1890)


MISCELLANEOUS PRIMARY MATERIAL

Ginswick, J. (ed.), *Labour and the Poor in England and Wales 1849–1851
    – The Letters to The Morning Chronicle from the Correspondents in the
    Manufacturing and Mining Districts, the Towns of Liverpool and
    Birmingham and the Rural Districts* (London: Frank Cass, 1983), vol. I
Head, (Sir) George, *A Home Tour Through the Manufacturing Districts of
    England in the Summer of 1835*, 2nd edn (London: Frank Cass, 1968
    [first published 1836])
Mann, Horace, 'Religious Census of 1851' in *Parliamentary Papers,
    1852–3*, vol. 89 (England and Wales)
Smith, James Elishama, *The Coming Man* (London: Strahan & Co., 1873),
    2 vols


SECONDARY SOURCES

SECONDARY SOURCES RELATING TO LOCAL HISTORY

Banks, William Stott, *Walks About Wakefield* (London: Longmans, 1871)
Baring-Gould, Revd Sabine, *Yorkshire Oddities, Incidents and Strange
    Events*, 5th edn (Otley: Smith Settle, 1987 [1st edn 1874])
Bowman, Winifred M., *Five Thousand Acres of Old Ashton* (Ashton-
    under-Lyne: 1950)

# Select Bibliography

Bowman, Winifred M. *England in Ashton-under-Lyne* (Ashton-under-Lyne: 1960)

Burnley, James, *Yorkshire Stories Retold* (Leeds: Jackson, 1885)

Butterworth, Edwin, *An Historical Account of the towns of Ashton-under-Lyne, Stalybridge and Dukinfield* (Ashton: T.A. Phillips, 1844)

Cannon, Michael, *Old Melbourne Town before the Gold Rush* (Loch Haven: 1991)

Chadwick, William, *Reminiscences of a Chief Constable* (Manchester: 1900)

Clarkson Henry, *Memories of Merry Wakefield*, 4th edn (Wakefield: Wakefield Historical Publications, 1985 [1st edn, 1887])

Cooper, A.N., *Round the Home of a Yorkshire Parson* (Hull: A. Brown & Sons, 1904)

Cudworth, William, *Round About Bradford – A Series of Sketches (Descriptive and Semi-Historical) of forty-two places within six mile of Bradford* (Bradford: 1876)

Cudworth, William, *Histories of Bolton and Bowling (Townships of Bradford) Historically and Topographically Treated* (Bradford: Thomas Brear, 1891)

Deighton, Elizabeth A., 'Prophet Wroe's Mansion', in *Yorkshire Life*, January 1967, pp. 24–5

Finn, Edmund, *The Chronicles of Early Melbourne 1835 to 1852* (Melbourne: Fergusson and Mitchell, 1888)

Glover, W., *History of Ashton-under-Lyne*, ed. Andrew, J. (Ashton: 1884)

Hewitt, J., *History of the Parish of Wakefield* (Wakefield: 1862)

Howcroft, A.J., *Tales of a Pennine People* (Oldham: 1923)

Lupton, Revd J.H., *Wakefield Worthies; or Biographical Sketches of men of note connected by birth or otherwise, with the town of Wakefield in Yorkshire* (Wakefield: 1864)

Owen, D., *History of the Theatres and Cinemas of Tameside* (Ashton-under-Lyne: Neil Richardson, 1985)

Parry, W. Augustus, *History of Hurst and Neighbourhood* (Ashton-under-Lyne: 1908)

Rose, E.A., *Methodism in Ashton-under-Lyne* (Ashton-under-Lyne: 1969), vol. 2

Scruton, William, *Pen and Pencil Pictures of Old Bradford* (Bradford: Thomas Brear, 1889)

Stainton, J.H., *The Making of Sheffield 1865–1914* (Sheffield: E. Watson & Sons, 1924)

221

Taylor, Kate, *Wakefield District Heritage* (Wakefield: European Architectural Heritage Year Committee, 1975), vol. 1

Walker, John William, *Wakefield Its History and People* (Wakefield: West
Yorkshire Printing Company, 1934)


OTHER SECONDARY SOURCES

Armytage, W.H.G., *Heavens Below: Utopian experiments in England*
(London: Routledge & Kegan Paul, 1961)

Baldwin, Ronald Arthur, *The Jezreelites: The Rise and Fall of a
Remarkable Prophetic Movement* (Orpington: Lambarde, 1962)

Balleine, George Reginald, *Past Finding Out: The Tragic Story of Joanna
Southcott and Her Successors* (London: Society for the Promotion of
Christian Knowledge, 1956)

Behagg, Clive, *Labour and Reform: Working Class Movements
1815–1914* (London: Hodder & Stoughton, 1991)

Blair, David, 'John Wroe' in *Notes and Queries* 3rd ser., vol. 5, no. 129,
18 June 1864, p. 493

Blunt, John Henry, 'Christian Israelites' in *Dictionary of Sects, Heresies,
Ecclesiastical Parties and Schools of Religious Thought* (London:
Rivingtons, 1874), p. 107

Briggs, Asa, *The Age of Improvement 1783–1867*, 2nd edn (Harlow:
Longman, 2000 [1st edn 1979])

Clark, Elmer Talmage, *The Small Sects in America* (Nashville: Cokesbury
Press, 1937)

Cohn, Norman, *The Pursuit of the Millennium*, rev. edn (London:
Random House, 1993 [1st edn 1957])

Davidoff, Leonore and Hall, Catherine, *Family Fortunes: Men and
Women of the English Middle Class, 1780–1850* (London: Hutchinson,
1987)

Featherstone, Guy. 'The Nunawading Messiah: James Fisher and Popular
Millenarianism in Nineteenth Century Melbourne', in *Journal of
Religious History* 26 (2002), pp. 42–64

Gilbert, Alan D., *Religion and Society in Industrial England – Church,
Chapel and Social Change, 1740–1914* (London: Longman, 1976)

Goldman, Lazarus Morris, *The Jews in Victoria in the Nineteenth Century*
(Melbourne: the author, 1954)

Gordon, Alexander, 'John Wroe' in Lee, Sidney (ed.) *Dictionary of
National Biography* (London: 1900), vol. LXIII, pp. 1073–5

222

Hammond, J.T. and Hammond, Barbara, *The Rise of Modern Industry*, 9th edn (London: Methuen, 1966 [1st edn 1925])

——, *The Skilled Labourer*, rev. edn (New York: Longman, 1979 [1st edn 1919])

Hardy, D., *Alternative Communities of Nineteenth Century England* (London: Longman, 1979)

Harrison, J.F.C., *Society and Politics in England 1780–1960* (London: Harper & Row, 1965)

——, *The Second Coming: Popular Millenarianism 1780–1850* (London: Routledge & Kegan Paul, 1979)

Harvey, A.D., *Britain in the Early Nineteenth Century* (London: B.T. Batsford, 1978)

Hobsbawn, Eric J., *Labouring Men* (London: Weidenfeld and Nicolson, 1964)

——, *Primitive Rebels* (Manchester: Manchester University Press, 1963)

—— and Rudé, George, *Captain Swing* (London: Lawrence & Wishart, 1969)

Holt, Peter, *Threats of Revolution in Britain 1789–1848* (London: Macmillan, 1977)

Hopkins, James K., *A Woman to Deliver her People: Joanna Southcott and English Millenarianism in an Era of Revolution* (Austin: University of Texas Press, 1981)

Inglis, K.S., *Churches and the Working Class in Victorian England* (London: Routledge and Kegan Paul, 1964)

Joyce, Patrick, *Work, Society and Politics* (London: Harvester Press, 1982)

Koditschek, Theodore, *Class Formation and Urban Industrial Society, Bradford 1750–1850* (Cambridge: Cambridge University Press, 1990)

Lewis, Samuel, *A Topographical Dictionary of England* (London: S. Lewis, 1831), vol. 1

Matthews, Ronald, *English Messiahs: Studies of Six English Religious Pretenders 1656–1927* (London: Methuen, 1936)

McLeod, Hugh, *Religion and the Working Class in Nineteenth Century Britain* (London: MacMillan Education, 1984)

Norman, E.R., *Church and Society in England 1770–1970: A Historical Study* (Oxford: Clarendon Press, 1976)

Numbers, Ronald L. and Butler Jonathan M., *The Disappointed: Millerism and Millenarianism in the Nineteenth Century* (Bloomington: Indiana University Press, 1987)

Oliver, W.H., *Prophets and Millenialists: The Uses of Biblical Prophecy in England From the 1790s to the 1840s* (London: Oxford University Press, 1979)

Roe, Michael, 'John Wroe' in Pike, D. (ed.) *Australian Dictionary of Biography* (Melbourne: 1966), vol. 2, p. 625

——, *Quest for Authority in Eastern Australia 1833–51* (Melbourne: Melbourne University Press, 1965)

Rogers, Philip George, *Battle in Bossenden Wood. The Strange Story of Sir William Courtenay* (Oxford: Oxford University Press, 1961)

——, *The Sixth Trumpeter. The Story of Jezreel and his Tower* (Oxford: Oxford University Press, 1963)

Rudé, George, *The Crowd in History: A Study of Popular Disturbances in France and England, 1730–1848* (London: Lawrence and Wishart, 1981)

Sandeen, Ernest R., *The Roots of Fundamentalism: British and American Millenarianism, 1800–1930* (Chicago: University of Chicago Press, 1970)

Stevenson, John, *Popular Disturbances in England 1700–1870* (London: Longman, 1979)

Taylor, Barbara, *Eve and the New Jerusalem; Socialism and Feminism in the Nineteenth Century* (London: Virago, 1983)

Thompson, E.P., *The Making of the English Working Class*, 2nd edn (London: Penguin, 1968 [1st edn 1963])

White, R.J., *Waterloo to Peterloo* (Harmondsworth: Penguin, 1968)

Wilson, Bryan Ronald, *Religious Sects: A Sociological Study* (London: Weidenfeld and Nicolson, 1964)

UNPUBLISHED SECONDARY SOURCES

Tobin, P.J., 'The Southcottians in England 1782–1895', MA thesis, religious studies, University of Manchester, 1978

# Notes

CHAPTER 1

1. *Divine Communications* or, to give it its full title, *The Life and Journal of John Wroe with Divine Communications Revealed to him, being the Visitation of the Spirit of God, to Warn Mankind that the day of the Lord is at Hand, when the Kingdoms of the World will Become the Kingdom of God and of His Christ* (Ashton-under-Lyne: Trustees of Christian Israelites, 1900) vol. 1, p. 17.
2. Wroe, *Divine Communications*, vol. 1, p .5.
3. The editions of *Divine Communications* used for the purpose of this book, unless otherwise stated, are: vol. 1, 2nd edn, Ashton-under-Lyne, 1900; vol. 2, 5th edition, Gravesend, 1861; vol. 3, Ashton-under-Lyne, 1902.
4. Wroe, *Divine Communications*, vol. 1, p. 3.
5. *Ibid.*, pp. 4–5.
6. Revd Sabine Baring-Gould, *Yorkshire Oddities, Incidents and Strange Events*, 5th edn (Otley: Smith Settle, 1987 [1st edn 1874]), p. 19.
7. Wroe, *Divine Communications*, vol. 1, p. 5.
8. *Ibid.*, p. 7.
9. *Ibid.*, p. 8.
10. *Ibid.*, p. 9.
11. *Ibid.*, p. 10.
12. *Ibid.*, pp. 15–16.
13. Baring-Gould, *Yorkshire Oddities*, p. 21.
14. Wroe, *Divine Communications*, vol. 1, pp. 16–17.
15. Baring-Gould, *Yorkshire Oddities*, p. 33.
16. Wroe, *Divine Communications*, vol. 1, p. 18.
17. *Ibid.*, p. 18–19.
18. *Ibid.*, p. 19.

225

19. *Ibid.*, pp. 19–20.
20. *Ibid.*, p. 20.
21. P.J. Tobin, 'The Southcottians in England 1782–1895', MA thesis, religious studies, University of Manchester, 1978, p. 156.
22. Wroe, *Divine Communications*, vol. 1, p. 25.
23. *Ibid.*, p. 27.
24. *Ibid.*, p. 29.
25. Chapelry records for the parish of Leeds, RDP25 3/1 (burials 1813–57), West Yorkshire County Records Office, Wakefield
26. Wroe, *Divine Communications*, vol. 1, pp. 33–4.
27. *Ibid.*, pp. 24–5.

CHAPTER 2

1. Hugh McLeod, *Religion and the Working Class in Nineteenth Century Britain* (London: MacMillan Education, 1984), pp. 18–20.
2. For a full account of the background to this particular outbreak of millennial religion, see J.F.C Harrison, *The Second Coming: Popular Millenarianism 1780–1850* (London: Routledge & Kegan Paul, 1979). For an outline of the succession of millennial leaders from Brothers to the twentieth century see George Reginald Balleine, *Past Finding Out: The Tragic Story of Joanna Southcott and Her Successors* (London: Society for the Promotion of Christian Knowledge, 1956).
3. Balleine, *Past Finding Out*, pp. 34–5.
4. This is only the briefest outline of Joanna Southcott's career. There have been several biographies written about the Exeter Prophetess, including: James K. Hopkins, *A Woman to Deliver Her People: Joanna Southcott and English Millenarianism in an Era of Revolution* (Austin: University of Texas Press, 1981); and Frances Brown, *Joanna Southcott: The Woman Clothed with the Sun* (Cambridge: Lutterworth, 2002).
5. Balleine, *Past Finding Out*, pp. 142–3.
6. John Stevenson, *Popular Disturbances in England 1700–1870* (London: Longman, 1979), p. 205.
7. Samuel Bamford, *Passages in the Life of a Radical* (London: Frank Cass, 1967 [1st edn 1839–41]), vol 1., p. 6.
8. Peter Holt, *Threats of Revolution in Britain 1789–1848* (London: Macmillan, 1977), p. 30.

9. Cited in James K. Hopkins, *A Woman to Deliver Her People*, p. 79 (ref. University of Texas Southcott Collection, ref. 370, 371, 372).

10. *The Life and Journal of John Wroe* is part of the title of *Divine Communications*, which is cited above.

11. Wroe, *Divine Communications*, vol. 1, p. 50.

12. J.T. Hammond and Barbara Hammond, *The Skilled Labourer* (New York: Longman, 1979 [1st edn 1919]), p. 181.

13. J.T. Hammond and Barbara Hammond, *The Rise of Modern Industry*, 9th edn (London: Methuen & Co. Ltd, 1966 [1st edn 1925]), p. 106.

14. George Rudé, *The Crowd in History: A Study of Popular Disturbances in France and England, 1730–1848* (London: Lawrence and Wishart, 1981), p. 79.

15. Holt, *Threats of Revolution*, p. 30.

16. Alan D. Gilbert, *Religion and Society in Industrial England – Church, Chapel and Social Change, 1740–1914* (London: Longman, 1976), p. 112.

17. Rudé, *Crowd*, p. 84.

18. Bamford's detailed description of a typical handloom weaver's life is reproduced in J.F.C. Harrison, *Society and Politics in England 1780–1960* (London: Harper & Row, 1965), pp. 54–8.

19. Hammond, *Skilled Labourer*, p. 153.

20. *Ibid.*, p. 154.

21. Eric J. Hobsbawn, *Labouring Men* (London: Weidenfeld and Nicolson, 1964), p. 5.

22. Gilbert, *Religion and Society*, p. 113.

23. Asa Briggs, *The Age of Improvement 1783–1867*, 2nd edn (Harlow: Longman, 2000 [1st edn 1979]), p. 181.

24. Hobsbawn, *Labouring Men*, p. 5.

25. Briggs, *Age of Improvement*, p. 184.

26. Briggs cites Abel Stevens, *History of Methodism* (1860–5).

27. Stevenson, *Popular Disturbances*, p. 229.

28. Hobsbawn, *Labouring Men*, p. 9.

29. E.P. Thompson, *The Making of the English Working Class*, 2nd edn (London: Penguin, 1968 [1st edn 1963]), pp. 411–40.

30. *Ibid.*, p. 428.

31. Theodore Koditschek, *Class Formation and Urban Industrial Society, Bradford 1750–1850* (Cambridge: Cambridge University Press, 1990); p. 64.

32. *Ibid.*, p. 76.

33. Elmer Talmage Clark, *The Small Sects in America* (Nashville: Cokesbury Press, 1937) p. 270.

34. J.F.C. Harrison provides comments on some of Smith's contemporary references in *The Second Coming*, especially p. 149.

35. James Elishama Smith, *The Coming Man* (London: Strahan & Co, 1873), vol. 1, pp. 274–5.

36. Patrick Joyce, *Work, Society and Politics* (London: Harvester Press, 1980), p. 80.

37. Balleine, *Past Finding Out*, pp. 86–7.

38. *Divine Communications*, Vol. 1, p. 235.

39. P.J. Tobin, 'The Southcottians in England 1782–1895', MA thesis, religious studies, University of Manchester, 1978, p. 141.

40. Balleine, *Past Finding Out*, p. 70.

41. Harrison, *Second Coming*, p. 137.

42. Balleine, *Past Finding Out*, pp. 77–8.

CHAPTER 3

1. Wroe, *Divine Communications*, vol. 1, p. 32.

2. *Ibid.*

3. Balleine, *Past Finding Out*, p. 81.

4. *Ibid.*, p. 82.

5. Wroe, *Divine Communications*, vol. 1, p. 35.

6. *Ibid.*, p. 40–1.

7. *Ibid.*, p. 53–5.

8. W. Anderson-Smith, *'Shepherd' Smith the Universalist: the Story of a Mind*, being a life of the Revd James Smith (London: Sampson, Low & Co., 1892), pp. 59–60. This is the biography of the Revd James Smith.

9. The Glasgow article was reprinted in the *Wakefield Free Press*, 28 February 1874, p. 6.

10. William Chadwick, *Reminiscences of a Chief Constable* (Manchester: 1900), p. 108.

11. *Leeds Patriot*, 18 December 1827.

12. Bill Williams, *The Making of Manchester Jewry 1740–1875* (Manchester: Manchester University Press), 1976.

13. E. Belfort Bax, *Reminiscences and Reflections*, p. 50, cited in Harrison, *The Second Coming*.

14. Smith, *The Coming Man*, vol. 1, pp. 277–9.
15. *Ibid.*, pp. 270–1.
16. Wroe, *Divine Communications*, vol. 1, p. 35–6.
17. 'Some of the Brighter Sides of Melbourne Life' in *Dunolly and Betbetshire Express*, 3 March 1891.
18. Wroe, *Divine Communications*, vol. 1, p. 55–6.
19. *Ibid.*, p. 56–7.
20. *Ibid.*, p. 98.
21. *Ibid.*, p. 104–5.
22. *Ibid.*, p. 96.
23. *Ibid.*, p. 189.
24. William Scruton, *Pen and Pencil Pictures of Old Bradford* (Bradford: Thomas Brear, 1889), p. 58.
25. Wroe, *Divine Communications*, vol. 1, pp. 216–7.
26. Balleine, *Past Finding Out*, pp. 72–3.
27. Wroe, *Divine Communications*, vol. 1, pp. 259–60.
28. *Ibid.*, p. 272.
29. *Ibid.*, p. 277.
30. *Ibid.*, pp. 66–8.
31. Baring-Gould, *Yorkshire Oddities*, p. 36.

CHAPTER 4

1. Hopkins, *A Woman to Deliver her People*, p. 79.
2. Wroe, *Divine Communications*, vol. 1, pp. 200–1.
3. William Cudworth, *Round About Bradford – A Series of Sketches (Descriptive and Semi-Historical) of forty-two places within six mile of Bradford* (Bradford: 1876), p. 389.
4. *Leeds Times*, 6 June 1857, p. 6.
5. Wroe, *Divine Communications*, vol. 1, pp. 128–9.
6. Tobin, *Southcottians in England*, p. 169.
7. Wroe, *Divine Communications*, vol. 1, pp. 201–2.
8. Smith, *The Coming Man*, vol. 1, p. 278.
9. Wroe, *Divine Communications*, vol. 1, p. 208.
10. *Ibid.*, p. 208.
11. *Ashton-under-Lyne Reporter*, 6 October 1972, p. 10.
12. *Leeds Independent and York County Advertiser*, 5 October 1824, p. 3.
13. From a report in *The Times*, reproduced by Richard Carlile in *The Republican*, vol. II, no. 12 (7 Jan–1 July 1825) pp. 353–63.

14. *Lancaster Gazette*, 19 March 1825, p. 3.
15. *The Times*, 17 March 1825, p. 3.
16. Richard Carlile, *The Republican*, vol. 11, no. 12, 7 January to 1 July 1825, pp. 353–63.
17. John Simpson, *Journal of Dr John Simpson of Bradford 1 January to 25 July 1825* (Bradford: Bradford Metropolitan Council Libraries Division, Local Studies Department, 1981), p. 19.
18. Wroe, *Divine Communications*, vol. 1, p. 352 (footnote).
19. *Ibid.*, p. 229.
20. *Ibid.*, pp. 227–8.
21. *Ibid.*, p. 229.
22. *Ibid.*, p. 350.
23. *Ibid.*, p. 229.
24. Transcribed in Wroe, *Divine Communications*, vol. 1, p. 230–2.
25. Wroe, *Divine Communications*, vol. 1, p. 235.
26. Simpson, *Journal*, p. 52.
27. Hammond, *Skilled Labourer*, p. 157.
28. Wroe, *Divine Communications*, vol. 1, p. 226 (footnote).
29. Wroe, *Divine Communications*, vol. 1, p. 304.
30. Brief newspaper item glued to a page of John Wroe, *The Word of God to Guide Israel to Eternal Life, Explained to John Wroe* (Wakefield: George Meredith, 1834), at Bradford Central Library, ref. B252 WRO.

CHAPTER 5

1. Gilbert, *Religion and Society*, p. 27.
2. M.H. Port, *Six Hundred New Churches: A Study of the Church Building Commission, 1818–1856, and Its Church Building Activities* (London: Society for the Promotion of Christian Knowledge for the Church Historical Society, 1961).
3. K.S. Inglis, *Churches and the Working Class in Victorian England* (London: Routledge and Kegan Paul, 1964), p. 6.
4. Port, *Six Hundred New Churches*, p. 5.
5. Inglis and Wickham both dismiss the problem as being merely a lack of space and focus on other ways in which the Church of England tried to redress the balance.
6. McLeod, *Religion and the Working Class*, p. 18.

7.  J. Thirsk (ed.), *The Agrarian History of England, vol. IV 1500–1640*, pp. 2–14, as quoted in Gilbert, *Religion and Society*, p. 99.

8.  Horace Mann, '*Religious Census of 1851*' in *Parliamentary Papers, 1852–3*, vol. 89 (England and Wales), pp. clix–clxi.

9.  Disraeli famously introduced the concept of 'two nations' in his novel *Sybil*.

10. Simon Dentith, *Society and Cultural Forms in Nineteenth Century England* (Basingstoke: Macmillan, 1998), p. 29.

11. Inglis, *Churches and the Working Class*, p. 9.

12. Gilbert, *Religion and Society*, p. 97.

13. *London Illustrated News*, 13 August 1870, p. 179.

14. William Kingo Armstrong, *Memoir of John Ross Coulthart of Ashton-under-Lyne, Forty years manager of the Ashton, Stalybridge, Hyde, and Glossop Bank* (Edinburgh: McFarlane & Erskine, 1876), pp. 104–5.

15. Nikolaus Pevsner, *The Buildings of England: South Lancashire* (Harmondsworth: Penguin, 1969), p. 69.

16. John Henry Blunt, 'Christian Israelites' in *Dictionary of Sects, Heresies, Ecclesiastical Parties and Schools of Religious Thought* (London: Rivingtons, 1874), p. 107.

17. Chadwick, *Reminiscences*, p. 108.

18. Information from Gay-Jeanne Oliver of Stalybridge.

19. The stables at the former Park Bridge industrial complex have been converted into the Park Bridge Heritage Centre.

20. Winifred M. Bowman, *England in Ashton-under-Lyne* (Ashton-under-Lyne: 1960), p. 475.

21. *Ibid.*, p. 239.

22. Richard Carlile, *The Republican*, vol. 11, no. 12, 7 January to 1 July 1825, pp. 354–5.

23. Carlile also recounts the case of the Lees baby in his 'Journal of Mr Carlile's Tour through the Country: Ashton-under-Lyne' in *The Lion* vol. 1, no. 4 (25 January 1828), pp. 99–100.

24. Baring-Gould, *Yorkshire Oddities*, p. 32.

25. A.J. Howcroft, *Tales of a Pennine People* (Oldham: 1923), p. 78.

26. Bowman, *England in Ashton-under-Lyne*, p. 238.

27. Wroe, *Divine Communications*, vol. 1, pp. 304–5.

28. Edwin Butterworth, *An Historical Account of the towns of Ashton-under-Lyne, Stalybridge and Dukinfield* (Ashton: T.A. Phillips, 1844), p. 69.

29. W. Glover, *History of Ashton-under-Lyne*, ed. J. Andrew (Ashton-under-Lyne: 1884), p. 315.
30. E.A. Rose, *Methodism in Ashton-under-Lyne* (Ashton-under-Lyne: 1969), vol. 2., p. 5.
31. Owen Mss, Manchester Public Library.
32. Carlile, 'Journal of Mr Carlile's Tour through the Country: Ashton-under-Lyne' in *The Lion* vol. 1, no. 4 (25 January 1828), p. 103.
33. Glover, *History of Ashton-under-Lyne*, p. 313.
34. Smith, *The Coming Man*, vol. 1, p. 283.
35. *Ibid.*, p. 269.
36. Chadwick, *Reminiscences of a Chief Constable*, p. 109.
37. *Ibid.*, pp. 109–10.

CHAPTER 6

1. The site of the farmhouse is now occupied by car showrooms for the Britannia Motor Company.
2. *Voice of the People*, 5 March 1831, p. 77.
3. Tong Mss 12a/220–1, Bradford Local Records Office.
4. Tong Mss 12c/37, Bradford Local Records Office.
5. Wroe, *Divine Communications*, vol. 1, pp. 393–8.
6. Although not named, Tillotson was probably Wroe's scribe who recorded the first part of the case of Martha Whiteley in *Divine Communications*.
7. Wroe, *Divine Communications*, vol. 1, p. 397.
8. *Ibid.*, p. 397.
9. Tong Mss 12g/126–30, Bradford Local Records Office.
10. Bell's Life in *London and Sporting Chronicle*, 13 March 1831, p. 4.
11. *Wheeler's Manchester Chronicle*, 5 March 1831, p. 3.
12. *Voice of the People*, 5 March 1831, p. 77.
13. Wroe, *Divine Communications*, vol. 1, p. 493.
14. *Sheffield Courant*, 4 March 1831, p. 1.
15. Wroe, *Divine Communications*, vol. 1, p. 521.
16. *Ibid.*, pp. 574–5.
17. *Ibid.*, pp. 521–2.
18. *Voice of the People*, 5 March 1831, p. 77.
19. Wroe, *Divine Communications*, vol. 1, p. 524.
20. *Ibid.*, p. 524.
21. *Ibid.*, p. 533.

22. The wording of the handbill as printed in the *Sheffield Courant*, 4 March 1831, p. 1. The precise wording of this handbill and the spelling of Wroe's aliases very between the newspapers that covered the story.

23. Wroe, *Divine Communications*, vol. 1, pp. 541–2.

24. Bell's Life in *London and Sporting Chronicle*, 13 March 1831, p. 4.

25. Wroe, *Divine Communications*, vol. 1, p. 328.

26. *Ibid.*, p. 542.

27. *Ibid.*, p. 543.

28. *Sheffield Courant*, 25 March 1831, p . 2.

29. *Voice of the People*, 26 March 1831, p. 101.

30. *Sheffield Courant*, 4 March 1831, p. 1.

31. *Wheeler's Manchester Chronicle*, 5 March 1831, p. 3.

32. Thomas Fielden, *An Exposition of the Fallacies and Absurdities of the deluded Church, generally known as Christian Israelites* (Rawtenstall: E. King, no date, *c.*1861), p. 15.

33. Baring-Gould, *Yorkshire Oddities*, pp. 31–2.

34. Fielden, *Fallacies and Absurdities*; Allan Stewart, *The Abominations of the Wroeites* (Melbourne: no date [1863]).

35. Notebook of one of Wroe's followers, probably Samuel Lees of Park Bridge, source: Tameside Local Studies and Archive Centre, Ashton-under-Lyne, ref. NCI2.

36. Chapelry records for the parish of Leeds, RDP25 9/4 (baptisms 1775–86), West Yorkshire County Records Office, Wakefield.

37. Wroe, *Divine Communications*, vol. 1, p. 522.

38. *Ibid.*, pp. 526–7.

39. *Ibid.*, p. 12.

40. *Ibid.*, p. 542.

41. Howcroft, *Pennine People*, p. 80.

42. *Voice of the People*, 9 April 1831, p. 120.

43. John Ward (1781–1837) founded and led the Shilohites millennial sect.

44. *The Times*, 11 April 1831, p. 3.

45. Wroe, *Divine Communications*, vol. 1, p. 552.

46. *Leeds Mercury*, 23 April 1831, p. 2.

47. *Voice of the People*, 23 April 1831, p. 136.

48. Baring-Gould, *Yorkshire Oddities*, p. 32.

49. Wroe, *Divine Communications*, vol. 1, p. 309.

50. *Leeds Mercury*, 16 April 1831, p. 3.

51.  *Voice of the People*, 23 April 1831, p. 136.
52.  Wroe, *Divine Communications*, vol. 1, p. 307.
53.  *Ibid.*, p. 308.


CHAPTER 7

1.  Sir George Head, *A Home Tour Through the Manufacturing Districts of England in the Summer of 1835*, 2nd edn (London: Frank Cass, 1968 [1st published 1836]), pp. 141–2.
2.  1851 Census, ref. HO 107/2328, sch. 309.
3.  1841 Census, ref. HO 107/1271/4, sch. 5–6.
4.  Accounts of the burglary taken from the *Leeds Conservative Journal*, 11 August 1842, p. 5 and the *Wakefield Journal and West Riding Herald*, 12 August 1842, p. 2.
5.  *Leeds Mercury*, 17 August 1844, p. 5.
6.  *Wakefield Journal and West Riding Herald*, 17 August 1844, p. 3.
7.  William Stott Banks, *Walks About Wakefield* (London: Longmans, 1871), pp. 120–1.
8.  Wroe, *Divine Communications*, vol. 1, p. 633.
9.  *Ibid.*, p. 542.
10.  Wroe, *Divine Communications*, Vol. 3, p. 275.
11.  John Wroe, *An abridgement of John Wroe's Life and Travels; also Revelations on the Scriptures, and various communications given to him by divine inspiration*, 4th edn (Gravesend: 1851), vol. 1.
12.  Wroe, *Divine Communications*, vol. I, p. 19.
13.  *Ibid.*, p. 235.
14.  *Ibid.*, vol. 2, p. 14.
15.  *Ibid.*, vol. 3, p. 444.
16.  *Ibid.*, vol. 1, p. 572.
17.  *Ibid.*, vol. 2, pp. 92–6.
18.  *Ibid.*, vol. 1, p. 30.
19.  Chadwick, *Reminiscences*, p. 106.
20.  Wroe, *Divine Communications*, vol. 2, pp. 5–6.
21.  *Ibid.*, pp. 401–2.
22.  *Ibid.*, p. 402.
23.  Henry Clarkson, *Memories of Merry Wakefield*, 4th edn (Wakefield: Wakefield Historical Publications, 1985 [1st edn, 1887]) p. 106.
24.  Wroe, *Divine Communications*, vol. 1, p. 33.
25.  *Ibid.*, pp. 33–4.

# CHAPTER 8

1.  Wroe, *Divine Communications*, vol. 1, p. 156.
2.  *Ibid.*, pp. 209–13.
3.  The account in *Divine Communications*, however, states that 'When within about 700 miles of New York, there came on very severe weather for about a week, so much so that the vessel was damaged, and could not proceed on its voyage, but returned to the Cove of Cork harbour.' This presumably is an error.
4.  B.R. Wilson, *Religious Sects: A Sociological Study* (London: Weidenfeld and Nicolson, 1964), p. 229.
5.  *New York Daily Times* 25 March 1854, as cited in Christian Israelite Church, New York, *Letter to the Editor of the Leeds Times on the Character of John Wroe* (Gravesend: Society of Christian Israelites, 1858), p. 22.
6.  Sheet of notes giving dates of Wroe's foreign travels and the locations of Christian Israelite Churches, Ref. 71D89/1, Bradford Records Office.
7.  *New York Tribune*, 4 June 1859, p. 2.
8.  Daniel Milton, *Abomination of Desolation, compiled from 12 Church Circulars by the Promised 'Shiloh'* (Wrenthorpe: Hebrew Press, 1890), p. 10.
9.  *Leeds Times*, 6 June 1857, p. 6.
10. Michael Roe, *Quest for Authority in Eastern Australia 1833–51* (Melbourne: Melbourne University Press, 1965), p. 127.
11. Wroe, *Divine Communications*, vol. 3, p. 23.
12. *Port Phillip Herald*, 18 August 1843.
13. *Ibid.*, vol. 1, 25 August 1843.
14. Howcroft, *Pennine People*, p. 76.
15. Wroe, *Divine Communications*, vol. 3, pp. 30–1.
16. *Ibid.*, pp. 480–2.
17. Roe, *Quest for Authority*, p. 127.
18. Lazarus Morris Goldman, *The Jews in Victoria in the Nineteenth Century* (Melbourne: the author, 1954), pp. 46–7.
19. *Melbourne Argus*, 10 September 1850, p. 4.
20. Wroe, *Divine Communications*, vol. 1, p. 571.
21. Edmund Finn, *The Chronicles of Early Melbourne 1835 to 1852* (Melbourne: Fergusson and Mitchell, 1888), vol. 1, p. 176.
22. Wroe, *Divine Communications*, vol. 3, pp. 493–4.
23. Roe, *Quest for Authority*, p. 129.

24. Stewart, *Abominations of the Wroeites*, p. 4.
25. *Ibid*. [the second pamphlet], p. 3.
27. *The Melbourne Age*, 12 June 1863.
27. *Ibid*., 15 June 1863.
28. *Latter Rain* (the quarterly magazine of the Christian Israelite Church), no. 22, p. 10.
29. Guy Featherstone, 'The Nunawading Messiah: James Fisher and Popular Millenarianism in Nineteenth Century Melbourne', *Journal of Religious History*, 26 (2002), p. 48.
30. *Imperial Review*, no. 33, 1892–1901, pp. 48–9.
31. *Melbourne Argus*, 11 July 1871, p. 4.
32. Featherstone, 'Nunawading Messiah', pp. 42–64.
33. *Christian Israelite Church, Singleton 1862–1986: 124 Years of History*, booklet at Bradford Records Office, ref. 71D89.

CHAPTER 9

1. *Dictionary of National Biography* 'Nayler'; Ronald Matthews, *English Messiahs: Studies of Six English Religious Pretenders 1656–1927* (London: Methuen, 1936), pp. 3–42.
2. Baring-Gould, *Yorkshire Oddities*, p. 35.
3. Michael Cannon, *Old Melbourne Town before the Gold Rush* (Loch Haven: 1991), pp. 452–3.
4. Fielden, *Fallacies and Absurdities*, pp. 19–20.
5. *Ibid*., p. 10.
6. As pointed out by religious studies postgraduate, Tobin in his 'Southcottians' MA thesis, p. 178.
7. Featherstone, 'Nunawading Messiah', p. 49.
8. Baring-Gould, *Yorkshire Oddities*, p. 34.
9. *Wakefield Express*, 5 July 1879, p .2.
10. *Leeds Times*, 6 June 1857, p. 6.
11. Christian Israelite Church, New York, Letter to the Editor of the *Leeds Times* on the Character of John Wroe (Gravesend: Society of Christian Israelites, 1858), pp. 11–12.
12. This is an abridged and amended version of the author's article 'Some Mute Inglorious Milton' in Kate Taylor (ed.) *Aspects of Wakefield 3* (Barnsley: Wharncliffe Books, 2001), pp. 108–20.
13. Milton claimed this in a newspaper interview in 1898, but officially there was no such position within the Society of Christian Israelites.

14. Dr John William Walker, *Wakefield Its History and People* (Wakefield: 1934), p. 486.
15. *Wakefield Free Press*, 28 February 1874, p. 6, quoting an article which appeared in the *Glasgow Weekly Mail*.
16. Baring-Gould, *Yorkshire Oddities*, pp. 35–6.

CHAPTER 10

1. Wroe, *Divine Communications*, vol. 3, p. 49.
2. Registry of Deeds records 1852 RH 473 557 and 1852 RN 145 158, West Yorkshire County Records Office, Wakefield.
3. Revd J.H. Lupton, *Wakefield Worthies; or Biographical Sketches of men of note connected by birth or otherwise, with the town of Wakefield in Yorkshire* (Wakefield: 1864), p. 257.
4. Built in the 1890s, this terrace survives and is now numbered 345–351 Bradford Road, although the end two houses, which included the house where Milton died (No. 353), were unfortunately demolished in about 1970.
5. *Notes and Queries*, 9 April 1864, p. 293.
6. Wakefield Local Studies Library, ref. box 4f.
7. Horridge was in business in Wood Street, Wakefield about 1849–91, and also printed material for Goodwyn Barmby (1820–81), the Wakefield Christian Socialist.
8. Potovens was the alternative name for Wrenthorpe, originating from the post-medieval pottery industry that once thrived there.
9. Mary S. Robertson, *Authentic History of the 'Great Box' of Sealed Writings Left by Joanna Southcott*, 1929, pp. 6–7.
10. *Yorkshire Post*, 19 December 1903, p. 7.
11. Newspaper article glued to a page of J. Wroe, *The Word of God to Guide Israel to Eternal Life, Explained to John Wroe* (Wakefield: George Meredith, 1834), at Bradford Central Library, ref. B252 WRO.
12. Late 19th–early 20th century newspaper cuttings books at Wakefield Local Studies Library, ref. 88/209.

CHAPTER 11

1. For some strange reason, in the incorrect description of the Ashton Christian Israelites as 'Southcottians' or 'Johannas', the latter word is almost always spelt with an 'h'.

2. Wroe, *Divine Communications*, vol. 1, pp. 399, 552.
3. Information from Gay-Jeanne Oliver.
4. *Ibid.*
5. Winifred M Bowman, *Five Thousand Acres of Old Ashton* (Ashton-under-Lyne: 1950), p. 175.
6. Gay-Jeanne Oliver.
7. Index of births and christenings at the New Jerusalemite or Christian Israelite Meeting House, Bowling Lane, Horton, Bradford, 1823–36, ref. RG4 1711, The National Archive.
8. William Cooke Taylor, *Notes of a Tour in the Manufacturing Districts of Lancashire*, 3rd edn (London: Frank Cass, 1968 [first published 1841]), pp. 234–5.
9. Harrison, *Second Coming*, pp. 147–8.
10. *Wakefield Free Press*, 28 February 1874, p. 6.
11. Society of Christian Israelites, *Tunes for the Use of the Society of Christian Israelites, adapted to the various meters in the 'Song of Moses and the Lamb'* (Gravesend: W. Deane for the Trustees of the Society, 1854).
12. *Leeds Times*, 6 June 1857, p. 6.
13. The date that the Christian Israelites ceased worshiping in the Sanctuary is unclear. It was certainly later than 1852, as volume 3 of *Divine Communications* records notes taken in the Sanctuary during that year.
14. D. Owen, *History of the Theatres and Cinemas of Tameside* (Ashton: Neil Richardson, 1985), p. 10.
15. *Ashton-under-Lyne Reporter*, 10 December 1954, p. 13.
16. Peter Leeming, 'The Buildings of the Christian Israelites in Tameside, Part 2' in *The Journal of Tameside Archaeological Society*, vol. 5, no. 7 (July 2002), p. 11.
17. Chadwick, *Reminiscences*, p. 106.
18. W. Augustus Parry, *History of Hurst and Neighbourhood* (Ashton-under-Lyne: 1908), p. 85.
19. John Wroe, *Divine Communications given to John Wroe During Ten Years from the beginning of the year 1823 to the end of 1832; with Accounts of Fulfilments of many of the Prophecies and of his travels during that period. Also an account of his life and prophecies previous to that period* (Wakefield: George Meredith, 1834).
20. The life story of Jezreel has been chronicled in two books: Ronald Arthur Baldwin, *The Jezreelites: the Rise and Fall of a Remarkable*

*Prophetic Movement* (Orpington: Lambarde, 1962), and Philip
George Rogers, *The Sixth Trumpeter: The story of Jezreel and his
tower* (Oxford: Oxford University Press, 1963).

21.  Baldwin, *The Jezreelites*, p. 64.
22.  Letter in the *Ashton-under-Lyne Reporter*, 7 January 1955, p. 6.
23.  Rogers, *The Sixth Trumpeter*, p. 137.
24.  Balleine, *Past Finding Out*, p. 123.
25.  William D. Forsyth, *The Bible Triumphant by Israel's Hope under
     Israel's Standard* (Littleborough: 1896), p. 51.
26.  Philip George Rogers, *Battle in Bossenden Wood. The Strange Story
     of Sir William Courtenay* (Oxford: Oxford University Press, 1961),
     pp. 210–11.
27.  Howcroft, *Pennine People*, pp. 89–91.
28.  Oral History Tape 49. An Interview with Miss Wood (aged 91),
     dated 7 December 1979, about the Christian Israelite Movement in
     Ashton. Source: Tameside Local Studies and Archive Centre, Ashton-
     under-Lyne.

CHAPTER 12

1.   Memories of Bernard Arundel, a childhood friend of Ben Wroe.
2.   *Wakefield Express*, 14 June 1969, p. 8.
3.   *Wakefield Express*, 23 January 1932, p. 5.
4.   *Ashton-under-Lyne Reporter*, 17 December 1954, p. 6.
5.   Mrs Hemingway died in 1995, aged 93.
6.   William Alfred Thackeray Synge, *The Story of the Green Howards,
     1939–1945* (Richmond: The Green Howards, 1952), p. 344.
7.   *Yorkshire Evening Post*, 11 September 1959, p. 15.
8.   It now forms part of the prestigious office accommodation of a major
     telecommunications employer.
9.   *Wakefield Express*, 10 February 1995, p. 9.
10.  Elizabeth A. Deighton, 'Prophet Wroe's Mansion', in *Yorkshire Life*,
     January 1967, p. 25.

# Index

Adwalton (Drighlington, near Leeds) 5, 127
Allman, Joseph ('Zebulon') 30
Alverthorpe (near Wakefield) 168, 169; church 117, 196; churchyard 176, 196, 197, 198
Anglican Church, *see* Church of England
Apperley Bridge (near Bradford) 54–7
Appleby, Benjamin 5
Appleby, Joseph 15, 125
Appleby, Mary, *see* Wroe, Mary
Ashton-under-Lyne 71–88, 89–90, 93–100, 108–111, 114, 125, 179–81, 182; Albion Congregational Church 74; Audenshaw 193; blue plaque for Wroe 186; cholera hospital 124, 185, 186; Black Lad (Black Knight ceremony) 110; Charlestown 43, 59; Church Street 80, 195; decline of the Christian Israelites 192–3; Droylsden 73; Fairfield Settlement 73–4; gasworks 59; Gate Street 84; as headquarters of the Society of Christian Israelites 168, 183, 193; Henry Square 77, 85; industrialisation 29; 'Johanna' Shops 87, 186–8; Ladysmith Barracks 180; Moss Lodge 83; Mossley Road 185; as the 'New Jerusalem' 68, 83–5, 87, 94, 114, 185; Nonconformity in the town 72, 73–4; the Odd Whim 83, 84, 95, 100, 109, 185–6; Oldham Road 59, 192; Park Parade 85, 100, 109, 185; Portland Basin 84; Richmond Street 193, 195; St Michael's parish church 47, 72–3; St Peter's Church 73; The Sanctuary 80–1, 181, 182, 184, 192, 195; fracas at the Sanctuary 99–100, 109, 185; Scotland Street 185; Shepley 84, 110; Southcottians 36; Southgate Street 84; the Stamford Park Hotel 185; Stamford Street 87, 187; Star Cinema 184; Taunton Lodge 84, 180; United Methodists 184; *see also* Park Bridge
*Ashton-under-Lyne Reporter* 73, 187

Bacup (Lancashire) 151
Balleine, Revd George Reginald 21
Bamford, Samuel 23
Banks, William Stott 119
Baring-Gould, Revd Sabine 10, 169
Barltrop, Mabel ('Octavia') 191
Barraclough, William 107
Barratt, Robert 162, 168
Bayley, Mr Justice 61, 62
'Beardies', *see* Society of Christian Israelites
Bell's *Life in London and Sporting Chronicle* 93, 101
Binns, Samuel 34
Bishop, John Laden 62, 133, 158, 162, 173
Bishop, Margaret 133, 162
Black Hill Foot (Peak District) 63
Blackwell, Robert 36
Blair, David 142, 167
Blake, Dr 6
Boon, Mary 30
Bossenden Wood (Kent), Battle of 192
Bowman, Winifred 180
Bradford 1, 5, 11, 42, 62, 91–2, 98, 111–14; Barkerend Road 174; Bowling 1, 168, 169; Christian

Israelites' meeting house 64–5,
111–12, 128; Cockpit 48; Dudley
Hill 48; Great Horton 66; Horton
182; industrialisation 4, 27, 29; New
Inn 112, 113; riots 64–6, 111–13;
Southcottians 16, 35, 36; Street House
4, 82, 84, 88 (and the virgins' scandal)
91–2, 93, 96, 97–8, 101; Sun Inn 65;
Tong Street 4, 6, 48, 91, 114; wool-
combing 4, 26; wool-combers' strike
29, 63, 66–7, 122; *see also* Apperley
Bridge
*Bradford Telegraph and Argus* 202
Brandy Carr, *see* Wrenthorpe
Brear, Joseph 65, 66
Brear, Mary 65
Brothers, Richard 17–19
Brown, Mary 126
Bruce, Revd Stanhope 18, 20
Brunton, John 55, 66, 126–7
Bullough, Mary 96
Burnley, Mary 178

Carlile, Richard 61–2, 86
Carr Gate (near Wakefield) 168, 169,
172, 198
Cartwright, John 138, 140, 148
Chadwick, William 75, 89
Chatham 188–9
Chetwode, Revd George 72–3, 74
Chilton (Buckinghamshire) 72
Christian Israelite Church (*see also*
Society of Christian Israelites) 193,
194, 205; in Australia 194, 195;
*Latter Rain* (magazine) 148
*Christian Times* 142
Church of England, decline of during
industrialisation 69–71; at Ashton-
under-Lyne 71–3
Church of the First Born, 147–8
Clark, Elmar 28
Clark, John 118
Clarkson, Joseph 64
Clayton, James 66, 126
Clunne, Cordelia, *see* Lees, Cordelia
Clunne, Sarah 78
*Collingwood Observer* 147

*The Coming Man* 28, 38–40, 87, 103,
105
Commissioners' (Waterloo or Million)
Churches 69–70, 117
Cooke, William 44, 45
Cooper, Canon A.N. 164
Corry, James 187
Corry, Joseph 169, 187, 189, 194
Corry, Sarah, *see* Wroe, Sarah
Courtney, Sir William, *see* Tom, John
Cudworth, William 56

*Daily Telegraph* 190
Davis, John 142
Day, Phyllis Sarah Catherine 205
Deane, Mary Ann, *see* Wroe, Mary Ann
Deane, William 168, 183
Dennison, Joseph 92
Devonport 23, 113
*Divine Communications* 2, 120–2
Dobson, John 64
domestic industries 10–11, 23–26, 28–9,
66–7, 75
Doncaster 95
Donnolan, Joseph 139
Dukinfield (Cheshire) 73, 84
*Dunolly and Betbetshire Express* 41,
145–6

Easterbrook, Isaac 148
Eccles, Abby 169, 178
Eddowes, Benjamin 158, 165
Elsworth, Elizabeth 65
Engels, Friedrich 38
Entwistle Samuel 132
Exeter, Helen 191

Farrand, Henry 188
Farrand, Mary Ann, *see* Wroe, Mary
Ann
Farrand, William 168, 183, 186
Farrow, Jesse 188
Fearnley, Susanna, *see* Wroe, Susanna
Field, Dr George 6, 58, 92
Field, Thomas 140
Fielden, Thomas 151–2, 155
Firth, Mary 5

Firth, Peter 5
Firth, Samuel 92
Fisher, James 147–8
*Flying Roll, The* 151, 189, 191, 194
Foley, Revd Thomas 18, 20, 30
Forsyth, William 191
Fox, Robert 34

Garland, Ann 96
Gill, John 152, 169, 187, 188
Gillingham (Kent) 23, 189
*Glasgow Weekly Mail* 37, 183
Goodman, Tobias 12
*Gospel Herald, The* 131
Gravesend 23, 47, 134, 183
Grimshaw, Daniel 60–1, 76

Hague, Sarah Lees 77–80, 179
Hague, William 77–8, 79, 80
Hainsworth, David 127, 132
Halhead, Nathaniel, MP 18
Hall, Ann 94, 95, 97, 98, 102, 104
hand-frame stocking making 24–5
handloom weaving 25, 75
Harling, Robert 43–4, 45, 130–2
Hartley, Sarah 118
Head, Sir George 115
*Hebrew Press, The* 171
Hemingway, Edith 200
Heywood, Peter 149
Hill, George 12
Hill, John 34
Hodgson, Harold 198
Hogan, James Francis, MP 147
Holgate, Ann 128
Holgate, Joseph 128, 148
Holmes, Abraham 11
Holt, J. 10
Horridge, George 173
Huddersfield 13, 63, 98
Hudson, James 118
Hudson, John 55
Hurst 185
Hutchinson, Revd John 72, 73

Idle (near Bradford) 23, 36, 54, 57
*Imperial Review* 147

Incorporated Church Building Society,
   The 69–70
Iveson, William 118

Jezreel, James Jershom, *see* White, James
   'Jezreel'
Jezreel's Tower 189–90
Jowett, John 174

Kettleshulme (Derbyshire) 67
Knight, Pastor David 148
Knowlson, Nancy 96

*Lancaster Gazette* 60–1
Laycock, James 128
Leeds 89; Bramley 15; Farnley 5, 15,
   106, 125; Queen Street Chapel 124,
   157; Woodhouse Carr 52
*Leeds Patriot* 37–8
*Leeds Times* 56, 157–8, 159
Lees, Cordelia (née Clunne) 47, 78, 179
Lees, Edward 76, 78
Lees, Esther 96
Lees, Hannah (Senior) 76
Lees, Hannah 76
Lees, Henry 59–61, 76, 180
Lees, Horace 77
Lees, Samuel (Senior) 76
Lees, Samuel 77, 78, 105
Lees, Sarah 77–9, 94, 106
Lees, Sarah (1824–1907), *see* Hague,
   Sarah Lees
Lees, Silas 100
Lees, William (Wroe's travelling
   companion) 46, 47, 49, 51; at Ashton,
   76, 97; departure from the Christian
   Israelites 179
Lindsay, Alexander 'Leban' 30, 49–52
*Lion, The* 86
Liverpool 43
Lockwood, Benjamin 4
Lost Tribes of Ancient Israel viii, 17, 19,
   31, 40, 190
Lovering, Edwin 121, 182
Lovering, Ephraim 120–1, 182
Lovering, Hannah 182
Lovering, Margaret 182

Manchester 13, 37, 38, 181

*Manchester Chronicle* 93, 101, 104

*Manchester Examiner* 127

*Manchester Guardian* 108, 174

Margrave, George 193

Margrave, Mrs I. 198

Masterman, Sarah 97

Masterman, William C. 95, 98–9, 100, 109–10, 159

Melbourne (Australia) 138, 139, 143, 144, 150, 165; Collingwood 138; Fitzroy Sanctuary 140, 165, 166; Old Town Hall 149–50

*Melbourne Age* 144–5

*Melbourne Argus* 138, 140, 155

Melbourne House 149–64, 166, 168, 195, 201–4; formal opening 157; funding scandals 150–3; furnishings 155, 158–9, 204; grounds 156–7, 197, 204; as headquarters of Christian Israelites 199; inspiration for Jezreel's Tower 189; interior decoration 156; local stories associated with 164, 176–8; Milton's ownership quest 160–3, 169–70, 172–3, 175; residential home 201, 203, 204; war damage (1941) 200

Melbourne House Farm 178, 203

*Melbourne Weekly Review* 166

Midgeley, William 130, 131

millenarianism vii, 17–19, 44, 50, 191, 205; socio-economic factors behind the popularity of 22–9, 75–6, 132, 145

Millerite Church (millennial sect) 160

Mills, Michael Keyfor 191

Milne, Mr (Coroner) 60

Milton, Dr John L. 145, 154

Milton, 'Judge' Daniel 133, 159, 160–3, 169–76, 178, 191

Moore, Sydney 199

Moravian Church 73–4

Mormons (Church of Jesus Christ of Latter-day Saints) 182–3, 199

*Morning Chronicle* 74

Morrison, Peter 18, 20

Mottram (near Ashton-under-Lyne) 87

Muff, Samuel 1, 9, 66

Muff, William 12, 35, 42–3, 66, 97, 98

Newchurch (Lancashire) 152, 187

New and Latter House of Israel, the 189

New Eve, the (millenarian community) 191

New House of Israel, The 189

*New Jerusalem*, *see* Ashton-under-Lyne

New York 131, 132, 162, 171, 173, 176

*New York Daily Times* 132, 159

*New York Sun* 161

*Notes and Queries* 167

*Nunawading Messiah*, *see* Fisher, James

Oakenshaw (near Bradford) 63

'Octavia', *see* Barltrop, Mabel

Odd Whim, the, *see* Ashton-under-Lyne

Ogden, Thomas 61

Outcasts of Israel, The 191

Panacea Society 20

Park Bridge (near Ashton-under-Lyne) 57, 67, 75, 114

Payne, Alexander 154

Perry, John 146

Pickersgill, Benjamin 118

Pickersgill, John 118

Pile, Sarah 94, 95, 97–8, 101, 102–3, 104

Pollard, Joshua 111, 112

*Port Philip Herald* 135, 136

Potovens (Wrenthorpe) 23, 117, 174

'Prince Michael', *see* Mills, Michael Keyfor

Prophet Wroe's Mansion, *see* Melbourne House

Pudsey (near Leeds) 67–8

Purnell, Benjamin 191

Quance, Mary 94, 95, 98, 102, 104

Queen Caroline Case, the 14

'Queen Esther', *see* Rogers, Clarissa

Raincock, Mr (prosecutor of Henry Lees) 60, 61

Ramsden, James 118
Ramsden, Constable William 162
Religious Worship, Census of (1851) 71, 75, 182
*Republican, The* 61
Robertshaw, Henry 152
Robertson, Charles 133, 134–5, 137, 138, 139
Rogers, Clarissa (Mrs Jezreel, *Queen Esther*) 190, 191
Rossendale 152

Sandal Magna (near Wakefield) 98, 106
Saxon, John 185
Seurat, Claude Ambroise (the 'Living Skeleton') 50
Shaker communities (in America) 171, 172
Shand, James Rephah 35, 99, 111, 113
Sharp, William 20, 30
Shaw, William 30
Sheffield 36, 102, 113
*Sheffield Courant* 101, 103
Shiloh (spiritual child of Joanna Southcott) 16, 21–2, 30, 41; George Turner's prophecy of 31–2, 33–4; birth of Sarah Lees 77–9; false claimants: (Mabel Barltrop) 191; (James Fisher) 147; (Daniel Milton) 161, 172–4; (John Ward) 109, 159, 161; as part of virgins' scandal 93–4, 103, 104
Sibley, Samuel C.W. 30
Simpson, Dr James 62
Skin, William 84, 100
Smith, Revd James Elishama 28, 38, 87, 95, 105, 180
Smith, Joseph, (Church of Jesus Christ of Latter-day Saints) 183
Smith, Joseph, (constable at Bradford), 111
Smith, Mary 163
Snell, John 169
Society of Christian Israelites: baptisms 57, 140, 182; beards and long hair 37–8, 51, 60–1, 147, 197, 199; beliefs 41–2; challengers for leadership

(Daniel Milton) 188, (James White) 188–90; christenings (the naming ceremony) 140, 181–2; church services 86, 183; circumcision 37, 59–62, 140, 144; cleansing rite 144, 153–4; decline 179, 182, 192, 193; differences between the Southcottians 36–7, 151, 180, 194; dress 38, 60, 85–6, 87–8, 105, 115–16; foundation of 36–7; Hebrew schools 87; hymn book 183–4; initiation rite 143–4; 'Johanna' shops 87, 159, 186–8; laws 37–8, 63–4, 88; marriages 181; music 59, 86, 148, 184; overseas congregations 133, 134, 145; printing press 109, 115, 134, 193; prohibition of images 63–4, 123; punishment 37, 88, 101, 104–5; trustees 169, 188, 189; utopian town planning 81–4; wealthy supporters 37, 75–6, 179; welfare 86–7; in America 62, 130–3, 159, 160; in Australia ('the Beardies') 133–148; in China 138, 139
Southcott, Joanna viii, 1, 19–22; box 20, 174; death 21; 'pregnancy' 21; *see also* Flying Roll, Shiloh
Southcottian congregations 16, 23, 34, 35–6, 37, 43; schisms (Joseph Allman) 30, (Mary Boon) 30, (Alexander Lindsay) 30, 49–52, (Samuel Charles Woodward Sibley) 30, (William Tozer) 30, (George Turner) 30, 31–4
Spencer, Thomas 100, 108, 109–10
Stalybridge 179
Stamford, 6th Earl of 72, 74, 83
Stanley, John (Junior) 84, 180
Stanley, John Strongi'th'arm 59, 75, 76, 81, 180, 186
Stanley, Mary 76
Stanley, Robert, 76, 186
Stewart, Allan 142–5, 152–4, 155, 166
Stewart, Robert 97
Stockport 36
Swire, Samuel 75, 86, 179
Sydney 135, 136, 137
*Sydney Morning Herald* 136, 137

Tameside Local Studies and Archive
   Centre 105, 194
Taylor, William Cooke 182
Teale, John Wroe (Wroe's grandson) 197
Teale, Mary Appleby 196
Teale, Sarai, *see* Wroe, Sarai
Thame (Oxfordshire) 73
Thompson, E.P. 28
Thornhill (near Wakefield) 64
Tillotson, John 12
Tillotson, William 92, 103, 109, 120
*Times, The* 79, 80, 110
Tobin, P.J. 77, 78
Tom, John 192
Tong (near Bradford) 58, 92, 93
Townley, Jane 21, 30, 48
Tozer, William 30, 51
Trickey, Daniel *see* Milton, 'Judge'
   Daniel
Turner, George ix, 16, 18, 20, 30, 31–4
Twigg, William 55

Underwood, Ann 21, 30, 48

*Voice of the People, The* 97, 101, 102,
   103, 108

Wakefield 113, 115, 119, 124, 149, 159;
   Clayton Hospital 198; Court House
   118; Flanshaw 169, 197; St John's
   129; Thompson's Yard 115; *see also*
   Alverthorpe, Carr Gate, Sandal
   Magna and Wrenthorpe
*Wakefield Almanack* 173
*Wakefield Express* 156, 166, 176
*Wakefield Free Press* 163, 166, 183
*Wakefield Journal and Examiner* 166
*Wakefield Journal and West Riding
   Herald* 119
Walker, Dr J. 163
Walker, Samuel 52, 98–9, 107, 110–11,
   159
Ward, John 'Zion' 109, 111, 159, 161
Webster, Revd Thomas 18, 20
Whitby 186
White, James 'Jezreel' 188–90, 191
Whiteley, John 171–2

Whiteley, Martha 92–3, 98
Williamson, Barbara Kemp 160
Wilson, Charles 133
Wilson, John 20
Wood, Ellen 193
Wood, Elsie 193, 194–5
Wood, Harold 190, 194, 195
Wood, John 188
Wood, William Deane 193
wool-combing 4, 10, 15, 25–6; wool-
   combers' strike 29, 63, 66–7, 122
Woollacott, Aaron 182
Wrenthorpe (near Wakefield) 116–19,
   149, 158, 168, 176, 198; Bradford
   Road 149, 157, 170, 198; Bragg Lane
   End 163, 168, 169, 170, 175; Brandy
   Carr 116–19, 149, 155, 168, 177,
   203; Prophet Wroe's Lane (Jerry Clay
   Lane) 116; St Anne's parish church,
   117, 200, 205; Silcoates School
   199–200; Snow Hill 168, 169;
   Springfield View 170; Trough Well
   Lane 200, 203; War Memorial 200;
   the Wheel 175; Wilson Hill 170; *see
   also* Melbourne House
Wroe, Benjamin (Wroe's 2nd son) 40
Wroe, Benjamin (Wroe's great-great-
   grandson) 199, 200–1
Wroe, Benjamin Appleby 'Asriel'
   (Wroe's 3rd son) 40–1, 118, 168, 183
Wroe, Ethel Grace 198
Wroe, George (Wroe's great-grandson)
   197, 200, 202, 203
Wroe, James (Wroe's grandson) 168,
   172, 176, 178, 187, 197
Wroe, 'Prophet' John, Anglican
   background of family 3; grandfather's
   prophecy 3; relationship with brother
   2–3, 4, 5; relationship with father 2–3,
   9; alleged poor literacy 1, 3; early
   financial difficulties 4–5; marriage 5;
   work as a wool-comber 4, 10–11, 15;
   early visions (pre-1823) 6–10, 12,
   13–14, 15, 16, 35, (other) 63, 82, 88,
   124, 163; trance scandal 10;
   leadership bid for the Bradford
   Southcottians 36; visitation 34–5;

early travels (Manchester) 13, (Liverpool) 12, 13, 43, (London) 14, 48–52; baptism (Apperley Bridge) 54–7, (Park Bridge) 57; circumcision 59; death of daughter Mary 58; wandering missions 62–4, 67–8, 82; 'Shiloh' Lees 77–80; the Martha Whitely allegations 91–3; the seven virgins 90, 91, 93–106, 159; trial 95–98, 129; relationship with wife 64, 106, 129; death of child 98; fracas at the Ashton Sanctuary (Feb 1831) 99–100, 185 (Apr 1831) 109; 'banishment' from Ashton 109–10, 125; riots in Bradford 64–6, 111–13; residence at Wakefield 115–16; burglary at Brandy Carr House 117–19; travels (America 1840) 132, (America 1859) 133, (Australia 1843) 135–7, (Australia 1850) 138–9, (Australia 1853–4) 139–42; (Australia 1859) 143, (Calais) 47, (Gibraltar) 43–6, (Milan) 47, (Paris) 46, (Spain) 45, (Strasborg) 46, (Trieste) 47, (Venice) 47; writing of *Divine Communications* 120; funding of Melbourne House 150–3; sale of gold rings 150–1, 190; opening of Melbourne House 157; cleansing scandals 153–5; peculiar punishments 101, 104–5; return to Ashton 180; conducts marriages 180, 181; appearance 64; nickname ('pudding Wroe') 52–3; excessively eccentric behaviour 52, 88–9, 158, 163; illness 3, 5–6, 7, 12, 16, 42; prophecies (death of brother-in-law) 15, (election results) 124, (flight) 135–6, (freak weather) 125, (harvests) 11, (industrial relations) 29, 63, 66, 122, (industrialisation) 122–3, (plague) 124–5, 186, (railways) 122–3, (retribution) 106–8, 125–6, (transport) 12, 121–2, 122–3; healing 64, 128; rivals (Fisher) 147–8, (Lindsay) 49–52, (Milton) 160–3, (Ward) 109, 159; death 165; burial 165; will 168–9, 170

Wroe, John (Wroe's great-grandson) 197, 198

Wroe, Joseph (Wroe's brother) 2, 4, 5

Wroe, Joseph (Wroe's father) 1, 2–3, 4, 9

Wroe, Joseph (Wroe's cousin) 9, 11, 12, 33, 42

Wroe, Joseph (Wroe's son) 64, 168, 172, 196

Wroe, Joseph (Wroe's grandson) 187

Wroe, Margaret 203

Wroe, Marion (Wroe's great-granddaughter) 172, 205

Wroe, Mary (Wroe's wife, née Appleby), birth 106; death 129; marriage 5; relationship with Wroe 64, 106, 129; at the Ashton Southern gatehouse 84, 110–11; and the virgins 97, 98, 102–3

Wroe, Mary (Wroe's daughter) 58

Wroe, Mary Ann (née Deane, later Farrand) 168, 183

Wroe, Muriel Doris 187

Wroe, Peter (Wroe's nephew) 197

Wroe, Sarah 98

Wroe, Sarah (Wroe's daughter-in-law) 196

Wroe, Sarah (née Corry), 187, 197

Wroe, Sarai (Wroe's daughter) 106, 129, 169, 196–7

Wroe, Susanna (Wroe's daughter) 169, 196

Wroe, Susanna (Wroe's mother, née Fearnley) 3

Wroe, Thomas (Wroe's brother) 3

*Yorkshire Life* 172